I'LL BE SEEING YOU

Letters Home from a Navy Girl

I'll Be Seeing You

Letters Home from a Navy Girl

Karen Berkey Huntsberger

KAREN BERKEY HUNTSBERGER

LUMINARE PRESS

WWW.LUMINAREPRESS.COM

I'll Be Seeing You: Letters Home From a Navy Girl
© 2018 Karen Berkey Huntsberger

Because of the dynamic nature of the Internet, any Web addresses or links contained in this book may have changed since publication and may no longer be valid.

Editor's Note: This is a work of nonfiction compiled from source documents. Some material in this volume has been lightly edited to improve readability. Obvious errors in spelling and usage have been corrected, and an internal house style has been applied for consistency in punctuation, spelling, and style.

Printed in the United States of America
Cover Design by Claire Flint Last

Luminare Press
438 Charnelton St., Suite 101
Eugene, OR 97401
www.luminarepress.com

LCCN: 2018944161
ISBN: 978-1-944733-71-1

For Lucy and every other woman
who did something
other than what they should

Also by
KAREN BERKEY HUNTSBERGER

WAITING FOR PEACE
The Journals & Correspondence of a
World War II Medic

TABLE OF CONTENTS

I'll Be Seeing You

LYRICS BY IRVING KAHAL

I'll be seeing you
In all the old familiar places
That this heart of mine embraces
All day through

In that small café
The park across the way
The children's carousel
The chestnut trees
The wishing well

I'll be seeing you
In every lovely summer's day
In everything that's light and gay
I'll always think of you that way

I'll find you in the morning sun
And when the night is new
I'll be looking at the moon
But I'll be seeing you

PREFACE

When I was writing *Waiting for Peace: The Journals & Correspondence of a World War II Combat Medic,* I discovered several letters to my father, Richard Berkey, from his sister Lucy. Her letters were so full of enthusiasm and life that I wanted to know more about my aunt and her service in the Navy Women's Reserve, WAVES, during World War II.

In 2014, I was able to learn more about Lucy's experience when I discovered a box of her World War II era letters among our family historical documents. More of her letters were found in late 2017.

I knew that Lucy's three brothers had to serve in the war, but why did Lucy choose to participate in military service? Curiosity about her experiences led me to do extensive research to understand women's participation in the military. I soon learned that very few books have been written by or published about the Navy WAVES, Women Activated for Voluntary Emergency Service. During World War II, there was an urgent and continual appeal for women to replace men in military and home front jobs. That appeal came through newspaper and radio advertising and prominently placed posters and billboards. Over 350,000 women answered the call to serve in the branches of the military, and 80,936 of them were WAVES.

Lucy was one of 30 women from her southern Indiana county who enlisted in a county where 12% of the population was drafted or enlisted. That 12% was a small fraction of the 12 million U.S. citizens who served during the war. Of that 12 million, 400,000 were killed, 670,000 were wounded and 73,000 went missing in action. Worldwide, 63 nations were involved and more than 60 million people died. Seventy years later, it is hard to fathom the enormity of world involvement and the exhaustion that accompanied years of war.

Virtually every family living in the United States today has a World War II story to tell—of a parent, grandparent, brother, sister, aunt, or uncle. Lucy's letters home give us a glimpse into a life altered by U.S. entry into World War II. This book is necessarily one-sided, as only Lucy's letters to her parents have survived. I know she wrote many more letters to friends and family in addition to her parents, but those letters have been lost to history. I have often wondered what Lucy wrote to others. As children rarely report all their troubles to their parents, it seems almost certain there was news that Lucy did not share. I can only guess about other aspects of her life and her feelings about women's issues of the time.

In the following letters, Lucy tells her own story of how a young woman, trapped by societal expectations, joined the Navy and became part of a larger, transformational movement for women at a pivotal time in history. Lucy's vivid descriptions of her training, assignments, and daily life help us to understand what it was like to be a young military woman in the U.S. during the war. It has been a tremendous gift and an honor to get to know Lucy and the women of the WAVES.

Karen Berkey Huntsberger
February 18, 2018

WHO'S WHO

FAMILY

Mother – Lucy's mother – Lennie Martin Berkey

Dad or Daddy – Lucy's father – James Garfield Berkey

Jonas (Jonie) – Lucy's older brother

Richard – Lucy's younger brother

Virginia – Lucy's younger sister

David – Lucy's youngest brother

Eleanor – Lucy's youngest sister

Mildred McBride – Jonas Berkey's wife

LUCY'S FRIENDS

Mildred Guthnecht – teacher in Columbus

Betty Patty – housemate in Columbus/friend in D.C.

Johnny Kooken – college boyfriend

Leonard (Len) Cunningham – boyfriend while teaching in Columbus

Bob – boyfriend while in D.C.

CHAPTER ONE
I'VE NEVER WORKED
SO HARD

EDITOR'S NOTE:

The first three chapters present background material to help readers understand how Lucy came to be a WAVE. Just three months out of college, Lucy started her first job as a public school art teacher. The first year of teaching is difficult for most young teachers, and during World War II, classroom teaching became even harder. A severe teacher shortage nationwide created unmanageable workloads with enormous class sizes. Seventy-five percent of the school districts across the country also had "marriage bar" laws preventing most married women from teaching. Many young women married quickly as soldiers headed off to war. As a result, schools were severely understaffed. Nonetheless, Lucy began teaching in fall of 1942 with high hopes and the ambition to work hard and be good at her chosen career.

September 8, 1942, Columbus, Indiana

Dear Folks,

There seems to be so much to do around here that writing letters is a luxury. I've drawn so many pictures in crayon that I can see them in my sleep. I've only taught two junior high classes so far, and that was this morning. My schedule hasn't been arranged yet. I'll have two junior high classes at McKinley that will meet every day. Then I'll have all the grades up to the seventh at different hours at different schools every day.[1] I've really worked since I've been here! Cleaned

---

1   Lucy was hired in August 1942 to teach art in the Columbus, Indiana, School District.

out cupboards and planned, planned, and planned!! Even on Sunday afternoon, Mildred Guthnecht and I worked like mad.[2] And of course I had to get a terrible cold and could hardly talk today.

Betty Patty arrived today at last, and she is going to take the single room because Martha got here first. Martha came Sunday and is sweet. I'd have preferred the single room, but then Betty does, too. However, I guess everything will work out somehow. There's a housing shortage here now because of Camp Atterbury.[3] Lots of wives have moved here to be near their husbands, even if it's for not very long.

One of the worst things about this house is no iron or ironing board. Guess we'll have to buy our own. And the bathroom is terribly hard to get into, I *must* say. And restaurants—actually, there's hardly a decent place to eat in, and the food is sky high. I'm certainly discouraged as far as saving any money is concerned. The bus situation is going to eat up fare, too, since that's the only way to get to all my schools.

Sunday I went to the Christian Church. It's beautiful, but odd—just that I'm not used to something like that being a church.

Daddy, they couldn't get the Hamilton, so I selected a Bulova watch, which I like very much. It's so nice and I'll be pleased with it. It's $42.50 and I had them lay it away. It's the nicest thing you could get me! Well, I must get to work. It really is work and I do mean *work*! So far I haven't met many of the teachers, but that won't last long. How's Jonie?[4]

Love,

Lucy

---

2   Mildred Guthnecht, art supervisor in Columbus schools, Lucy's co-worker.

3   Camp Atterbury was a combat training facility for the U.S. Army during World War II.

4   Lucy's oldest brother, Jonas (Jonie) had joined the Navy in January 1942.

September 21, 1942

Dear Folks,

At long last I am getting around to writing you again. Boy, I've never worked so hard in all my life! If I thought college was wearing, I take it back—at least most of it. I work all day, every day, with no hours off. They said the previous art teacher used to have three hours and one afternoon per week to plan her work, but there is no time off for me. Mildred and I plan constantly with just about 15 minutes off for lunch. At noon on Mondays, I walk from McKinley to Garfield because I can't make bus connections—and it's 15 blocks! Tuesday noon I walk 12 blocks from McKinley to Jefferson. Wednesday and Thursday afternoons I am at Wilson, the junior high in the same block as the high school, so I ride the bus from McKinley to Hook's Nook where I eat, then walk three blocks home, and then two blocks to school. Friday I'm at McKinley all day, thank goodness. Every morning at McKinley I have junior high—7B and 8B—and one grade school class, so my afternoons are worse, with five classes one after the other. It's always after 4:00 before I can get home. Bus fare amounts to at least 50¢ per week, and this morning when it was so cold, I thought the bus would never come!

Whew! Do I sound gripey! Teaching does have its good side. All the teachers have been swell to me, even though I don't know much about grade school teaching. Next week I'll have to go to Indianapolis to get a specially made pair of shoes. Every night my legs and feet swell so terribly I can hardly stand at all.

I've eaten less and spent more for food than ever before in my life. Couldn't find a clothes iron here, so I ordered one from the Montgomery Ward store. Guess I was lucky to get it, because all the hardware stores said I wouldn't be able to find one. Well, I'm beginning to wonder if I'll save any money at all! Besides, all teachers are required to pledge so much of each check to buy war bonds.

I wish I had taken the single room, because I'm so tired that I like to be alone when I have to draw at night. Besides, I already have so many pictures to grade that they're running all over the place. Mildred is one swell girl! She has helped me so much—I really couldn't do it without her. Certainly everyone who knows her loves her. I want to bring her home with me some weekend. She's 26 but acts as if she's 20! She really knows her stuff and is a plenty good artist from some of the things I've seen at her home. Miss Voland, the last high school art teacher, died last year. I just found that out the other day. She thought so much of Mildred that she gave her practically all of her art materials and books.

Have you heard from Jonie lately? And will Richard get to stay in school?[5] Johnny is now a thing of the past, so I guess I'll start looking for someone else.[6] I knew it this summer, but refused to believe it. Life sure is funny. Johnny was always swell to me and did everything to make me happy, so I can't complain.

I must plan tomorrow's lessons—eight of them—so I'll write more later. Daddy, the watch is swell! It runs fine—keeps perfect time! And I need it constantly for this teaching business. Thanks a million!!

Write me—maybe I'll be more used to teaching by then and won't sound so droopy.

Love,

Lucy

P.S. Eleanor, write me—remember? You're a much better artist than most of my frisky 8Bs![7]

---

5   Richard—Lucy's younger brother.
6   Lucy graduated from Indiana University in May 1942 with a degree in art. Johnny is John Kooken, her college boyfriend, who graduated from IU in 1941. Commissioned as a second lieutenant in the Army and called to active duty July 1, 1941, he was promoted to captain in October 1942. While a lieutenant, he served as an aide to the Fort Knox commandant.
7   13-year-old Eleanor, Lucy's youngest sister.

> Miss Lucy Berkey eldest daugh-
> ter of Mr. and Mrs. J. G. Berkey,
> has been named assistant art sup-
> ervisor in the Columbus city
> schools.

August 26, 1942
Courtesy of The Salem Leader

Lucy with Johnny Kooken—Bloomington, Indiana, April 1940
Photographer unknown

I'll Be Seeing You

October 1, 1942

Dear Mother & Daddy,

Maybe sometime I'll get used to teaching school! Both Mildred and I are so swamped we can barely drag around.

I'm so glad to hear that Jonas and Mildred are really going to get married at last.[8] I envy them, but it doesn't do me much good. To get married during wartime is so hard. Many girls go ahead and marry knowing they could be widowed. Others wait, and then end up alone when their fiancé is killed. None of it is fair.

Last Sunday, Mildred [Guthnecht], Major Simpson, 2nd Lieutenant Leonard Cunningham, and I went to Bloomington in the major's car. We met the fellows through Lieutenant Paul Kundra, Udena's fiancé. Udena lives here at Dr. Teal's.[9] We went out to the Officers Club at Camp Atterbury two Saturday nights in a row to dance and had so much fun. Then we went to the show a couple of times. Sunday, Leonard went to church with me then we ate at the Officers Mess, and was that a thrill! Then in the afternoon we four went to Bloomington. We sat in the Commons and listened to the orchestra, ate at Boxman's, and then went to see Virginia.[10] Leonard is really nice and I'm so glad I can go with someone, 'cause otherwise this job would drive me insane.

Wasn't that a mess of laundry I sent home![11] I'd keep forgetting to send it and it's so hard to find time to do any washing here. This town is so expensive I'm getting skeptical about saving anything per month.

---

8   This is a different Mildred, Mildred McBride, engaged to Jonas.
9   Dr. Dorothy Teal, one of the first women physicians in Columbus, began her obstetrics practice in 1933 and worked for more than 40 years. During World War II, she performed physicals for servicemen and delivered their wives' babies. Lucy rented a room above her office at 728 Franklin Street.
10   Virginia—Lucy's younger sister, a freshman at Indiana University.
11   Sending laundry through the U.S. mail in specially designed cases was a common practice from 1910–1960. Most users were college students and military personnel. Self-serve laundromats starting appearing in the mid 1930s but were not in common use until the 1950s. It was less expensive to send laundry home than to have it professionally done.

Food is my biggest expense. You can't get a meat meal for less than 45¢ and vegetables are so much higher.

In my 8B class I have two terrible problem boys. They nearly upset the whole class this morning. I asked one of them to move and he flatly refused. My discipline is pretty bad, I'm afraid, because I'm so young the kids take advantage of me. Mildred [Guthnecht] says I should ask Mr. Reece, the principal, to straighten them out for me, for that's his job.

I'm looking forward to tomorrow—payday again! But after I pay room rent and board, it fades away. Still, that check really looks good and boy, have I earned it and more!

I'm pretty anxious to come home, and will whenever I can get time. Mother, don't hurry with that laundry, 'cause I'll do okay for a while.

Love,

Lucy

October 6, 1942

Dear Mother & Daddy,

Saturday Betty Patty and I went to Indianapolis and I got my feet examined at Ayres by a Dr. Warren, the Scholl representative. He said he didn't see how I'd been standing up at all. Seems that my arches are bad and that's what throws the weight on my heels. He got a pair of steel arch supports and fitted them to my feet and said I should come back in two weeks and have them readjusted. The shoes he gave me are nice looking brown oxfords. It cost plenty, but it's worth it. Right now the shoes feel clumsy, but he said they would for a while. Anything to get my feet fixed up!

Betty and I saw more kids we'd known at IU. Saw Bonnie Bouchard and she said Margie Reeves was teaching at Sharpsville, near Tipton. She's making $165 a month! Am I burned! I bet she doesn't work half as hard! Betty and I had loads of fun just going around. I also got a purse and a hat. Thought you all might come up Sunday as it was so beautiful. All the rest of the kids here went picnicking in Brown County Park, but I was without a date, since Leonard had gone to New York, so I stayed home.

I'm surrounded by hundreds of kids drawings, and grades must be made out by the end of next week. Mother, you knew I was teaching beginners! I have all the grades from 1–8 in all the schools except the junior high at Wilson. I can't imagine Richard putting pies in his suitcase! Sometimes I get so hungry for good pie, though, I don't blame him. Food here is punk and expensive.

Love from,

Lucy

October 19, 1942

Dearest Folks,

I was so glad to see you, Daddy! I wish you could have stayed longer. That teacher's meeting lasted only half an hour and was about teachers helping in defense work. Tonight I've been grading papers. I sorta dread Teachers Association. All the teachers say it's a rat race and that you have to stand up during all the sessions. We'll go up on Thursday morning and come back Friday night. I can just see my bank account after all this! My ticket to the Association costs $2.50 and then $4.50 for two organizations all teachers have to belong to. Then my room rent and I'd like to get a few things in Indianapolis. Oh well, I guess life is more enjoyable if you enjoy a few extra things once in a while. Mildred [Guthnecht] and I will go to art sessions at John Herron all day and then there is a luncheon at noon.[12]

Leonard Cunningham is transferring into the parachute troops soon and will go to Fort Benning, Georgia. Seems as if lieutenants and I weren't suited or sumpin'! We went to the show at Camp Atterbury Saturday night with another lieutenant and his wife. I saw General

---

12 John Herron Institute of Art at the Indianapolis Museum of Art.

KAREN BERKEY HUNTSBERGER

Millikin—the first general I've ever seen in person! In the movie they had one of those sing-alongs and you should have heard Leonard! He loves to sing and he about brought the house down!

Love,

Lucy

October 27, 1942

Dear Folks,

I went to Teachers Association in Indianapolis over the weekend. The sessions I went to were okay, but not very wonderful. I was really disappointed in the Association. I stayed at the Claypool Hotel with four teachers, all young and one married. We had lots of fun together!

Monday I got a letter from Richard! I about fell over dead! It was the craziest thing. He was teasing me about teaching and hearing that I was going with another soldier. Told me 80% of teachers never married. Said he was sorry I wasn't going to ever marry, and a lot of other junk!

Heard from Johnny and he's still doing the aide's work until the new one arrives but thinks he'll be transferred to a company soon. Thanks for the photo of Jonas. He looks really ritzy in his uniform, doesn't he? Whew! Guess I'll join the WAVES![13] I read Mrs. Roosevelt's article in the paper about the tea she gave for the leader of the Canadian women's military. She says that Americans shouldn't be afraid that military work will make women less feminine. The paper here is full of ads looking for women to work and lots of them are working in factories now. Teaching has still got to be better than that! I must get to work now.

Love,

Lucy

---

13   WAVES—Women Activated for Volunteer Emergency Service, the women's reserve of the Navy. Elizabeth Reynard, professor of English at Barnard College, was charged by the Navy with creating a design for the women's reserve program and is credited with coming up with the acronym.

November 5, 1942

Dear Folks,

Just finished grading my Halloween pictures for the seventh and eighth grades. Some of them are pretty nice. But the kids got so bad Tuesday I had the principal come in and talk to them about keeping order. I was so discouraged I felt like quitting right then. Today they were still pretty rowdy. But I guess I can live from day to day. I don't think I like teaching even as moderately as I did at first.

All of the teachers had to help with kerosene rationing at the different schools last Thursday and Friday nights. Thursday was bank night, so not many people came.[14] Consequently, Mildred and I sat there and worked out all our grade lessons for this week. This last Saturday I went with Cunningham to the football game at IU. We rode over with two of his lieutenant friends. Cunningham yelled so much everyone in the stadium was looking at us! He was for the Seahawks! Said he was for anyone in the service, which after all is right, I guess. Did he have fun razzing the Indiana fans! Then we went over to see Virginia. She was just leaving to go to the show, so I didn't see her long. On Sunday, Len came down in the afternoon with a Lieutenant Hasell whose wife is visiting her folks in Chicago. We all went to the show and had fun.

I got my laundry today. Thanks so much for the fruit—it's swell! Monday night I went to Indianapolis with Betty and I bought a dark green suit. It cost quite a lot, but I'd decided it would be worth it and I need one so badly. Everywhere I go I really need a suit worse than a coat right now. I just love it, and am so pleased, and it looks swell on. Right now I don't know just when I will be home. Prob-

---

14   The Office of Price Administration was established April 11, 1941, to control prices and rents after World War II began. Schools were responsible for enrolling families in the rationing program and distributing ration books. One of each ration book was given to every man, woman, and child in the U.S., approximately 130,000,000 people. Teachers were not paid for this extra duty. They were considered volunteers, whether they did this work willingly or not.

ably within two or three weeks. I want Len to come home with me when he can get off. He's so nice and I know you'd like him. He's in Chicago now, bringing back some Army transport trucks. Wish I could see Jonie's pictures!

All my love,

Lucy

November 12, 1942

Dear Mother & Daddy,

So glad to hear from you today. This week has been so awful. This Betty Clark who lives here is a pain and she and Udena can't stand each other. They really got into it the other night and did some real word-lashing. And Miss Gibbs got mad at us because Paul and two of his friends tracked in some mud when they came in to get us Sunday afternoon. Said she'd kick us out if they did it again. And teaching gets worse every day. Honestly, I try to like it, but the more I teach the more I realize I was never cut out for teaching. It makes me tired, and not because I lack sleep. Now, Mother, I *don't* go out every night. I usually see Leonard on Saturday and Sunday. After all, he has classes at night and plenty of work to do.

I've felt terrible all afternoon after what you said about Leonard. After all, I don't run around up here—I just *date* him and he's the nicest fellow I've ever known in all my life, even nicer in some ways than Johnny. You couldn't find a guy with finer ideals, and an orphan at that. Anyway, Johnny and I aren't going together anymore and never will, and I don't see why I can't bring Leonard home. I want him to meet you. He gets Thanksgiving off and I so want to ask him to come home with me, but I certainly *won't* if you don't want him. I don't care, I think he's swell, and but for his pep talks I don't think I could stand teaching sometimes. You just don't know him.

Sunday we went to Major Kane's home to a buffet supper for all the lieutenants in the Signal Corps. The Kanes have a three-week-old baby and it's the sweetest thing! We had lots of fun.

I'd like to bring Mildred [Guthnecht] home, but both of us have to work at gas rationing on Thursday and Friday nights, and on Saturday, so that's out! I'm anxious to come home, too!

Wasn't Sam's death tragic?[15] I knew even before Aunt Minnie wrote me because I read it in the *Star* on Saturday.[16] Right away I thought about that night he brought us home. This war is awful.

I'm sorry I'm a disappointment about teaching, but I can't help it—I try. About affecting my later life—I think my happiness and health is more important than any job. I'm just a dope, don't mind my raving! I'll be home when I can get away from here.

Love,

Lucy

November 19, 1942

Dear Mother & Daddy,

After teaching all day and then helping with gas rationing from 4:00 to 6:30, I am plenty tired. My goodness, but I'm ashamed and sorry for what I wrote before! I was just upset anyway and of course I'm not mad at anybody. Yes, Grandmother is a good backer-upper! Now Len doesn't think he can get off for Thanksgiving since this speed-up program started, though he isn't sure yet. He says to thank you for asking him. After I practically begged you to!

My junior high classes have been so rowdy this week I about went nuts. I'm determined to send about eight of them into the office in

---

15   Sam Mitchell was from Lucy's hometown. An attorney when he entered the U.S. Army Air Corps, he died November 6, 1942, in a flight training accident in the U.S. He was 25 years old.

16   *The Indianapolis Star* newspaper.

the morning. Wednesday I was so blue I had to come home and cry and brood about being such a failure as a teacher, but today things went better.

Guess I'll come on the bus on Wednesday night. I certainly am determined to come to Jonie's wedding! I'll just have to make the school board let me off. After all, I might not see him for a long time. I'm sorry Richard will have to go so soon.

All I do is work, eat, and sleep, have a few dates, and feel pretty bad and gripe about it, so I don't have much news right now. Some life! Len says it's some life compared to the Army!

Richard wrote me about withdrawing from IU. I feel so sad that he has to go, too. I hope they'll train him to be a medic because it's what he wants. All those pre-med classes he's had already should count for something![17]

I'll see you Wednesday. I may or may not have Len with me. He'll have to find out about a leave at the last minute.

All my love,

Lucy

> Miss Lucy Berkey, art instructor in the Columbus schools, accompanied by Lt. Leonard Cunningham of Evanston, Ill. who is stationed at Camp Atterbury, was here Sunday afternoon, for a few hours' visit home. Miss Berkey will arrive today, Wednesday, to spend the Thanksgiving holiday with her parents Mr. and Mrs. J. G. Berkey.

November 25, 1942—Courtesy of The Salem Leader

---

17   Richard was a third-year pre-med student when he was drafted in December 1942. He reported to Camp Atterbury on January 16, 1943.

December 13, 1942

Dear Mama & Daddy,

It was so good to be home for Jonas and Mildred's wedding—everything was perfect![18] I'm so glad all of us got to be there. It's so unfair that Mildred won't be rehired at the end of the school year just because she got married. Unlike me, she really loves teaching school! I still haven't gotten a wedding present for them. After seeing all their gifts, I hardly know what to get them. Do you think a satin comforter would be okay?

Jonie and I talked a little the night before the wedding about women in the service. I know several girls from school who are joining. There've been so many articles in the paper by people who say women can't do the jobs men have done. I even read that a Michigan congressman who is against women in the service said, "Who will raise the children and make men of them so that they too may march away to war someday?" *Is war to be endless?* Jonas said he thought women were needed and if I was seriously thinking about joining, the WAVES would be his choice for me. Of course, he'd say his branch was best!

Tonight Martha and I went to the Teachers Federation supper party down at the Girls Club. We had to pay 65¢ for our meal, and we were so hungry afterwards we went down to the Greeks and got some ice cream. All they talked about at the meeting was what all was to be taken out of our paychecks—victory tax, income tax, and teachers retirement fund. Honestly, I won't have any paychecks anymore. We found out the other day we all got a $10 per month raise. But it doesn't mean much when they take out so much for taxes and stuff.

I saw Roger Rudder downtown tonight and he said he got his draft card today to report for his physical. So many of the men teachers here in Columbus are going to the Army that pretty soon there won't be anyone left but old maids!

---

18   The wedding was held Friday afternoon, December 4, in Jeffersonville, Indiana.

My classes have been really rowdy this week, and I got so mad I shook one boy yesterday, moved four, and sent one out of the room. The principal told me to come to him next time and he'd spank the boy so the class could hear it and maybe they'd behave. He said I shouldn't let the classes run away with me or I'd be a nervous wreck. I'm practically a nervous wreck now from those rowdy classes and cut paper lessons!!

We get off for Christmas vacation on the afternoon of the 23rd and I'll be home sometime that night.

Love from,

Lucy

December 20, 1942

Dear Mother & Daddy,

Mildred [Guthnecht] is so busy now with Christmas work she asked me if I'd plan the lessons for this week. Of course I said I would. All day yesterday I worked on my lessons and then for two hours this afternoon. Then for an hour and a half I've been addressing Christmas cards. Leonard is so busy he hasn't been in for over a week. He says he thinks he will not get Christmas off. They are planning a nice dinner and program for the men. They've been on 20-mile hikes and have had battles in which they fire actual guns, etc. for a week. One day I could hear those big guns vibrating—11 miles away!

I've never been so embarrassed in my life as over this money business. Here I thought I had $30 more than I really did. What a manager I am! I couldn't even sleep for two nights just worrying about it. This last week has been hectic, anyway, what with cut paper lessons, grading hundreds of pictures, and discipline so bad because of Christmas excitement.

I heard from Johnny this week—got a Christmas card and letter. He's still at Fort Knox, and at the time he wrote didn't know where he would be sent. At first they were going to send him to school, a basic tactics course, and he wanted that. Then they said he'd be with an armored division that was going overseas soon.

Yesterday afternoon, it snowed and snowed—almost like a blizzard. Today the snow is just beautiful with the sun shining on it—about 2½ inches deep, too. I'd love to paint a snow scene!

We get off at 2:30 Wednesday so I'll probably be home at 9:00 if I can get on the bus. I'm so anxious to come home! Monday night we girls here at the house are having a little Christmas party.

Love,

Lucy

CHAPTER TWO
STACKS OF DRAWINGS
TO GRADE

January 11, 1943

Dear Folks,

This last week has been the busiest time I've had since I came up here. All weekend I drew and painted an alphabet in old English letters on large papers—one for each letter. Boy, last night when I finally went to bed my eyes jerked and burned like they used to in college. Then today Frances Smith informed me that I had to make or print 50 names on diplomas for the eighth grade—in Old English letters! They have to be done by Monday. Then—grades for my two adjustment classes and my two junior high classes have to be in by Friday.[19]

Thank you for everything you did to make a wonderful Christmas for us, even with rationing on. The stockings were hung by the chimney with care and St. Nicholas did arrive! I wish I could have done more for everyone, but with my meager salary I did the best I could. It was a perfectly cozy Christmas Day, except for missing Jonas and Mildred. Who knows how many will be at home next Christmas? The war drags on with no end in sight and now Richard is going. It seems like a lot of our boys from Salem are going, although I suppose it's the same amount everywhere. Have you heard from Jonas? Honestly, it seems years since I was home and we heard from him.

Leonard called me up as soon as he got back Monday night to say he'd see me Tuesday. Then he called and said he was sick and so bad

---

19   Adjustment: In order to lower the dropout rate, educators in the 1940s developed the Lifestyle Adjustment Curriculum, intended to be less taxing than a standard course of study. Experts estimated that 60% of students were not smart enough to attend college and needed basic skills to make a useful contribution to society and live a happy life.

he had to eat an orange in order to swallow enough to talk to me over the phone. He got a cold in Chicago—and then Tuesday they had to go on a 15-mile hike and sleep on the cold ground. It developed into a severe cold in his head and chest. He said he hasn't felt so bad for 15 years! They tried to make him go to the hospital, but he wouldn't do it.

I had quite a time getting back here after Christmas. Had to stand up on the bus all the way from Seymour to Columbus.[20] The bus station here was filled with recruiting posters, including the ladies room! I'd like to meet the artists who draw them—they are really beautifully done with such wonderful color. I don't feel like I'm doing vital work at all. Maybe they need artists in the service![21] The price of meals raised 15¢ while I was home. Surprise![22]

Love,

Lucy

---

20   Due to gas and rubber rationing, driving a car was impractical during the war. In May 1942, the speed limit was set at 35 miles per hour nationwide, which made any kind of motor vehicle transportation very slow. Travelers turned to buses and trains to conserve the precious gasoline they were allotted. Greyhound Bus Lines advertised their role in transporting people "between their homes and military camps and bases" and helping "millions of other Americans in their everyday pursuits." Ads in newspapers asked travelers to "Put Your Wartime Travel on a 4-Day Week" to make room for soldiers on furlough. Because Lucy lived so near Camp Atterbury, buses were often packed, and uniformed personnel had priority for seats.

21   John Falter, a Navy artist, created the majority of images used on WAVES recruiting posters. He designed over three hundred recruiting posters during the war years.

22   Food prices had risen 12% in both 1941 and 1942. The rationing program curbed inflation by fixing prices of goods. During the remainder of the war, food prices only increased 4%.

World War II recruiting posters

January 28, 1943

Dear Folks,

Received my laundry case this afternoon and decided to sit right down and write you a letter. Thank you for the lovely cookies, Mother. They were really swell and they sure went in a big hurry. I really hadn't sent that chocolate home for myself, but I didn't mind getting it back in the form of cookies! They seem to have loads of semisweet chocolate up here. I hear they're going to ration clothes. My college coat is getting threadbare and I'm wondering if I'm going to be able to get a new one for next winter. Maybe I should get it pretty soon.

I imagine Virginia told you that I was in Bloomington weekend before last. I decided to go home with Betty Saturday morning. We didn't do very much, as it rained so hard it was hard to go anyplace. Virginia went to the show with us to see *Hitler's Children* and we all thought it was swell.[23]

Today was the first school day I've ever missed—upset stomach. I'm so disgusted that I had to miss a day because I really need that pay. Betty just brought me some hot soup and does it taste good!

Guess what? You know I told you my name was in the *IU Alumni Magazine*. Well, my address was also there, and it brought results! I got a letter last week from Cpl. David Compton who is at Fort Bliss, Texas. He said he graduated from IU Business School last year. He's from Hope, which is 15 miles from here. He knew Virginia from a guy she had a couple of dates with, also from Hope. I wrote back and he sent another letter yesterday with a small picture. He's not bad looking—blond and 6 feet tall. Says he enjoys writing to an IU alumnus. Guess it's fun, and maybe I'll get a letter once in a while.

23　*Hitler's Children* plot: Sensationalistic expose of the Hitler Youth program follows the sad tale of an American girl who is legally declared a German.

Has Richard gone yet? I've been wondering about him. I hope he won't be sent too far away. And how is Jonie? I still haven't gotten a wedding present for those kids.

Love,

Lucy

February 5, 1943

Dear Mother & Daddy,

Wednesday night, Mildred [Guthnecht] asked me to go with her to the Auditorium Series at Bloomington. We got Virginia at the dorm, and we all went together. The violinist was really good and we had good seats.[24] After the program, we started home and it was really hailing. I got a cold from the weather and lost my voice! Today, in all my classes, I just drew and they copied me. I hardly said a word because I sound like a foghorn!

Paul and Udena have moved to an apartment, so we don't have quite as many people wanting in the bathroom at the same time. Did I tell you she had moved? I think I forgot to tell you that she and Paul got married in January in Louisville. Cunningham and I have split up, and I suppose all of you will be glad to hear it. He calls me up occasionally, but that's all. I don't mind, but I do get bored never having any dates.

I'm anxious to know where Richard is being sent. Honestly, Jonie probably about passed out when he received a letter from me. Last Sunday I was so lonesome because everyone else went home that I wrote more letters. I'm sending my laundry tomorrow with a headscarf for grandmother and a couple of boxes of semisweet chocolate for you to use. I'll see you next Friday unless something unexpected comes up.

Love,

Lucy

---

24 The performer was French violin virtuoso, Zino Francescatti.

February 22, 1943

Dear Folks,

This weekend I visited Virginia in Bloomington and when I got back I found your card, Mother. So I'm sending my ration book back home because I don't understand about all that food junk. All morning I've been writing all that stuff on the new No. II Ration Books until my arm is about paralyzed. I have to work at rationing again tonight from 6:00–9:00. Then Tuesday, Wednesday, and Thursday we teach all morning and have to ration from 1:00–5:00 and 6:00–9:00. I'll be so glad when all this is over.

Saturday night I went to Bloomington to see the Indiana-Minnesota game with Virginia and Phil and Marilyn and some drip.[25] I saw so many kids I knew and had such a good time! Came back on the bus at 5:00 last night. I was disappointed about a sailor I met on the bus. I tried calling the Naval Training Station and they said there wasn't any such name as he gave me, so I must have gotten his name wrong.

I've got stacks of drawings to grade. Today it's so beautiful that I feel more like walking outdoors than anything else. Betty isn't back yet, as she went home especially to see Bill and he hasn't come home yet. He was in Officer's Training School at Fort Monmouth, New Jersey, and had pneumonia twice. He was in the hospital so long that they discharged him.

Will you send the ration book back so I can get shoes? Thanks for letting me know that Robert Walden had died at Guadalcanal. So terribly sad.

Lots of love,

Lucy

---

25   Phil—Virginia's boyfriend.

March 12, 1943

Dear Folks,

This last week has really been a busy one, and this weekend I could work straight through and still not be done with my work. I have about three hundred drawings on hand to be graded.

An article in today's *Herald* that says our school staff handed out 2,027 ration books last week! Whew—I can believe it! We were absolutely on the go every minute. Our first blackout drill was last night. I didn't have time to grade drawings last night as grading by candlelight would be too difficult. Lights out was 8:30. Are you having blackout drills at home?

Martha and I were out to Udena's Monday night, and she had a good meal for us. She thinks she and Paul will be sent back to Fort Monmouth very soon, although Leonard and Bealor will stay here until June.[26]

Martha is thrilled to death because today she's getting a diamond from Claude. He had an 18-day furlough and was here last weekend. Then he went home to see his folks and came back last night. Sunday he leaves for San Diego, and from there he'll go to Samoa. He and four other Marines are going to relieve men who have been there a long time. Martha and Claude almost got married, and then decided it was best not to. She got today off and Betty Patty taught in her place. Claude is a wonderful person.

Today at noon, I saw two WAACS over at Hook's Nook.[27] Their uniforms are so neat and becoming. I expect we'll see more of them this weekend. Hope we hear from Jonas soon and know where he's going to be sent.

Love,

Lucy

---

26   Paul served with the 83rd Infantry Division in Europe from June 1943–December 1945. While he was away, Udena went back to New Jersey to live with her parents.

27   WAACS—Women's Auxiliary Army Corps.

March 18, 1943

Dear Folks,

I was glad to hear about orders for Jonas, although I can't understand why he's pleased about being on a sub chaser. However, I suppose it's best to like whatever you're doing. Would that I could! Did he say what part of the ocean? I suppose he'll be on the Atlantic, since his address is New York City.

Onya and Monya LaTour left here yesterday, really kicked out by Miss Gibbs because she said no children were to live here—and Monya a senior in high school! They got a room on the west side of town. Monya's nice, but conceited, and rather a pest to bother you when you don't exactly want her around. She speaks French fluently because she lived in France for 18 months and attended school there.

Last night I went to Circle Meeting at the church. Hardly anyone came and the refreshments were one cup of cold tea and one very, very small cupcake. Also, they elected me to make a scrapbook about South America, as if I didn't have anything to do!

Went out to Udena's for dinner Saturday night and Leonard was there.[28] Afterwards we all went to the show and had a nice time. Bealor was married Saturday in New Jersey. He and Winnie will be here today. Udena is a swell cook and I ate there again Monday night and did I stuff myself!

Don't know just when I'll be home again. Next weekend we have to help at the grade school basketball tourney. Fun!

Love,

Lucy

---

28   This is the last time Lucy mentions Leonard. The nature of wartime dating made relationships transitory. Their relationship clearly was not important enough to continue during the remainder of the war, or Leonard may have died in battle.

March 26, 1943

Dear Folks,

I'm writing this at McKinley School at noon because it seems to be the only time I'll have to write to you today. I've been under such an emotional strain at home, it's a wonder I've been able to teach at all. Betty Patty accused me of telling some things about her that I absolutely know nothing about. I don't know who it came through, but at any rate, someone's doing me dirt. Then Betty Clark got so mad at Betty Patty about a number of things, especially noise, that she's moving out next week. I feel the only friend I have in that house is Martha, and it worries me crazy. I decided if Betty was so angry, I'd better move in that back room, the one the LaTours moved out of. When I asked Miss Gibbs, she said Betty Patty had asked to move two hours before I did. After Betty Clark leaves I'll move into her room, for it's nicer, although I'd rather move someplace else and find peace, quiet, and someone who trusts and respects me, but rooms are hard to find. The whole thing is silly and childish and I don't see why people have to act like that.

I went to the doctor at Shelbyville last Saturday. The doctor said I was so nervous that I'd have a breakdown if I didn't do something about it. When I told him about my job, he said it was too much of a strain for anyone with my nervous setup. He said I should have a job I could forget about at night. Then another doctor, who specializes in skin diseases, looked at my face, shoulders, chest, and back and said my rash was pretty bad and would scar me if it didn't clear up soon. So I have to have seven or eight ultraviolet treatments. I had the first one Saturday and even that one treatment helped. It's going to be frightfully expensive, but they inspired me to take care of myself so I am determined to get entirely well. As soon as I'm through the school year, I can begin to really get better and I'll be so glad. With open house coming up, life is jumping from one place to another, from one job to another. Tonight is the grade school basketball tournament, and I have to work and take tickets at the door.

I was so glad to hear more about Jonie. Am so glad Richard got to come home and wish I could've seen him. Got a letter from Sergeant David Compton in Texas who was happy to have been promoted. He sent me an anti-aircraft artillery insignia and it's so pretty. He's in the hospital now, with a bad throat caused by the dust storms. He said he thought he might get a furlough the last of April. Thanks for the checkbook, Daddy.

Love,

Lucy

CHAPTER THREE
THE NAVY CRUISER

May 7, 1943

Dear Mother & Daddy,

I managed to sit down on the bus this time all the way back! Thank goodness, as I was sure stuffed full of your wonderful Easter dinner, Mother! I thought sure the bus would be mobbed with people.

Betty Patty and I walked downtown after supper tonight to see the Navy "cruiser." I've never seen anything like it before, kind of a trailer with a large canopy that rolls out on one side. Girls were actually being sworn in right there under the canopy! Inside the cruiser, they were showing newsreels and had brochures about joining. We talked to a lieutenant who's been in the WAVES since they started and a couple of other WAVES answered our questions. They were all such lovely girls and looked so sharp in their uniforms. Maybe Jonas was right in December—the WAVES could be the best choice for me.

This past week the teachers in adjustment and Mr. Lind wanted me to finish grading their work and make out grades. As if I don't have enough to do. I tendered my resignation this morning. Principal Reece was not happy. He announced in the staff meeting today that the next ration book will be issued by mail. Thank goodness—no more rationing work for overworked teachers! Of course, I'll soon be out of the teaching business! Ahem! All for now.

Love,

Lucy

What happens when you join the Waves

1. First, go or write to the nearest Navy Recruiting Station or Office of Naval Officer Procurement for application blanks. Give the information required, and return papers to office of origin.

2. If your application papers are satisfactory, you'll receive free transportation to the nearest Office of Naval Officer Procurement. There you'll be interviewed and take the simple aptitude test.

3. Then comes a physical check-up by Navy doctors. Requirements are thorough but not too difficult. Any young woman in sound health should be able to pass the examination with flying colors.

4. It's a thrilling moment when you raise your right hand and are "sworn in." From then on you're in the service of Uncle Sam, ready to do a man-size job for your country!

— 12 —

From WAVES recruiting booklet Lucy picked up at the Navy "cruiser"
Courtesy of the United States Navy

5. Off for training school! The Navy takes care of all expenses. Transportation. Meals in the dining car. And you'll find comfortable quarters ready for you when you arrive.

6. Yes, it's really you! You'll feel proud — and rightly so — when you first see yourself in trim Navy blues. Complete outfit — $200 worth of clothing — is furnished you free as an enlisted WAVE.

7. Training schools are located at some of the country's finest colleges. Typing, radio operation, communications, mechanics are only some of the skills you may acquire.

8. At training school you'll follow an interesting schedule. Athletics, games, recreation with friendly companions are yours to enjoy in addition to the valuable training under expert Navy teachers.

9. And now — a full-fledged member of the service — you go on duty at one of the big Naval bases. You'll be in the thick of all that's exciting and important in America at war.

10. Yes, your salute will be recognized even by an Admiral. And you deserve recognition! For yours is a big job — a service to your country you will be proud of the rest of your life.

— 13 —

From WAVES recruiting booklet Lucy picked up at the Navy "cruiser"
Courtesy of the United States Navy

I'll Be Seeing You

Picture yourself in

It's a proud moment when you first step out in brand new Navy blues. The trim, smart uniform was especially designed to flatter every figure and make you look— and feel—your best.

When you arrive at recruit school as an enlisted WAVE, you will be provided with an allowance of $200 for uniforms and other clothing. The official uniform consists of "everything that shows," except shoes and gloves. The cost—about $180 —is paid from the $200 allowance. The balance of about $20 is given you for shoes, underclothing and anything else you may need.

After one year's service you will get $50 a year for clothing replacements.

The regular uniform for enlisted WAVES consists of the following articles:

Soft hat, rolled brim, black band.

Navy blue wool suit. Jacket has slightly built-up shoulders, rounded collar and pointed lapel. Flattering six-gored skirt.

*Summer white dress uniform, same design.

White and dark blue shirts.

Black and reserve blue seaman's ties.

Over-shoulder leather pouch bag.

Cool, gray-and-white, pin-striped seersucker work uniform for summer.

White gloves and black gloves.

Beige hose.

Black oxfords (heels not over 1½") or *pumps (heels not over 2").

Rain-proof havelock and raincoat.

*Overcoat.

Blue denim work coverall, slacks or reserve blue smock — for special jobs.

*Optional.

— 18 —

From WAVES recruiting booklet Lucy picked up at the Navy "cruiser"
Courtesy of the United States Navy

these smart Navy Uniforms

Light-weight whites for summer dress

Summer gray-and-white seersucker shirtwaist dress and jacket

Navy blue wool winter work uniform

Attractive raincoat and rainproof havelock

Blue work smock

— 19 —

From WAVES recruiting booklet Lucy picked up at the Navy "cruiser"
Courtesy of the United States Navy

Many Waves enjoy better incomes than they earned in civilian life

You enlist in the WAVES as an Apprentice Seaman at $50 a month. Not high by civilian standards. But remember, that $50 is just your beginning pay — it's only your base pay — and it's all yours, because all your living expenses are paid. You get good food, comfortable quarters, the finest medical and dental care, and $200 worth of clothing — all free. And in those cases where government food and quarters are not provided, you get the equivalent in cash allowances — $1.80 a day for food, $1.25 a day for quarters — an average of $92.42 a month. So your beginning base pay of $50 becomes $142.42. A pretty good starting salary in any job! And as you can see by the table below, you can increase that income to more than $230 a month.

"Extras" you are entitled to

Under the present income tax law, no enlisted WAVE is required to pay a tax on her Navy income, because of a special exemption granted to members of the armed forces. You can buy life insurance at low government rates. And, like any other member of the uniformed services, you will get the privileges of free mail, reduced rates on transportation, theatre tickets where granted, and you may benefit from USO, Red Cross, and Navy Relief.

The Navy wants you to become skilled in your job. You don't have to ask for promotion. If you are willing and able, you will be recommended for advancement.

HOW YOUR NAVY PAY GOES UP

RATE	Monthly Base Pay—Clear	Food Allowance*	Quarters Allowance*	Total Income
Apprentice Seaman . . .	.$ 50	$54.50	$37.92	$142.42
Seaman, Second Class . . .	54	54.50	37.92	146.42
Seaman, First Class	66	54.50	37.92	158.42
Petty Officer, Third Class . .	78	54.50	37.92	170.42
Petty Officer, Second Class .	96	54.50	37.92	188.42
Petty Officer, First Class . .	114	54.50	37.92	205.42
Chief Petty Officer, Acting Appointment . . .	126	54.50	37.92	218.42
Chief Petty Officer, Permanent Appointment .	138	54.50	37.92	230.42

* Or equivalent provided by Navy.

From WAVES recruiting booklet Lucy picked up at the Navy "cruiser"
Courtesy of the United States Navy

Your family will be proud of you
—your friends will look up to you

You couldn't ask for a bigger thrill than a girl gets when she comes back home on leave wearing her smart Navy uniform. Your friends crowd around. Your folks beam with pride. They all want to know where you've been, what you've done. And do you have stories to tell!

You're proud. And you should be! *You're* not sitting this war out on the sidelines. You're in it, helping to win it — and all your friends realize it.

Your parents are proud, too. The Navy receives hundreds of enthusiastic letters from mothers and fathers of Navy women. They speak in glowing terms of the splendid training their girls are getting in the WAVES and of the fine life they're leading. Here are some typical comments:

"I've never seen my daughter look or feel so well in her life. Her WAVES training has done wonders for her, and her Dad and I are mighty proud."—*Mrs. Douglas McGinnis, Stockton, Calif.*

"It is gratifying to realize that our daughter, Katherine is an officer in an organization that is playing a vital part in the restoration of world peace. We feel that her Naval training and experiences are enriching her life and will be invaluable to her in post-war times."—*Mr. and Mrs. W. Bruce Luna, Dallas, Texas.*

"We feel that aside from giving our daughter an opportunity to serve our country that the Navy is giving her a training and education that will be invaluable to her in later life."—*Mr. and Mrs. Fred C. Taylor, New Orleans, La.*

"Nathalie says she would not exchange her job for a million dollars in cash. Personally, I think it is a wonderful opportunity for any young woman and I am very pleased to know that Nathalie wanted to join and do her part."—*Mrs. Miriam H. Willey, Victoria, Virginia.*

"We're so glad that Peggy can still go to the same church she always has. As president of the Twin Cities WAVES Mothers Club, I know other parents feel the same way."—*Mrs. Louis F. Shaw, St. Paul, Minn.*

— 31 —

From WAVES recruiting booklet Lucy picked up at the Navy "cruiser"
Courtesy of the United States Navy

MOST WOMEN 20-36 CAN MEET THESE REQUIREMENTS

Check your qualifications for enlistment

TERM OF ENLISTMENT—You will enlist for the duration of the war and up to 6 months thereafter.

CITIZENSHIP—You must be a native-born American, or if you are not native-born, you or your parents must have naturalization papers. You must show written proof of citizenship when you apply.

AGE—On the date of enlistment, you must be at least 20 years old and not yet have reached your 36th birthday. If you are under 21, you must have the written consent of your parents or guardian.

MARRIAGE—A married woman may enlist in the WAVES, provided her husband is not in the Navy. You may not marry while you are at Recruit School. In special cases permission may be granted to marry during specialist's training. However, after this training is over there are no marriage restrictions whatever.

DEPENDENTS—Women with children under 18 will not be accepted in the WAVES.

CHARACTER—The Navy wants women of good character. When you enlist, you will be asked to furnish three references.

EDUCATION—You must have at least two years of high school or business school.

EXPERIENCE—You will be asked to submit a record of your occupation since leaving school.

PHYSICAL—You must be able to pass a physical examination to show you are in sound health.

HEIGHT—You must be at least 5 feet.

WEIGHT—Your weight must be in proportion to your general body build.

EYES—Eyes must be correctable with glasses to 20/20 vision.

HEARING—You must be able to distinguish whispered words at 15 feet.

TEETH—Natural teeth must be in sound condition, or you must have satisfactory replacements.

PRESENT EMPLOYMENT—Women employed by the Federal Government or in certain essential war industries, or who have voluntarily terminated such employment within 60 days, will not be accepted for the WAVES without a release from their employer or a certificate of availability from the U. S. Employment Service.

— 37 —

From WAVES recruiting booklet Lucy picked up at the Navy "cruiser"
Courtesy of the United States Navy

May 15, 1943

Dear Folks,

I just got back from the doctor in Shelbyville. I've hardly begun on the diplomas that must be done by Friday, but would rather write to you. I may have to get help on those diplomas, for it takes ages to do even one.

Mildred [Guthnecht] said she'd have enough gas to bring me home, so I guess you won't have to come. I just hope we can get all of my stuff in her car, for I certainly have scads. I'll probably come on Wednesday, the 26th, because it will take some time to get everything together.

Naomi Ney, a teacher at Wilson High School, met me at Edinburg and took me over to Shelbyville today. She lives at Mt. Auburn where Betty Patty taught school last year. She's really swell and is going to join the WAVES this summer. About eight people I know here are joining the WAVES or the Marines. I still want to join the Marines. I've read a great deal about it and talked to the recruiting officer, who says I'd have a good chance of getting in officer's training. He says your education is important, but special training isn't so much so because they figure out what you're best fitted for from your aptitude test and personal interview and train you the way they want to.

I got a letter from Richard and he said he'd be going home this weekend. Told me about amputating a leg, and it just about made me sick the way he told it. He says he'll be leaving Darnell soon and will be transferred to Ohio State for the ASTP program.[29] I didn't even know what that was until I asked our school librarian and she showed me an article in the

---

29   Richard had been receiving medical training at Darnell General Hospital in Danville, Kentucky, since January 30, 1943. Reclassified in May 1943, he was assigned to the Army Specialized Training Program (ASTP). The program sent over 200,000 soldiers to 227 colleges throughout the U.S., where they took accelerated courses in foreign languages, medicine, engineering, psychology, dentistry, physical education, and military studies. The program ended by April 1944, as these troops were needed as replacements in Europe and the South Pacific.

paper explaining it. So back to school for Richard—he's safe from the fighting for now.

Teaching is not worth the time spent on it with all the kids so excited about school getting out. My 8Bs are so dumb I can't tell what they know, so I made out a test and had it mimeographed over at the office. I'm giving it tomorrow to both the 8Bs and 7Bs to see which group does better. I think the 7Bs will, for that's the best class I've had all year.

Dave Compton says he will be sent across very soon and he's very glad because he's tired of training. Udena invited me over the other night to eat fried chicken and I was so busy I couldn't go.

I must get to work. Sorry I couldn't give you something for Mother's Day, but I'm pretty broke with medicines, going to Shelbyville, and a couple of birthdays.

Love,

Lucy

Miss Lucy Berkey, who taught the past year in the Columbus schools, has returned home. She was accompanied by Miss Mildred Guthnecht of Columbus, art supervisor, who remained for a few days' visit.

June 2, 1943
Courtesy of The Salem Leader

CHAPTER FOUR
AT HOME—SUMMER
OF 1943

On May 26, Lucy rode home to Salem with Mildred, as planned. There would be no more letters until Lucy left home again in the fall. She was still considering whether to enlist, and if she did, whether to join the Marine Corps or the WAVES. Lucy's miserable year of teaching made her reluctant to commit again too quickly. Perhaps her lack of experience and small stature had made classroom discipline a struggle, but there were larger factors at play, including low pay, heavy workload, and overfilled classes.

While Lucy was relieved to be rid of a job she hated, she couldn't help feeling like a failure. Her college boyfriend, Johnny Kooken,[30] had graduated ahead of her and enlisted in the Army, where he met another girl. If the U.S. had not gone to war, it's likely Lucy and Johnny would have married soon after Lucy graduated, like so many other young couples.

As young men enlisted or were drafted in the early 1940s, marriage rates soared. Couples married quickly in simple ceremonies, so they could be together before the young husband was sent abroad. Societal norms dictated that a wife's place was in the home, even if her husband of a few weeks was serving overseas and she had no children. Due to restrictive "marriage bar" laws enacted by three-quarters of U.S. school districts in the 1940s, married women could not be hired

---

30   By this time, Johnny was dating Martha Childress who he later married December 1943. She was a flying instructor in the aviation training program at Columbia, Tennessee. He was promoted to major in January 1944 while serving with the 708th Amphibious Tank Battalion in the Pacific. He was promoted to lieutenant colonel in January 1946 at 26 years of age. Highly decorated after two years of active duty in the Pacific, he was granted terminal leave in 1946 and went back to IU to attend law school.

to teach, and if a single teacher got married during the school year, she was to resign immediately.

The result was a severe teacher shortage, resulting in the enormous workloads and overfilled classes that made Lucy's job so difficult. Young, inexperienced teachers found they couldn't manage the heavy workload, low pay, and poor conditions. Like Lucy, many grew discouraged and resigned from teaching. When they spoke with recruiters, such as the one Lucy had visited aboard a Navy cruiser back in May, these women learned that they fit the requirements for wartime service.[31] They were young, educated, hard working, and not tied down with a husband or children.

After unloading her things from Mildred's car and settling into her childhood bedroom in Salem, Lucy had a few days to readjust before going to church, across the street, on May 30. When asked by churchgoers when she would go back to teaching, she probably changed the subject. Lucy's parents still had reservations about their daughter joining the military, and she wouldn't have discussed her future until her decision to enlist was definite.

In those weeks of early summer, as the days lengthened, Lucy helped her mother with housecleaning, meal preparation, laundry, making and repairing clothing, and gardening. Rationing limited available food, and anyone with the space was urged to plant a Victory Garden.[32] Having lived through the Depression, the Berkeys already had a large garden situated at "the farm," a mostly wooded piece of land with a creek, 11 miles southeast of Salem, a 30-minute drive from town down country roads. During gardening months, Lucy's father worked a half-day on Thursdays, came home for dinner (lunch), then drove them all down to the farm to do the necessary planting, weeding, and, as the season progressed, harvesting. By August, the women would be getting up early in the morning to preserve what

---

31 Married women were permitted to enlist, so long as they met the qualifications. See photo on page 34.
32 Many commercial crops were diverted to military use. Besides providing locally needed food, the Victory Garden campaign also served to boost morale, express patriotism, and ease the burden on commercial farmers.

they had harvested the day before. Canning in the summer humidity of southern Indiana was a not a comfortable task but was necessary if the family was to have food on the table during the winter months.

The Berkey family also complied with the government's request to citizens: "Don't waste anything; buy only what is necessary; salvage what you don't need; and, share what you have." In addition to rationing restrictions, this included conserving electricity, recycling any kind of metal, as well as recycling newspapers and paper cartons. Fat drained from cooking was even saved and recycled to make dynamite.

Some evenings, Lucy, her mother, and her sisters did volunteer work for the war effort by knitting bandages and garments for soldiers. A booklet published by the Red Cross called "Knitting Instructions for War Work" provided patterns for sweaters, socks, mufflers, fingerless gloves, toe covers, stump covers, and other clothing to be made with olive drab or navy blue yarn. Knitted bandages were 100% cotton and 15–20 feet long. Women and girls across the country supported the war by producing thousands of knitted items for the comfort and warmth of soldiers, while providing a needed distraction for themselves.

On June 12th, Lucy celebrated her 23rd birthday. She enjoyed social time with friends who were home for the summer, often congregating at the Sweet Shop in downtown Salem, owned and run by two of her father's sisters. Extremely popular and a great hangout for youth, the Sweet Shop made candy and had a modern ice cream plant and soda fountain, as well as an outdoor seating area called The Palm Garden. They bottled the first soft drinks in Salem in the basement of the store. Lucy occasionally worked there to help out her aunts when they were short on staff.

But through it all, the war was a constant presence. Lucy learned about soldiers who had been wounded, listened to stories from those who had returned, and lived in fear of hearing that someone she knew had died. When the town learned that one of their own boys had been lost, Lucy grieved along with the rest of the community. Three times a day the family gathered around the radio to hear the national news broadcast. Daily articles reported on the progress in the war in Europe, Africa, and the South Pacific. Newspapers ran articles about men who were drafted and where new enlistees and draftees were training. Even a night of escape at the movie theater was thwarted by the war newsreels preceding the feature film.

Controlled by the U.S. government, all war news had to go through the Office of War Information (OWI) before it was released to the public. The OWI felt that people on the home front would panic if they were given detailed accounts of the war. Nearly two years after Pearl Harbor, the American public would finally be shown the first image of a dead American serviceman. That photograph appeared in the September 20, 1943 issue of *LIFE* magazine. That first shocking image was only released because the OWI speculated that Americans had become complacent about the war. With the subsequent release of graphic images in newsreels and photographs, the true horror and cost of war became a daily fact of life to those on the home front. As a result, enlistment decreased and bond sales escalated.

During the summer of 1943, recruiting posters were located in the street level windows of stores, post offices, and government buildings across the nation, imploring young women to fill holes left by the men who had gone off to war. Recruiting slogans were emotional and patriotic:

The More Women at Work the Sooner We Win

Save His Life and Find Your Own

Enlist in a Proud Profession—Join the U.S. Cadet Nurse Corps

Your Duty Ashore…His Afloat

Share the Deeds of Victory—Join the WAVES

Don't Miss Your Great Opportunity—The Navy Needs You in the WAVES

He'll Be Home Sooner… Now You've Joined the WAVES

To Make Men Free—Enlist in the WAVES Today

I'd Rather Be With Them Than Waiting

Lucy would have seen these posters everywhere, urging her to serve. And these posters may well have influenced her parents, helping them to resolve any lingering unease.

WAVES posters were specifically designed to convince mothers, fathers, husbands, and brothers that serving in the Navy was respectable work for women. Posters showed an idealized version of what a woman could become. The propaganda appealed to women's emotions by suggesting it was their duty to enlist and that if they didn't help, soldiers would die. Again, the OWI was involved. With the same theme materials being distributed nationally to magazines, newspapers, and radio, the OWI used a coordinated appeal to market war work to women. Then they encouraged media outlets to report on women who had joined the military and women who had taken on traditional male jobs while men were away at war. By this time in Britain, women war workers received pay equal to a man's, but that was not the case in the United States. The American Women's Policy Committee of the War Manpower Commission estimated that, by the end of 1943, 5 million women would be needed to serve in war related industries.

Appeals to women through recruitment advertising used an emotional, patriotic approach and generally did not emphasize wages for fear of causing inflation. Instead of promoting economic gain, recruitment posters urged women to help out while their husbands, brothers, or fiancés were away at war. Policy makers did think ahead to what post war America would look like. All along, the recruitment of women made it clear that their war jobs would be temporary and that men would return to their customary roles after the war. Many women, especially single breadwinner mothers, worried that they would lose their jobs as men returned.

Other women believed that they would be perceived as masculine if they joined the military. The Navy extensively used media coverage in magazines and newspapers to assure women that competence and professionalism could exist side by side with beauty and femininity. Short newsreels preceding feature films also promoted this aspect of women in the military, featuring glamorous members of the women's services. During the first three years of the war, Hollywood produced 1,313 feature films. Of those films, 374 were war related and many had idealized female characters.

Fear was another powerful tactic used to recruit women. The following statement appears in the opening section of *Prepare for the Official Tests for WAACS, WAVES, SPARS and Marines—A Complete Guide and Instruction Book for Women in Military Service*: "Every American woman knows that in the horrible plan of our Asia enemies, women will be relegated to a secondary place in the life of a nation, to domestic slavery, and denied the privileges of education and suffrage which every American woman considers her natural heritage." Many American women already felt that way about their own country.

Labor saving devices such as dishwashers, freezers, and automatic washers and dryers did not exist during the war years. Housework took most of a woman's time during the day. Food was cooked from scratch, laundry was put through a ringer, hung out to dry then ironed, and women were expected to care for their own children. Women who did go out to work were still expected to manage housework and childcare.

Surely the urgent voice of the recruitment call was ever present in Lucy's mind that summer. June slipped into July, and Lucy's brother, Richard, came home on leave from the ASTP program in Cincinnati July 10th–12th. Their youngest brother, David, would leave on July 14th for Navy training at Great Lakes Naval Training Station.[33] David had graduated from high school just a month earlier, knowing he would soon be drafted into the Army. Rather than wait for the draft, he chose instead to enlist in the Navy, as his eldest brother Jonas had. David would train as a radio operator. And it wasn't just the boys of the family who would serve. Their sister Virginia planned to join the Cadet Nurse Corps when she graduated from college. Although the idea of women serving in the military was gaining acceptance,

---

33   A thousand miles from the nearest ocean, Great Lakes Naval Training Station is located in North Chicago, Illinois. This facility supplied around a million soldiers during World War II.

most women who worked served in "acceptable" professions, such as teacher, secretary, or nurse. Lucy's desire to use her artistic gifts put her outside these expected roles, and her desire to enlist also pushed against prevailing attitudes of her time. Many Americans still believed that women should not be recruited to the military unless a dire need arose. Others were concerned that women's safety or virtue would be compromised.

When the Women's Army Auxiliary Corps (WAAC) first began recruiting enlistees in 1942, lots of rumors spread about the "type of woman" that would join the Army. Embracing the kind of abrupt societal change that included women in the workplace, specifically the military, was difficult for the majority of Americans. Rumors led to bad reputations and the military struggled to turn around public perception. Damon Runyon's editorial in the Louisville Courier Journal on June 23, 1943, refers to these rumors.

> I think the utterance or circulation of slanderous rumors about the WAAC, WAVES, WAFS or any other women's service corps should be deemed as much a crime against morale as unfounded and discreditable tales about our soldiers and sailors. I have heard both men and women civilians tell villainous stories they professed to have heard from others reflecting upon the members of the service corps. If a lady wishes to be unchaste why the hell should she want to don a uniform that detracts from her attractions, and work and drill and sweat and slave all day long, and cut herself off from theaters and other amusements and from the pleasures of civil life? And all for fifty slugs per month? Does that make sense?

To stave off possible rumors, those responsible for generating WAVES recruitment materials decided to present the image of an elite Navy that was better than other branches of the service. Recruiting offices were located in the better parts of town and parents were assured that their daughters would have constant supervision, training for a good career, fine housing, and moral and religious guidance. The Navy, wishing to avoid the same kind of bad press received by

WAACs, designed an enlistment process in which a woman had to first write a letter of intent to the local recruiting office. If she looked like a promising recruit, she was sent an application form and an appointment time.

Summer was nearly half over, and still Lucy had not made her enlistment decision. Having already spoken with a Navy representative on the cruiser, Lucy now paid a visit to a Marines recruiter. There she learned that most of the Marine Corps jobs designated for women were clerical. When she mentioned her poor typing and said she'd like really like to use her art skills, the recruiter suggested she consider joining the Navy, where roles for women were expanding. The question Lucy had been asking herself all summer was finally answered. Lucy would apply to the WAVES.

She submitted her letter of intent the following week and received a reply later that month letting her know that her application was satisfactory. The letter contained an official application form and an appointment time on August 16th at the Office of Naval Procurement in Cincinnati, Ohio. She was advised to obtain a copy of the book, *Prepare for the Official Tests for WAACS, WAVES, SPARS and Marines—A Complete Guide and Instruction Book for Women in Military Service.*

Lucy read the book carefully, knowing that despite the message of the recruitment posters, women serving in the military were not always seen as noble. Prejudice abounded regarding women taking over "men's jobs." Soldiers who had safe jobs in the United States resented being placed in the infantry while women took their jobs. The paradox was that women were recruited to help save soldier's lives, but in reality many of these men went to the front and died. Reaction by servicemen, in general, was very negative toward women in the service and many women experienced condescension, teasing, or harassment while in uniform. A 1943 defamation campaign consisting of cartoons, dirty jokes, obscenities, and the suggestion that servicewomen were deviants nearly derailed recruiting efforts. Men questioned whether women were smart enough or physically strong enough to do certain jobs. There was tremendous resistance to women scientists serving in war industries, women physicians were barred from the Army Medical Corps, and black women were initially prohibited from entering the WAVES.[34] However, they were desperately needed and they were wanted for their minds and their skills.

Other Americans were upset when they were displaced from their homes due to the urgent need for housing near training centers. In the Bronx alone, the United States government took over 17 apartment buildings to house WAVES training at nearby Hunter College.[35]

Despite major resistance, women became a part of the military, worked in war industries, and replaced men in virtually every profession during the war. Congress approved the Women's Army Corps, WAACS, in May 1942. The Women's Flying Training Detachment, WFTD, and the Women's Auxiliary Ferrying Squadron, WAFS, were created in September 1942 and merged in August 1943 to form the Women's Air Force Service Pilots, WASPS. The Women's Reserve of the Coast Guard, SPARS[36], came into being in November 1942, the Women's Navy Reserve, WAVES, in June 1942 and the Marine Corps Women's Reserve in February 1943. July 30, 1943, marked the first anniversary of the formation of the WAVES with 27,000 enlisted women already serving. Lucy would soon become one of them.

---

34   Black women were finally allowed into the WAVES on October 19, 1944. New York City councilman Adam Clayton Powell Jr. had sponsored a successful resolution to end racial discrimination in the Hunter College buildings and other training facilities in the area. WAVES director Mildred McAfee and Dr. Mary McLeod Bethune helped Secretary of the Navy Forrestal push through the admittance of black women.

35   In February 1943, The U.S. government selected 281 colleges across the U.S. that were suitable for training of soldiers and women in the reserves of each branch of service. These colleges were in addition to the 600 non-federal training locations already in use. Hunter College, where Lucy trained, was authorized as a boot camp for the Navy on December 30, 1942. Located in a major city, with access to two subway lines, Hunter was considered an ideal location. As a commuter college, its main drawback was the lack of dormitories.

36   SPARS—a contraction of the Coast Guard motto, *Semper Paratus*—Always Ready.

On August 16, 1943, Lucy travelled to Cincinnati for her appointment at the Naval Procurement Office there. She submitted her application, three letters of recommendation, and a certified transcript of her college record. She was given a physical exam and aptitude tests. Her enlistment application states that she was 5'2½" tall, 102 pounds, with brown hair. Her enlistment physical shows a medical history of measles, mumps, chicken pox, whooping cough, and an appendectomy at the age five. She was deemed "physically qualified for enlistment in the United States Navy Reserves, Class V-10" and was sworn into the WAVES. She signed an application affidavit stating she was unmarried, had no children, would not marry before training was completed, did not draw a government pension, and would be available for active duty when called.[37] Lucy enlisted as an apprentice seaman earning $50 per month, the same as a man. She was advised that anyone entering the WAVES was a member of the Navy first, and a woman second. "Remember to be a lady, forget you are a woman," was one of the first pieces of advice given to a new WAVE. When Lucy enlisted she swore the following oath: "I oblige and subject myself to serve during the present war and for six months thereafter, or until such earlier time as the Congress by concurrent resolution or the President by proclamation may designate." The recruiter made it clear to Lucy that joining the WAVES was a privilege, not a career. She was asked to report on September 9, 1943, to the United States

---

37   Women who joined the WAVES had to be between 20 and 36 years old, submit three references, have a high school diploma, pass a physical, be at least five feet tall, and weigh at least 95 pounds. Women over 36 were only eligible for service when their qualifications were of specific value to the Navy. They enlisted for the duration of the war plus six months. Many women joined to help the war effort, others joined because they were widows, fiancées, or sisters of men who had been killed, and many were daughters of Navy men. Others enlisted because military work appeared easier than the drudgery of war work in shipbuilding and defense plants. At first, WAVES assignments were limited by law to the continental U.S. In 1945, WAVES were finally allowed to serve in Alaska, Hawaii, the West Indies, and Panama.

Naval Training School at Hunter College in The Bronx, New York.[38]

For many women, joining the military was an odd sort of freedom. They traded "just waiting" and the toils of home life for the regimented life of the service. But, it was service with other women. These military women would later reflect that their unique camaraderie during the war years would not be duplicated during the rest of their lives. For many young women from rural areas enlisting was a way to travel, to see big cities, and to experience a life that would not have been available any other way. These women had a myriad of emotions as they headed to training stations—apprehension, relief, excitement, pride, and determination coupled with homesickness.

The few weeks Lucy had remaining at home were spent preparing to go and learning more about the WAVES. She was given a list of what she could bring to training. She was to keep her luggage to a minimum and sew name labels on her clothing. Allowed items on the list were simple dresses or skirts, sweaters, winter coat, raincoat, boots, lisle or wool stockings, underwear, a gabardine rain hat, gloves, scarf, slacks, pajamas, robe, flashlight, and a mending kit. Travel to training was paid for by the Navy. Lucy departed Salem on the 9:32 a.m. train on September 8, 1943.

---

38   85,885 WAVES trained at Hunter College, now Lehman College, from February 1943 through August 1945. 80,936 of them graduated from boot camp and went on to their assignments. Every two weeks, a new group of 2,000 women would come in for a six-week training course. Lucy's boot camp was only four weeks long due to the dire need for personnel during September 1943.

APPLICATION AFFIDAVIT
(WAVES)

August 16, 1943
_____
Date

Lucy Marian BERKEY 768581, A.S., V-10 USNR, hereby swear the following statements to be true, and I understand that should any of my statements in connection with my application be established to be false, I may be discharged from the United States Naval Reserve without recourse on my part:

1. (a) I am (not) married.
      My husband is not serving as either an officer or enlisted man in the United States Navy.
      I have no children under eighteen (18) years of age.

   (b) I agree not to marry after the date required to report at a training school and prior to the completion of any other indoctrination or special instruction courses to which I might be assigned.

2. I am not drawing, nor have I a claim pending for, a pension, disability compensation, or retired pay from the Government of the United States.

3. I will be available for active duty when called, and I understand that the Bureau of Naval Personnel shall in no way be obligated to place me on active duty.

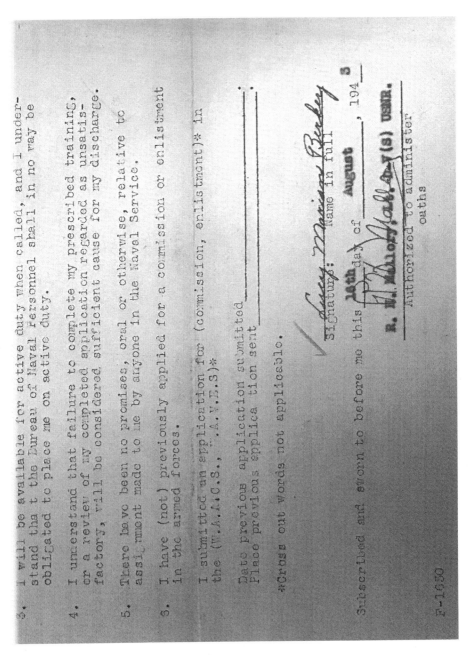

3. I will be available for active duty when called, and I understand that the Bureau of Naval Personnel shall in no way be obligated to place me on active duty.

4. I understand that failure to complete my prescribed training, or a review of my completed application regarded as unsatisfactory, will be considered sufficient cause for my discharge.

5. There have been no promises, oral or otherwise, relative to assignment made to me by anyone in the Naval Service.

6. I have (not) previously applied for a commission or enlistment in the armed forces.

I submitted an application for (commission, enlistment)* in the (W.A.A.C.S., W.A.V.E.S)*

Date previous application submitted _____
Place previous application sent _____

*Cross out words not applicable.

Signature: _Lucy Maria Berky_ Name in full

Subscribed and sworn to before me this 10th day of _August_, 194_3_

R. W. Khopffallavy(S) USNR.
Authorized to administer oaths

F-1650

Courtesy of the National Archives

MISS LUCY BERKEY

Another Salem girl has taken the oath of allegiance for the Navy's WAVES according to information from the U. S. Navy Recruiting Station, Salem.

The new WAVE is Miss Lucy Marian Berkey, daughter of Mr. and Mrs. James G. Berkey, 306 E. Walnut St., Salem, Ind., who was enlisted in the WAVES August 16. Miss Berkey at home on inactive duty, will report to Hunter College, New York City in the near future for her recruit training.

Miss Berkey is a graduate of Indiana University and was employed last year in the Columbus, Indiana public schools as assistant art supervisor. She has three brothers in the service: Jonas, who is an Ensign in the Navy; Richard in the Army Engineering School at Cincinnati, Ohio; and David in the Navy, Great Lakes, Illinois.

August 25, 1943
Courtesy of The Salem Leader

Enlists in WAVES

SALEM, Ind., Sept. 25 (Spl.)—Miss Lucy M. Berkey, who left Saturday to begin her training as a member of the WAVES at Hunter College, New York, is the daughter of Attorney and Mrs. James G. Berkey.

Miss Berkey has three brothers in the armed services, Ensign Jonas M. Berkey, on sub-chaser duty with a San Francisco postoffice address; Private Richard J. Berkey, enrolled in specialized training at the University of Cincinnati and Apprentice Seaman David B. Berkey, United States naval training station, Great Lakes, Ill.

A graduate of Salem High School in 1938, Miss Berkey attended Indiana University, graduating in 1942, where she was one of four Berkey children to be enrolled at the same time. She taught art in the Columbus schools in 1942-43.

September 25, 1943—Unknown newspaper

I'll Be Seeing You

CHAPTER FIVE
BOOT CAMP

September 10, 1943

Dear Folks,

Rather a long, tiresome train ride, but I finally arrived. Met Ruth on the train, and was I glad. Got to see quite a bit of New York City on the bus from Jersey City to New York subway. The subway ride was noisy, but interesting! Ruth and I are both on the fifth floor, but in different rooms (or *billets*, as the Navy calls them). There are three other girls in my room. They are all from Texas. I have an upper bunk, but it isn't bad. We've had drill, and are being stuffed with information. We all have real trouble making our beds neat and tight—hospital corners! Shoe fittings are this afternoon. I'm sure it will be a wonderful time.

Love,

Lucy

NAVAL TRAINING SCHOOL (W.R.)
BRONX, NEW YORK, N. Y.

September 9, 1943
(Date)

PLEASE ADDRESS MAIL FOR:

Lucy   *Marian*   *Berkey*   A.S.
(First Name)   (Middle Name)   (Last Name)   (Rank or Rating)
(Print or Write Legibly)

REGIMENT # *14*   BUILDING # *M*   APARTMENT # *5 2*

NAVAL TRAINING SCHOOL (W.R.), BRONX, NEW YORK

It is essential that she be addressed by her FULL NAME, RANK or RATING, and UNIT as above. Addressing her only with her initials and merely "U. S. NAVAL TRAINING SCHOOL (W.R.)" is not sufficient. There may be other women on the Station with the same name and initials.

NRB—35667—4-19-43—50M.

COMMANDING OFFICER

September 12, 1943

Dear Mother & Daddy,

It's only Sunday, and yet I feel as if it's been years since I came here! As far as feeling as if I were in New York—well, I might as well be in Africa! The subway close by clanks along every so often, but otherwise we seem to be removed from the city. Our building is not on the campus proper, but is about four blocks away.[39] I can see the campus from my window. It's very beautiful. We march near the mess hall building three times a day. The sick bay is in the gym building. Next to it is the Ship's Store, where everyone wants to go because there is a soda fountain there. Yesterday was my first day to have a Coke there, and boy, did it taste good! Sounds silly, but it seems as if we've been here weeks instead of days.

I about died waiting to board the train in Mitchell and finally ate at a Bluebird Restaurant.[40] Finally the train came and I got on. The conductor was able to get me an upper berth, so I was in the Pullman car. When I went in and sat in the club car for a while, I really felt funny because there were so many rich people. I sat down by an Army captain who was slightly crippled. Beside him there was a major. At 7:00 p.m. I went into the dining car and found Ruth. The train jiggled around so much I could hardly eat, but it was fun.

Ruth and I talked until 9:30 then went to bed. An experienced lady traveler told me it'd be much easier to dress in the lady's room instead of the berth, so I followed her advice. The berth wasn't bad, since I'm small. However, about 10:00 I became sick as a dog and called the porter with his ladder. I rushed to the rest room and threw up all

---

39   Lucy was assigned to Regiment 14, Building M, Apartment 5J. Her apartment, on University Avenue, was in one of the 17 apartment buildings taken over for housing by the government via the Second War Powers Act. A total of 1,860 people were displaced. Early in February 1943, apartments were quickly converted to house WAVES and SPARS. Walls were painted eggshell white, furniture was taken from passenger liners, bedspreads were taken off the U.S. Lines, and linens were new.

40   Lucy switched trains in Mitchell, Indiana—30 miles from her hometown of Salem.

over the place. Went back to my berth, and before I could ring for the porter, I drenched my sheets! He called the train nurse and she came and gave me a medicine especially for train sickness. It only made me worse and I vomited about 10 times. Hot water and soda helped some, and by 11:30 the nurse said she thought I could go back to bed. The train was one of the nicest around, just beautiful inside, but boy did it go fast! It rolled and rolled, but I finally slept a little bit. Since they couldn't get me a berth on the cars going to New York, they put me on the Washington car. I had to get up at 6:30 a.m. and change cars for the train that was going to Washington. In Washington, the nurse had me walk up and down the platform since I'd gotten sick again. My biggest disappointment of the whole trip was not being able to see any of Washington but a train station! I started vomiting again and continued until a few hours out of New York. The nurse got off at Washington, so poor Ruth rushed around getting the porter to get me medicine. I took Bromo-Seltzer first and it came up, then Alka-Seltzer and it came up. I finally decided I had been poisoned by that lousy food in Mitchell. I'd had a plate lunch—wieners that were cooked to death, cottage cheese half spoiled, a roll that had a bluish mold on it, a few syrupy pears, and half spoiled milk. It's no wonder I got sick. Besides, I shouldn't have eaten so much on the train.

We arrived in Jersey City about 1:30 Thursday afternoon, and took the bus from Jersey City to the subway. Ruth and I both thought the subway hard on the ears, but a nice way to go for a nickel. We came straight from the subway across the street to the Armory. There were hundreds of girls going through lines to tables, just like college. We had to turn in unused meal tickets and be assigned to buildings, etc. Also, we were issued two pairs of lisle hose and a blue hat with a blue crown. This hat is worn until we graduate. We have to have it on at all times, except when indoors and at ease. The worst thing of all was carrying our suitcases three blocks to our building, and uphill at that! I was so tired I could hardly stagger, but I finally made it. Of course, I'm on the fifth floor! Steps really wear you out around here. I have discovered that there is a sixth floor and an attic, so I feel better.

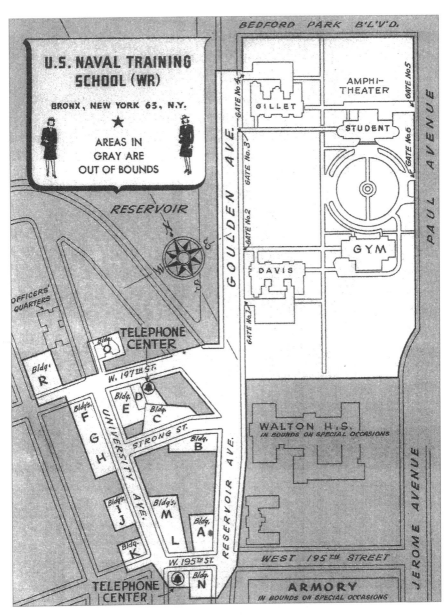

Map of Hunter College WAVES Training School
Courtesy of the U.S. Navy

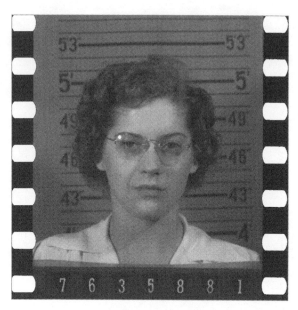

Lucy's induction photo
Courtesy of the National Archives

Today at noon mess I met a girl from East Chicago who lives on the sixth floor and she's wonderful. Plays the trumpet and is a laboratory technician. She went with a guy from the IU swimming team for six years. A girl from Indianapolis is down the hall.

We were shown how to make beds and put away our gear, first thing. They mustered in our section, about 40 girls, and we were shown simple drill rules, which got everybody thoroughly confused. Then we marched to mess where I fell over a board and dropped my tray! Anyway, the day ended somehow.

We were issued gym shoes to keep and GIs. They didn't have my size in, so it'll be several days before I receive my clodhoppers. Truly, though, I'm lucky, because now I'll get the worst over before my feet hurt. Sally Ball, who has the bunk below me, has a sore on the side of her foot. So far, even with all the marching, my feet haven't hurt one bit! Only the muscles in my legs surely are sore. Wow!

We're all green as grass, and do so many things wrong. Today we've been in suspense all day because our room hasn't been inspected. Three times we mopped the floor and dusted and scrubbed the bathroom floor. Now I believe the ensign won't even come, and our bunks look the nicest they've ever looked. The first day we had the nicest apartment in our section. Those hospital corners really are hard. Yesterday, the ensign wrote that our bunks looked beautiful!

The very first day of marching, Friday, Ensign Wilson picked me out of our section to be right guide—said I'd kept a good cadence. However, it's a hard job because you have to set the pace for the whole bunch. The next day, a new guide started because everyone has to do it, and I was glad. It's quite a responsibility and I'm not good enough for that yet. One thing that none of us like is this—if a girl faints when marching, the girl behind is supposed to catch her, lie her down on the ground, and keep marching or standing at attention, depending on what we're doing. We all think that's just not right, but it is expected of us. Thank goodness no one has fainted so far!

Outside of mess, drill, two meetings—one about recreation and the other a song fest—and a general company meeting, we've done little but hear about demerits. It seems as if every minute is full—yet we have time off now and then. All in all, this so far has been a strain because of the trip, the hurry, and the new things to learn; however, I'm liking it more and more as we go along. I believe by the time we leave, after six weeks, we'll all love being WAVES. They certainly make us realize *why* we're here. There are such wonderful girls here. Zonia Tucker is one of the other girls in my room—she's so fine and so much fun.

I'm so sorry I won't get to see David when he's home on leave. So far, I've no idea about a furlough. I sure miss all of you! "Now be good, and eat your beans," as Toby used to say. Write when you can and tell me all the Salem news.

Much love,

Lucy

P.S. We had church outdoors this morning and it was so nice!

U. S. NAVAL TRAINING SCHOOL (W. R.) BRONX, N. Y.   HC 1

Rock Garden, U. S. NAVAL TRAINING SCHOOL (W. R.) BRONX, N. Y.   HC 4

Postcards of Hunter College collected by Lucy

Outdoor church service at Hunter College
Courtesy of the National Archives

September 18, 1943

Dear Mother & Daddy,

Two days ago, I received your letter dated September 13, so of course today's news about David coming home was old. Anyway, no matter how old news is, it's *wonderful!*

Martha Ellis wrote me from Rockville because Columbus High School isn't starting until September 20 because of the farm kids being so necessary. She says Naomi Ney is going to teach after all, but she had planned on going into the WAVES. She was worrying about Claude since he'd written that they'd been bombed frequently. She was happy about his promotion to first lieutenant.

The reason I'm writing at last is because we have a free afternoon for once. Only on Saturday afternoon and Sunday do we have station liberty when we can go away from the building by ourselves or in twos to the Ship's Store, to Student Hall for recreation or to visit one of the other buildings.[41] Other times, if we have free time at all, we must log out and go in groups of five. They're terribly strict and you get demerits for even one little thing wrong. If we leave money "floating" around—that's 5 demerits. So we bought moneybags to hang around our necks and keep our money on us at all times. If we get any demerits and have to work them off on our weekend in New York, which is the last weekend before we leave, we can't go. I'm holding my breath and hoping I don't lose my chance to see New York.[42]

So many things have happened since I last wrote, I hardly know where to begin. Last Monday we were fitted for our uniforms, summer and winter. Tomorrow we have a second fitting and on Thursday we go into uniform.[43] I'll really be glad because the weather is so crazy here you never know what's going to happen. Besides, we never have time to wash our clothes out, and mine are filthy. My raincoat has food all over it from those trays at the mess hall. We march in, grab an enormous tablespoon (no teaspoons allowed!), knife and fork, and a regulation metal tray with compartments. We pick up an enormously thick cup

41   There were two "Ship's Stores" set up by six department stores—Saks Fifth Avenue, Abraham & Straus, Bloomingdale's, Loeser's, Wanamaker's, and Macy's. Each shop was operated by a different store for a week at a time. Originally stocked with low-cost items due to the salary of WAVES & SPARS, retailers soon discovered that the trainees preferred more expensive items. As the women had no liberty for the first three weeks of training, any needed items had to be purchased at the "Ship's Stores."

42   The women were not allowed to leave the "USS Hunter" until a short one-day leave to see New York City on their final weekend. They were also not allowed to read newspapers, listen to the radio, or have visits from family or friends except at prescheduled times.

43   The WAVES uniforms had been designed by Mainbocher, an American from Chicago who had opened a fashion house in Paris in 1929. The uniform consisted of a soft-crowned hat with rolled brim and black band, navy blue jacket with rounded collar and blue and white insignia, six-gored skirt, reserve blue and dark blue shirts, black seaman's tie, over the shoulder leather purse, white gloves in summer, black gloves in winter, beige lisle hose, and black oxford shoes with heels no higher than 1½ inches. As umbrellas were not allowed, the hat could be covered with a havelock that protected the head, neck, and shoulders from the elements. Summer and winter versions were available. Women were allotted $200 to acquire uniforms initially with stipends of $50 annually for replacements.

without a handle and pass along a line where food is dumped into several compartments. Sometimes the food is good and sometimes it's pretty punk. There are so many thousands of girls here it's amazing how they feed them at all.[44] I'll be here only four weeks instead of six. Every two weeks a new regiment comes in.

This week we signed up for insurance and had gym three times—general, volleyball, exercises, etc. I wanted swimming, but very few could be accommodated. We've had two lectures a day on learning Navy ratings, health talks, and lectures on diseases. We had an orientation selection talk, selection interview, movies on prelude to war, movies showing saluting and life aboard ship, several company meetings, drill once a day, and yesterday our medicals.[45] On Monday evenings we have a variety show called "Happy Hours" at the nearby high school and Friday evenings there are Captain's Concerts there, too.[46]

The medical was extensive, but not bad. We had a vaccination for small pox on the left arm, a tetanus shot also on the left, and a typhoid shot on the right arm all at the same time. Last night two girls in our section fainted and many were sick. I have awfully sore arms, but I don't feel badly. They haven't informed me otherwise, so I guess I passed okay. However, I've lost eight pounds. Yet that may not be bad. I weighed 100 pounds yesterday and my eyes were 4/20 in each eye without glasses. One lieutenant doctor told me I had good posture! The doctor who took our blood for the Wasserman was really handsome!

---

44   With five seatings and two hours allotted for each meal, 5,000 women were fed three times a day. Each regiment had approximately 17 minutes to eat a meal. The supply officer at Hunter estimated that he could feed 25 men in one minute, but doubted whether women could eat that quickly.

45   The 36 hours of WAVES classroom instruction included courtesy, law, records, chain of command, recognition of officers and enlisted in all branches of service, Navy equipment, ships and planes, communication, traditions and customs, and security. Another five hours were devoted to war orientation, ten hours to training films, and two hours of orientation to special devices such as the Link Trainer.

46   During training, WAVES were treated to shows by many top performers of the day. Entertainment was also provided by a dance orchestra, a military band, and the Singing Platoon. Various WAVES radio broadcasts originated from the campus and were an effective recruitment tool.

Today we witnessed a Regimental Review of the 12th Regiment. It was very short, but very impressive. All of our company stood there and wondered if we'd ever be that good in drill. For me, drill isn't very interesting so far—probably because I'm so clumsy. All of the girls who've been here three weeks tell us we'll like it after the worst is over. At 11:00 today we had Captain's Inspection, and did we ever work. We nearly went crazy cleaning up! Every speck of dust had to be *incognito!* We even scrubbed one wall that looked fingerprinty. Our gear had to be laid out on our bunks in regulation order. Contrary to what I'd thought, we don't have to scrub our floors, but we wipe them with damp rags to keep down dust. We *do* scrub the walls and everything in the head (bathroom) and galley (kitchen).

The lieutenant who came this morning swiped his glove over the venetian blinds and the top of the locker. He didn't say a word. He looked us over as we stood at attention to see if our hair was short enough and our shoes were shined. The hardest thing is to *not* look at them when they ask you a question, but look straight ahead at a spot on the wall! We have inspection every day and so far we've done very well, even getting Shipshape and Seamanlike one day, which is the best you can get. Ensign Wilson inspects our rooms during the week and she's the sweetest person here. I don't care much for our specialist who drills us—she seems bored. However, she's good in her work.

About our selection interviews yesterday: First, we took quite a few tests—general, teaching opinions, mechanical, arithmetic (ugh!), reading, etc. Then yesterday, different people interviewed us concerning jobs. Lieutenant Kincaid interviewed me, and I was lucky to get her. She was the second WAVE, Miss McAfee being the first.[47] Her personality is outstanding—she's very businesslike and yet very sweet, too. She feels very confident that I will get some sort of artwork. However, there are very few girls who are sent out in art, for most of it is confidential stuff. At first she said there was one *new* job that was to be filled concerning intricate diagrams. She took me in to see a big shot lieutenant, who

---

47   Mildred McAfee, president of Wellesley College since 1936, was recruited in August 1942 to become the director of the newly established WAVES.

was as gruff as gruff can be, and was I scared! He decided I hadn't had enough art school (commercial mainly) experience and besides, my eyes weren't strong enough to take the job. I really don't want it because I wouldn't be fitted. I'm afraid my type of artwork isn't what they need. If I do get in art, I'll be sent out on a direct assignment. Where, I don't know. If I don't get in art, no telling where I'll be sent—maybe on a general assignment. Time will tell. They say it would help my recommendation to report to Student Hall every Tuesday and Wednesday to help make posters, etc., for they're swamped with work. If the head people there like my work they will recommend me to the selection board. Most of the time we have is filled and those are free nights (usually!) to wash, iron, clean up, and study, so I hate giving them up. But, I'm going over if it'll help me get a good assignment. No matter what, Lieutenant Kincaid will help me get something I'm interested in. The yeoman who was there also was so sweet and said her sister was in Storekeepers School at Bloomington and liked it fine. According to my tests, I'm punk in math—ha, ha, ha!—and have little mechanical ability. Most of our regiment will go to Yeoman, Storekeeper, and Link Trainer schools.[48] A large number will be in the Hospital Corps. There are no schools for artists! You must have previous training. I'm sorry, because I'd feel more fitted for a job if I had training.

I feel terribly bad because I didn't get to come see David when he was home. He's probably leaving today. Radio school sounds good and I'm glad he's in that kind of work. Today I had my first confection, a sundae, at the Boot Shop in Ship's Store. That store has everything! Also had heel caps put on my shoes, since my size in GIs hasn't come in yet. You can also buy luggage at the store that's WAVE type and very nice. I'm considering it.[49]

---

48   The Link Trainer was a flight simulator used for learning navigation.
49   The Ship's Store area included a shop that carried over one thousand items from necessities to luxuries. Other services included a beauty shop, shoe shine area, cobbler shop, photo studio, film developing service, dry cleaning and laundry service, a small bank for cashing checks and purchasing travelers checks, three canteens, and the "Betty Boot Smokehouse."

By the way, Daddy, I was glad to get your letter on Tuesday. Yesterday my social security card came. I do wish my nametags would come! Tell me where David goes, so I can write him. How does Eleanor like high school? I have a million things to do! We have a tough schedule, but I like it. Of course, all of us will be glad when boot's over.[50]

Much love,

Lucy

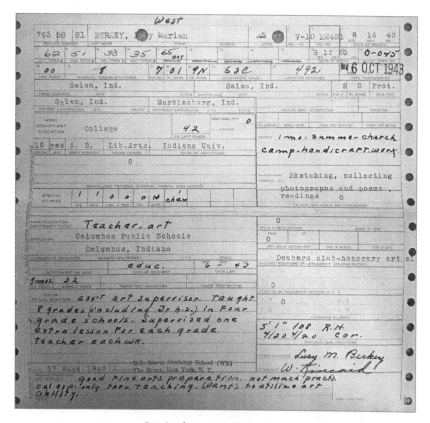

Lucy's selection interview form
Courtesy of the National Archives

---

50   The typical daily schedule ran from 5:30 a.m. to 9:30 p.m. with marching taking up two hours each day.

A Boot's Eye-view

U. S. NAVAL TRAINING SCHOOL (WR) NEW YORK, N. Y.

 WAVES

Courtesy of the United States Navy

WELCOME ABOARD THE U.S.S. HUNTER

...WHERE buildings stand in patriotic splendour!

...WHERE by threes you march in marked precision and amid laughter and chatter take all you can eat and eat all you take!

...WHERE, through supervised drill, your tottering walk becomes a firm, determined step and forty steps sound as one!

...WHERE your heart pulsates with action as you don perfection-fit Navy blues and take your place in the fight for freedom!

...WHERE learned officers bring forth a world of military knowledge in exciting, understandable manner!

...WHERE you relax and enjoy planned recreation in the genial atmosphere of great artists.

...WHERE physical education brings firm beauty to your figure!

...WHERE specialists in personnel selection give you the assurance that you are the most important person in the world and aid you in choosing the job you like best and can do best for the NAVY!

...WHERE, on Sunday, regardless of your faith, you may worship God according to the dictates of your own conscience!

...WHERE at bargain prices you may shop to your heart's content for trinkets for those you love and buy necessities for yourself.

...WHERE you stand amazed as you review a great white wave — two thousand feet beating down in unison and two thousand white-gloved hands swinging in rhythmic motion as the band plays on!

...WHERE station and shore liberty are given for your personal pleasure and enjoyment to do as you please.

...WHERE movies and models of planes and ships, graphs, pamphlets, and booklets show you the way of the NAVY!

THIS IS THE U.S.S. HUNTER
WHERE YOU LIVE . . . WORK . . . AND PREPARE . . . FOR THE GREAT JOB THE NAVY AND THE NATION EXPECTS YOU TO DO.

Courtesy of the United States Navy

WELCOME ABOARD THE U.S.S. HUNTER

... WHERE buildings stand in patriotic splendour!

... WHERE by threes you march in marked precision and amid laughter and chatter take all you can eat and eat all you take!

... WHERE, through supervised drill, your tottering walk becomes a firm, determined step and forty steps sound as one!

... WHERE your heart pulsates with action as you don perfection-fit Navy blues and take your place in the fight for freedom!

... WHERE learned officers bring forth a world of military knowledge in exciting, understandable manner!

... WHERE you relax and enjoy planned recreation in the genial atmosphere of great artists.

... WHERE physical education brings firm beauty to your figure!

... WHERE specialists in personnel selection give you the assurance that you are the most important person in the world and aid you in choosing the job you like best and can do best for the NAVY!

... WHERE, on Sunday, regardless of your faith, you may worship God according to the dictates of your own conscience!

... WHERE at bargain prices you may shop to your heart's content for trinkets for those you love and buy necessities for yourself.

... WHERE you stand amazed as you review a great white wave—two thousand feet beating down in unison and two thousand white-gloved hands swinging in rhythmic motion as the band plays on!

... WHERE station and shore liberty are given for your personal pleasure and enjoyment to do as you please.

... WHERE movies and models of planes and ships, graphs, pamphlets, and booklets show you the way of the NAVY!

THIS IS THE U.S.S. HUNTER

WHERE YOU LIVE . . . WORK . . . AND PREPARE . . FOR THE GREAT JOB THE NAVY AND THE NATION EXPECTS YOU TO DO.

Closeup of image (opposite)

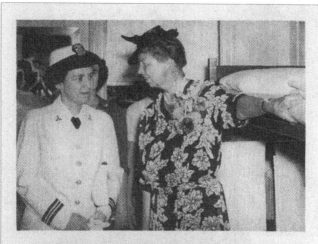

Above: CAPTAIN MC AFEE (THEN LT. COMDR.) AND MRS. ROOSEVELT
INSPECT BARRACKS . . . . *Below:* A QUIET EVENING "AT HOME"

WE DO "A HEAP O' LIVING"
TO MAKE OUR BARRACKS A HOME

Fresh tang of "Navy air" smacks the recruit when, shortly after arrival, she finds herself in company with thirty-nine other girls marching through barracks and "falling out" at the apartment she will share with other shipmates during "boot" training. The fascinating change from civilian individuality to Wave uniformity starts as soon as bunks are claimed and mysteries of their making unfolded. Feminine garments with laces and ribbons suddenly become known as "gear." The familiar long mirror gives way to a pocket mirror which must answer all needs. The tub loses its status as a bubble-bath haven and turns into a "bigsome thing" to be scoured. The "boot" finds she must bunk with more room-mates than she has ever lived with before, "stow her gear" in closer quarters . . . but when all is said and done, she knows these experiences in the Navy will take their place with such treasured memories as "the first date."

Courtesy of the United States Navy

WE DO "A HEAP O' LIVING"
TO MAKE OUR BARRACKS A HOME

Fresh tang of "Navy air" smacks the recruit when, shortly after arrival, she finds herself in company with thirty-nine other girls marching through barracks and "falling out" at the apartment she will share with other shipmates during "boot" training. The fascinating change from civilian individuality to Wave uniformity starts as soon as bunks are claimed and mysteries of their making unfolded. Feminine garments with laces and ribbons suddenly become known as "gear." The familiar long mirror gives way to a pocket mirror which must answer all needs. The tub loses its status as a bubble-bath haven and turns into a "bigsome thing" to be scoured. The "boot" finds she must bunk with more room-mates than she has ever lived with before, "stow her gear" in closer quarters . . . but when all is said and done, she knows these experiences in the Navy will take their place with such treasured memories as "the first date."

Closeup of image (opposite)

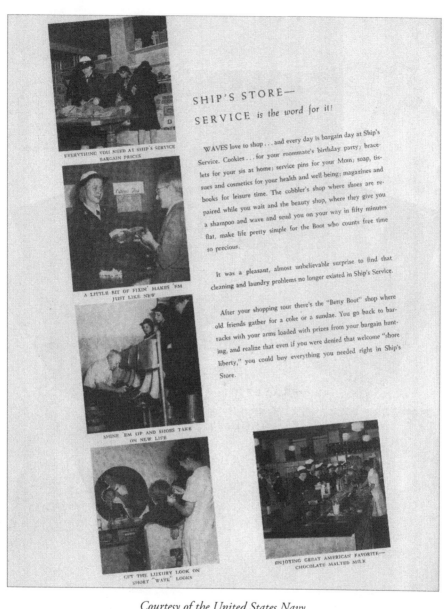

SHIP'S STORE—
SERVICE is the word for it!

WAVES love to shop . . . and every day is bargain day at Ship's Service. Cookies . . . for your roommate's birthday party; bracelets for your sis at home; service pins for your Mom; soap, tissues and cosmetics for your health and well being; magazines and books for leisure time. The cobbler's shop where shoes are repaired while you wait and the beauty shop, where they give you a shampoo and wave and send you on your way in fifty minutes flat, make life pretty simple for the Boot who counts free time so precious.

It was a pleasant, almost unbelievable surprise to find that cleaning and laundry problems no longer existed in Ship's Service.

After your shopping tour there's the "Betty Boot" shop where old friends gather for a coke or a sundae. You go back to barracks with your arms loaded with prizes from your bargain hunting, and realize that even if you were denied that welcome "shore liberty," you could buy everything you needed right in Ship's Store.

EVERYTHING YOU NEED AT SHIP'S SERVICE
BARGAIN PRICES

A LITTLE BIT OF FIXIN' MAKES 'EM
JUST LIKE NEW

SHINE 'EM UP AND SHOES TAKE
ON NEW LIFE

GET THE LUXURY LOOK ON
SHORT "WAVE" LOOKS

ENJOYING GREAT AMERICAN FAVORITE—
CHOCOLATE MALTED MILK

Courtesy of the United States Navy

SHIP'S STORE—
SERVICE is the word for it!

WAVES love to shop . . . and every day is bargain day at Ship's Service. Cookies . . . for your roommate's birthday party; bracelets for your sis at home; service pins for your Mom; soap, tissues and cosmetics for your health and well-being; magazines and books for leisure time. The cobbler's shop where shoes are repaired while you wait and the beauty shop, where they give you a shampoo and wave and send you on your way in fifty minutes flat, make life pretty simple for the Boot who counts free time so precious.

It was a pleasant, almost unbelievable surprise to find that cleaning and laundry problems no longer existed in Ship's Service.

After your shopping tour there's the "Betty Boot" shop where old friends gather for a coke or a sundae. You go back to barracks with your arms loaded with prizes from your bargain hunting, and realize that even if you were denied that welcome "shore liberty," you could buy everything you needed right in Ship's Store.

Closeup of image (opposite)

THE JOB'S THE THING

The opportunity to express your personality, talents, intelligence, experience, and desires comes in SELECTION. Tests are given which discover hidden qualifications you didn't know you had, and bring out those you're sure you have. You are interviewed by experts in personnel classification whose attentive ears listen as you discuss the job you would like to follow in the Navy.

You know the Navy's needs come first — the quotas must be filled. But more often than not a seaman's desire for a job coincides with the quota and her qualifications.

Photographs of WAVES at their jobs from California to New York, and from Maine to Florida, with vivid descriptions of these jobs, enable you to make an intelligent choice of a job for which you prefer to train.

FROM THE SELECTION INTERVIEW SHOWN ABOVE COME ASSIGNMENTS TO ESSENTIAL NAVY JOBS

There's scarcely any sort of work a WAVE cannot be trained for. Sixteen special training schools include Hospital Corps, Link Trainer School, Parachute Rigger's School, Yeoman School, Storekeeper School, Aviation Machinist's School, Radio School, Aerographers School — the list continues to grow.

Selection officers give careful consideration to every reason for your choice, and your mind and energies are directed to the important job you can do as a WAVE and as a representative of the nation that believes in you and your ability to help bury the Axis!

Courtesy of the United States Navy

THE JOB'S THE THING

The opportunity to express your personality, talents, intelligence, experience, and desires comes in SELECTION.

Tests are given which discover hidden qualifications you didn't know you had, and bring out those you're sure you have. You are interviewed by experts in personnel classification whose attentive ears listen as you discuss the job you would like to follow in the Navy.

You know the Navy's needs come first — the quotas must be filled. But more often than not a seaman's desire for a job coincides with the quota and her qualifications.

Photographs of WAVES at their jobs from California to New York, and from Maine to Florida, with vivid descriptions of these jobs, enable you to make an intelligent choice of a job for which you prefer to train.

There's scarcely any sort of work a WAVE cannot be trained for. Sixteen special training schools include Hospital Corps, Link Trainer School, Parachute Rigger's School, Yeoman School, Storekeeper School, Aviation Machinist's School, Radio School, Aerographers School — the list continues to grow.

Selection officers give careful consideration to every reason for your choice, and your mind and energies are directed to the important job you can do as a WAVE and as a representative of the nation that believes in you and your ability to help bury the Axis!

Closeup of image (opposite)

Courtesy of the United States Navy

KAREN BERKEY HUNTSBERGER

CHOW TIME

Muster for "Mess" is a welcome note to all seamen at "U.S.S. Hunter" for we know that at the end of a brisk march to Mess Hall our ravenous appetites will be fully satisfied.

Thousands go in and thousands go out with clock-like precision three times a day — 21 times a week — and no one ever fails to take advantage of the sign which warns those whose eyes are bigger than their stomachs — "Take all you can eat. Eat all you take."

Cafeteria style we go down the line, tray in one hand, tableware in the other, past steaming pans of Navy "chow," and if anyone has the idea that we always eat beans in the Navy, he ought to see our trays piled to the limit of our capacities with potatoes, fruit and green vegetables, meats, salads, desserts — all selected and prepared with an eye to palates, vitamins and our strenuous days.

How we keep slender in spite of it all is a question that's answered in drill and gym.

Closeup of image (opposite)

I'll Be Seeing You   75

CHAPTER SIX
A WAVE IN WASHINGTON!

October 10, 1943

Dear Mother & Daddy,

At last I can write you news of where I am and what I'm doing. Of course, from the envelope you can see I'm in Washington, which already has nine thousand WAVES! At first I was quite disappointed about this assignment because I'd heard so much about how crowded this place is.[51] My work is in the Hydrographic Office, and there is only one—in Suitland, Maryland.[52] So you see I'm really in Maryland, although the address is Washington. It takes about 30 minutes to ride the bus into the heart of Washington, so it isn't bad at all. Because Hydro is so new, this place is really in the country with a woods on the left. There is the Census Building, the Hydrographic Building, and our Barracks H. Besides these there is a recreational hall where dances are held every two weeks. Upstairs there is a beauty shop, ping-pong table,

---

51   More than half of the uniformed Navy personnel in Washington, D.C., during the war were women.

52   The Hydrographic Office prepared and published maps and charts required for navigation. By mid 1943, the office was printing more than two million charts each month. Rear Admiral G.S. Bryan was the Hydrographer of the Navy during the war. During his tenure, the office went from a peacetime facility with less than two hundred employees to a vast organization in a new building that employed over 1,800 people, many of them WAVES. Hydrographic Office records include around 90,000 published charts. About 9,000 of these were printed during World War II and included an array of information depending on the specific need. Many specialty charts were made such as maps designed for rafts and lifeboats. These maps were 26" x 36", yellow nylon, and waterproof. They could be used to catch rain for drinking water, as sun protection, as a distress signal, and they were strong enough to be used as a small sail.

and a craft room. The recreational setup is wonderful! Outside the hall are targets for archery. They have riding, badminton, bowling, and swimming, too. To swim, we'll have to take a bus to the new pool at the Anacostia Receiving Station on this side of the Anacostia River. I'll have to buy a suit so I can go two nights a week and learn to swim. Maybe this time I'll really learn, since the instructor is supposed to be so wonderful. The barracks is very empty because the Marine girls just moved to their new barracks in Arlington, Virginia. They had been using this one until theirs was finished. Everyone says we are lucky to have the newest and nicest barracks in Washington. Also, Hydro is an enviable working place because the officers here are more lenient than on most stations. I suppose that is because most people here are artists. You should see the barracks—it's gorgeous! It's done modernistically, with yellow and green drapes predominating. The lobby is large, with blond furniture and little booths built on each side where you can eat, write, or entertain friends. On the main floor off the lobby is a small store where we can get necessities and a few things to eat such as fruit juices, coffee, milk, breakfast rolls, pie, cake, ice cream, and occasionally hot dogs. This store is open till 11:00 at night and is convenient to use to get a bit of breakfast when we don't want to walk clear to the Census Building, which is quite a distance away.

The Hydrographic Office—Suitland, Maryland 1944
Courtesy of Scuttlebutt magazine

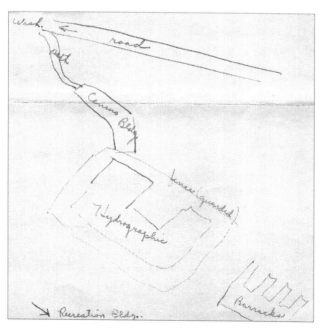

Lucy's sketch of the Hydrographic Building and her barracks

It's so lovely here. We weren't expecting much and were amazed when we came out here on Friday. Best of all, we all have our own rooms. To live alone is sheer heaven after living so jammed up at Hunter! There are venetian blinds at the window and a medium size rug on the floor. A nice closet, a lounge chair and hassock, a cute desk, chest of drawers, a cabinet for toilet articles with sliding mirror doors, an indirect lamp, and a nice soft bed complete the picture. All the furniture is blond wood and very attractive. Upstairs there's a beautiful library stuffed with good books, and a writing room. And there's a modern infirmary with nurses on duty 24 hours a day! I wish you could see it all. Twenty-five of us came from Hunter and we fill up the C wing. All of our rooms are pastel colors and the doors are the same. It looks so pretty to see a green door, then a pink, then blue, yellow, etc. Mine is pink, with a brownish red rug and flowered tan and green drapes and pillow. Our beds resemble studio couches because there is no head or foot piece, just a base, but soft! The first night I got here I could barely sleep. I was so used to my hammock affair top bunk. Here I don't have to hang onto the sides. It all seems too good to be true—very much like a college dorm, with lovely laundry rooms and washrooms. The ironing situation is bad and they say after this barracks is filled, and it will be soon, you'll hardly be able to get an iron at all. So I think I'll have you send my iron. Since I have my own room it will be safe. We always lock our rooms no matter where we go. I've decided to not let anyone use my iron—it's just too hard to get one. Every day there are shirts to iron, so I do need it.

By the way, I do need so many things—I hope you can send them. I'm sure we'll be here for the duration, as everyone is who comes here. Mother, most of the things I intended to put in originally I want now, especially my manicure set and bath powder. Could you also please send my three-piece dresser set, hand mirror, alarm clock, my brown radio, photo album, pictures and corners, an old pillowcase, and my sketchbook?[53] I forgot—hangers—I need them badly. About six or eight more if you can spare them. This is a lot to send and if it costs

---

53   Three-piece dresser set: comb, brush, and mirror.

too much, just send the radio and clock, which I want most of all. I thought maybe you could send all but the radio in my large suitcase. Boy, will I be glad to get some mail!

Probably you're wondering what I do—I don't know yet, and haven't the slightest idea. We came Friday evening, saw the ensign in personnel, filled in papers on Saturday morning and had liberty the rest of Saturday and today. Yesterday Helen Koenig and I went into Washington. I tried to find dress shoes to fit me, but was unsuccessful. My feet have spread so much it's pitiful. However, my feet seldom hurt and I really believe marching has helped them. We went to see *For Whom the Bell Tolls* with Ingrid Bergman, and it was wonderful.[54] The movie price is 50¢ for service people—for others $1 and up! We were so tired we decided not to go up in the Washington Monument or do any sightseeing since we'll be here for some time. I do like Washington very much—it's so interesting. Hope I can see Josephine and the Crims soon.[55]

All the girls here are swell! I'm so anxious to find out what I do—Monday I will undoubtedly know. The food at the cafeteria is delicious, but high-priced. It's a relief because the food at Hunter got pretty poor. They are to give us subsistence of $1.50 per day for meals. I guess they do that to save money, so we can eat where we please. However, if food is high we lose money. Besides, we don't get paid for some time, and I'm afraid I may run pretty short. Maybe it will work out.

Last Sunday I had a wonderful time seeing New York with Claire Patterson and Zonia Tucker, friends I met at Hunter. They were assigned to Jacksonville, Florida, to the Hospital Corps. We took the subway to the end of the island. We saw ships of all kinds, and were

---

54   *For Whom the Bell Tolls* plot: The story of an American soldier finding love during a risky mission to blow up an important bridge during the Spanish Civil War.

55   A happy coincidence, several of Lucy's cousins were living in Washington. Josephine Berkey and Cecil Cantrell (a widowed woman) were both schoolteachers. Margaret Ann Crim was a nanny for 8-year-old Warren Gordon Cantrell, Cecil's son. Margaret Ann's sister, Kathryn, often visited.

they large! It was a gorgeous day and sailors and soldiers were feeding pigeons, just as I've always read and heard about. We just wandered around in the warm sunshine taking it all in—the beautiful view, the fascinating water, and the different kinds of people. Soon the ferry came and we rode out to see the Statue of Liberty. We got off the boat and ran up to take a look then back again. If we'd stayed, it would've been 45 minutes and we couldn't waste so much time. The statue certainly is impressive and I was astonished to discover it is green! On the ferry ride back, a convoy of returning soldiers passed us. It really made a lump in my throat to see how excited these boys were at seeing America again. Next we went to an Automat to eat and had fun seeing the little doors pop open. I got a roll that had jelly with it instead of butter and was asking Zonia why when the man next to me got another roll with butter and said he'd be glad to exchange with me. People really treat you nice when you wear a uniform.

After eating we went up in the Empire State Building and it was wonderful! The city is laid out so perfectly. Next we went into St. Patrick's Cathedral and it's positively breathtaking—that gold altar and those beautiful statues. You've seen all this, so you'll know what I mean. Before the cathedral, we walked down around Times Square and then it did seem like the New York I'd heard about, with people pushing and jostling you. On main streets there was little activity and almost no cars because of gas rationing. It seemed peculiar in such an enormous city. Our tour of Rockefeller Center was the nicest of all. The guide really knew his business. Isn't the lobby in the Music Hall gorgeous with the gold ceiling and beautiful murals and chandeliers? We didn't have time to go inside the theater and see a show, but since I'm not too far away perhaps I could go over on a weekend and see the Rockettes.

Our tour ended on top of one of the tall buildings in Rockefeller Center. I could see much better from there than from the Empire State Building. There was a powerful telescope we looked through for a dime and had fun seeing a man out fishing just as plain as day, although he was miles and miles away. I bought some postcards, and we had a soda on top of the skyscraper. The sunset, as viewed from the top there, was one of the most beautiful things I've ever seen. The sky was brilliant, and the fiery sun was reflected in the water of a river a long way off. I'll never forget it. By the time we ate it was time to go back to boot camp—to be in at 9:00 p.m. We decided we'd seen a lot of New York from 10:00 till 7:30! Now I'll get to see Washington!

Monday we drilled, and that night we saw Cornelia Otis Skinner give some skits on our variety show. She was splendid—and I've never laughed so much in my life. The next day most of the kids left and we were really blue. Then Wednesday morning we set out to walk to the subway. We had to carry our small bags and my overnight case was so stuffed, even it was heavy. I was glad and sorry to leave Hunter. In spite of it all, it was fun and I learned so much. Also, we had such swell leaders.

I almost am forgetting to tell you about us, Building M of Regiment 14. First, we won the Navy E for excellence in our very first regimental review, so we got to be the color company and be up front. The flag we had was a red flag with a white E. This meant we had the cleanest rooms, the neatest girls, and the best marching of all. Even fire drill discipline counted. One captain who inspected us said building M had the neatest cleanest rooms and the prettiest girls! Then, last Tuesday we were told to muster out front unexpectedly. Big shots were there, and Lieutenant Knuckle presented us the Navy E for the second time. It was the first time it had ever been presented twice in succession to the same company and building. It's a blue flag with a white E. We yelled and marched down the middle of the street, with all the officers beaming. They were more excited than we were! That's really an *honor*, and I was proud to be part of the company!!

It takes only four hours to come from New York to Washington, so we got here in the afternoon—about 275 of us in all. We waited in the station several hours and finally were taken by bus to the Anacostia Receiving Station, which is lousy. Our beds creaked and I got an upper bunk again. We stayed there until Friday. However, on Thursday evening we had liberty and Ruth Wickersham from Indianapolis and I went into Washington and ate at the Shoreham Hotel. It's so beautiful there. We ate in the Grill Room and had $1.15 meals, which was reasonable. The main dining room price would have been horrible. We felt we could splurge after that awful receiving station. Wednesday night we did see *So Proudly We Hail* at the receiving station, so that was something.[56] During those few days, all we did was just wait around—it was awful because we weren't allowed to write letters until we got our new address. Hope you all are fine.

Write!

All my love,

Lucy

Miss Lucy Berkey, seaman second class, who received her training at Hunter college, New York, has been assigned to the hydrographic office in Washington, D.C., where she entered upon her new duties Monday. Her brother, David Berkey, seaman second class, who has been in training at Great Lakes, has been transferred to Chicago university, where he is taking training for radio and signal corps work.

October 21, 1943
Courtesy of The Salem Leader

---

56 *So Proudly We Hail* plot: WWII nurses returning from the Philippines reminisce about their experiences in combat and love.

October 18, 1943

Dear Mother & Daddy,

It was so wonderful to hear some news from home! I'd been feeling rather lost after not getting any mail for over two weeks. Also, I got a letter from Aunt Fannie—brought right to the room where I work in Hydro. The address hadn't been straightened out, so that letter really traveled. And was I proud to see my picture in the clipping you sent! Sixty-seven WAVES from Indiana, and there's little me, the only one from Salem!

Monday morning, we began work and I confess I was terrified at the complications; however, it isn't that hard at all and is becoming easier all the time. Unfortunately, I'm not allowed to say much about what I'm doing because it's too vital and important and secretive. Even I know little about what happens to my work. I can say the work is painstaking and very tiny and hard on the eyes. We have ample time in which to get things done, which is wonderful. Very fine people work along with us, a great many of them civilians. We were all surprised to discover so many civil service men and women here, but then they were there long before we were. Our barracks has WAVES on one side and civilians on the other. In quite a few ways that isn't good, but we get along. The man who is training us in our work and getting us started is so fine and patient. He says my work is nice and gave me one of the most tedious jobs the other day. It made me feel good to know he had confidence in my ability, because most of the other girls have had three times the training I have. He talked to me a long time the other day, and he really can pep you up and make you feel like doing your best. There are only four of us in my section. We were all assigned before we reported for work, so there were no choices. But if you hate what you're assigned, then you can be transferred to a different section. There are very few WAVE officers here—mostly men officers. We were assigned according to results of our interviews at Hunter plus our past experiences. I was amazed to find I'd been assigned to one of the most difficult jobs.

Later I discovered it was due in part to my college training—so it helps—always! At first I was worried about my eyes, but it seemed better by the third day. I'm just getting used to something new. Now I love the work and feel I'll do well in it. Everyone here is so extremely helpful and cheerful. And guess what? I work beside a boy from Indiana—Terre Haute. He's married (as they all are!), very talented, and is swell to help me.

Saturday we had to work all day. From now on we have our choice of every other Saturday off or every Saturday afternoon off. I haven't decided which to do. We work from 8:30 to 5:00 and on Thursday afternoon at 5:00 have to drill. Friday morning is Personal Inspection, Saturday morning is Captain's Inspection and every day, Room Inspection! Monday after work is a muster meeting to explain the week's activities. At muster we also hear a war orientation lecture that keeps us up on the developments in every theater of operations around the world. Nights we're kept busy washing and ironing clothes and cleaning our rooms. Every two weeks we go on the night shift, and our turn will come soon. The girls on night now say it's fun and not bad at all. The coffee shop is next to our room at Hydro, and we can get coffee and rolls if we don't have time to eat breakfast before we come. Anytime during the day, we can get up and go out and get anything we want to eat, even bring it to our table and eat as we work if we so desire— it's wonderful! This shop is good for noon lunch if it's raining or too cold to go to the cafeteria next door. Or, if we want to eat at the barracks at noon we can—three places to choose from! Only trouble is, food is high, but I guess it is any place. We're all practically broke because we haven't been paid since we left Hunter and won't be paid until Thursday. No subsistence money has been given to us, and we've had to eat on what we had with us when we came.

Saturday night we certainly had fun. The sailors invited us to a dance at the Solomons and 50 of us went from Suitland.[57] They were six charter buses from various WAVE barracks. We had steaks and all kinds of good things to eat and then a marvelous orchestra to dance to. There were about 10 sailors to one WAVE and, of course, that was nice for us. I met some very swell boys who'd really seen action. They showed us their recreation hall and bought me Cokes and 7-Up. All of these boys were short and very good dancers. However, they were disappointed I couldn't jitterbug. I've never met such well-mannered boys! After the dance, we had cake and coffee. The baker had gone hog wild and put rosebuds and green leaves on the chocolate cake—and all for us!! We sang all the way home and decided we had a marvelous evening. On our bus I met two girls from Fort Wayne who knew some kids from IU!! Today I got acquainted with the girl who said she'd fix my coat that's too long for a very small sum. It'll be such a relief to get my coat up off my ankles so to speak. My jackets have to be fixed, too.

I think I forgot to tell you that at Boot Camp we had several Happy Hour programs, variety shows, movies, etc. I have a picture of our section to send home if I ever get around to it. My face sorta ruins the scene, but otherwise it's a good picture. The worst day we had was when it poured all day. As you know, WAVES are not allowed to carry umbrellas, so we had water running from our hat brims onto our coats and dripping from our coats into our shoes! All day we had to sit in classes, drill, stand colors, etc. in those soppy clothes. We left at 5:45 and got back at 9:00 p.m.!! Boy, you should have seen me marching. Because I'm short, I had to march toward the end of the section and all I did was run because those tall girls really set a pace! We always sang as we marched and I learned some crazy songs, as well as some really nice ones.

---

57   Solomons—U.S. Naval Amphibious Training Base located at the mouth of the Patuxent River, 53 miles from the Hydrographic Office. Chosen in March 1942 and rapidly built, close to 70,000 men trained there.

Today I got a letter from Richard and one from Betty Patty. Betty is now at Fort Des Moines, Iowa, and just loves it all. She had a furlough and saw Martha Ellis in Indianapolis. Richard's letter was funny, as usual, with all those ahems! I'm glad David's in radio school—it's a terribly good field to get into. I must write him, and Jonie, too. I'll bet Jonie's quite the boy with that beard! Every time I show his picture to any of the girls they go into spasms! "*Is he married? Yes? Oh phoeey! Gee, is he handsome*!" I have millions of things to tell Mildred [McBride Berkey], and have meant to write since my first week at Hunter. All I've written is to you. Virginia should feel glad to be in college, for I've learned it certainly pays no matter what you do or where you go. Besides, when she gets out, she'll be helping as much or more than I am. It does feel good to know my work is essential, that an error on my part would be drastic, and that my good work means victory is that much closer. It's really aerial navigation, the charting of waters, but includes so awfully many departments, every one as interesting as can be. That is absolutely all I can say about Hydro, much as I'd like to explain.

We have to show identification cards every time we enter or leave the building. It's thrilling and very, very nice. Hope you're all fine and I do wish I could see you and talk a while. Furloughs are things we don't get for a while. Be good and write.

All my love,

Lucy

Regiment 14, Building M—Hunter College—October 1943
Lucy is in second row from bottom—second from left

KAREN BERKEY HUNTSBERGER

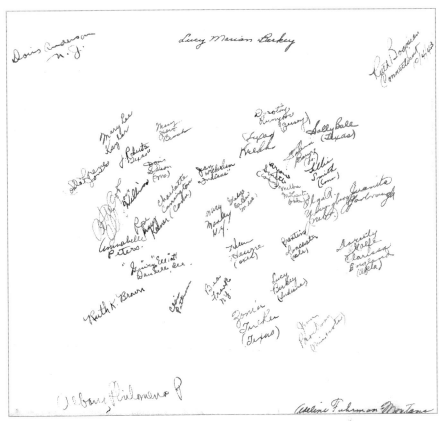

Back of Regiment 14 photo—Hunter College—October 1943

October 25, 1943

Dearest Daddy,

It was so good to hear from you again. I wrote Jonie today and heard from Richard and David. The main reason I'm writing this in a hurry before I go to work is about this railway express business. This place is outside their delivery limits and they refuse to deliver this far. Consequently, I had to go down and hire a taxi to bring the heavy box here—cost me $2. The ensign here said I should have only paid $1.25, as that's the usual rate. Anyway, taxi fare is too much anyway, since we're so far out, so I always ride the bus for 15¢. The worst of it is—there is another package coming, evidently my radio, so I'll have to go get it. I'll try to bring it back on the bus if it isn't too heavy. Parcel Post is delivered right here, so if you ever send me anything else (ahem!) please send it that way.

About the money situation—they say it's always a problem when being transferred in the Navy. I know that now! They had told us at Hunter we'd be paid in two weeks after we got here, but we have found out differently since. Finally, the personnel officer at Hydro said our pay numbers hadn't come through, and also, they'd taken out three month's insurance! I certainly didn't spend anything for luxuries, but all my money's gone for food since we haven't been paid subsistence. We're all broke and it's almost funny. Anyway, I was down to my last dime last Thursday and here came the card saying that box was waiting. I finally decided I'd better cash a check since they said we wouldn't be paid until November 5th. Daddy, I certainly hated to do it, but I also hate to owe money. I'm glad I went ahead and wrote the check now that there's a rumor it may be a week more until we're paid. All the WAVES who've been here for a long time have told us it always takes ages at first, and then soon it's regulated. I hope!

This week has been about the same—except for a Navy dance Friday night at the Arena—Vincent Lopez's orchestra. This coming week we have a Halloween dance on Wednesday, but I won't get to go because I start on the night shift tonight—4:30 p.m. to 1:00 a.m. It lasts for two weeks and most of the girls like it.

Well, I must get ready for work. That iron is so wonderful! I really needed it! And it's so good to have my other things, too. Hope you're all well.

All my love,

Lucy

October 31, 1943

Dear Mother & Daddy,

Thanks so much for sending my radio, Mother! Today I feel as if I'm back at IU because I'm listening to the game between Brooklyn and Washington and it's exciting. It's a beautiful day—sun shining, um! Someone bought a newspaper, and I got to read the funnies for the first time in weeks.

Washington certainly was the last place I expected to go, but since I'm here now, it seems very nice. In fact, everyone is so friendly I believe I'll really love it here. The climate is not nearly as healthy and invigorating as it was at Hunter in New York. Here it's so moist and muggy that either heat or cold is very penetrating and uncomfortable.

Since last Monday, I've been on the night shift, from 4:30 p.m. to 1:00 a.m. At first I was terribly sleepy and thought it would be awful, but now I'm getting used to it and it isn't so bad. The worst thing is we haven't been paid since September 20 and I've been broke for two weeks. Our pay numbers haven't come through and it's a mess because all of us are starving practically.

Last Sunday I had a date with a fellow at Camp Springs Army Air Base. I met him at the first dance we had here. He's from Detroit and is really okay. Yesterday he went home on a four-day furlough. They really have some swell dances for us. So far, I haven't gotten around to seeing a lot of Washington, but hope to if we get paid and have some nice weather. I really enjoy my work and like it better than anything I've ever done. Really something, no?!

Thank you for letting me know about Paul McLemore being lost in the North Sea. I had to sit right down and cry. Of course, we hear about boys dying every day, but they're usually not one of the kids I grew up with. I feel so sad for his family.

Much love,

Lucy

CHAPTER SEVEN
SETTLING IN

November 7, 1943

Dear Mother & Daddy,

It's such a perfect day I hated to come in at all, but there's so much to do before Monday, it's best. It was terribly expensive to call as I did, but it meant a lot to me. It was so good to hear your voices! Mother, you sounded exactly like yourself, but Daddy, you didn't sound like yourself—more like Frank Neal. Isn't that funny? I felt so much better after I hung up that I called Margaret Ann and told her about calling you. We talked for half an hour.

This morning I decided to go into town to church instead of attending services here. Every Sunday we have a chaplain. He and his assistant conduct services here and it's very nice. I went into Washington with a WAVE who saw that I got on the right streetcar to go to the National City Christian Church. It's a beautiful church, as you know. You were right, Mother, when you said I'd find it more homey than the one in Columbus. The thick green carpet and the drapes behind the pulpit seem to absorb sound and make the place more reverent. The minister, J. Warren Hastings, is very fine and had a good sermon, to the point. He's one of the best speakers I've heard in a long time. When I first went into the church a Mrs. Moser welcomed me, had me register, and then asked if I would like to go home with someone for dinner. I said okay, thinking of a free meal, of course! Then I sat down and heard someone call my name, and there was Josephine sitting in front of me! I sat with her in church and she invited me to dinner. So I canceled my previous dinner date. It was so swell to see Margaret Ann and Kathryn. Margaret Ann had prepared a lovely meal and boy, did that home cooking taste good! Dear Warren Gordon was about the same. I really was ashamed to go to dinner anywhere because my face is so horribly broken out. However, they didn't say anything. I think the night shift and the peculiar hours and food it necessitates are responsible. Thank goodness we start on the day watch tomorrow. Night work isn't bad, in fact, it's much more quiet.

After eating, Cecil, Jo, and Warren took me across the street to see the Washington Cathedral and grounds. The Bishop's Garden was closed. Cecil was especially disappointed since she thought it was one of the nicest things I could see. We saw the school where Warren goes. Daddy, Cecil wanted me to be sure and tell you I saw Warren's school, since you had asked about it. It seems very nice inside with plenty of playground outside. The grounds there cover four city blocks and include many school buildings, prep schools for girls and boys, the bishop's home, various other buildings, and the cathedral. The cathedral is simply magnificent! It has been under construction for 35 years and has 50 years to go because it's all been built by hand, no machines whatsoever. The intricate carvings on columns, statues, etc. are particularly noticeable. Below the main floors are various rooms with altars for certain purposes. There are many paintings, including the "Sistine Madonna" and "Madonna of the Chair." On the main floor is the children's chapel that is so sweet. It was made possible by the contributions of a couple that had lost their only son when he was four years old. The grillwork surrounding the chapel has animal heads molded into the design. Also on the main floor is a chapel dedicated to war and service people. The altar is carved wood that has a history. We tried to get a guide to take us through so we'd know all these things, but the place was awfully crowded. All the altars are real gold.

After straining our eyes staring and admiring everything, we went downtown. As we rode along, Cecil pointed out different embassies to me, ones located along Massachusetts Avenue. Once downtown, we went to the Mellon Art Gallery on Constitution Avenue. I had seen the building before, but didn't realize it was an art gallery. I really enjoyed myself there! The floors are so shiny it seems as if you'd fall down any minute. Upstairs there is a central court with a circle of very tall black marble columns with a fountain in the center. The central part of the fountain is a beautiful bronze figure. I enjoyed looking at the sculpture almost more than the paintings. We saw only part of the exhibit, because we were getting tired. After all, you can't enjoy art in a gulp! So, I intend to go back one of these days and look some more. Truly, I was surprised to find the place crowded and most of those present were service people. Next we rode the streetcar back to 11th and Pennsylvania, where I got off to catch the bus and they went on home. They were all swell!

Tonight I'm pretty tired and lonesome for Sally Bracken. Somehow I've come to really love that girl—she is so sweet and so genuine. She's from Rye, New York, and is going home to a girlfriend's wedding this weekend. She invited me to go home with her the weekend of December 4th, and I'm so excited! She's engaged to a fellow who is an aviation cadet in the Navy, now in training in Texas. Her father is also a Navy flier, and left for overseas last week. After her father left, she brought home two lovebirds in a cage. She was going to give them to a fellow over at the office who said he'd care for them for her. Those birds really made a racket while they were here that one night, and the ensign came down to find out what kind of bird had gotten into Sally's room! Poor Sally's nerves were on edge the next day because those birds woke her at 6:00 a.m. with their chattering! The louder you talk, the louder they twerp and chirp. Sally said she loved the darn things but was glad to be rid of them because every time she looked at them she was reminded of her father and felt like crying.

Daddy, you asked about Geri Knight. She's fine, even after her birthday Friday on which day she became 25. She's a large girl—must weigh over 200—but lots of fun and a good sport. She received three cakes on Friday—a chocolate one from her mother who lives in Kansas, a white one from her sorority sisters back at Kansas University, and a caramel one from other friends. She took two of them over to the office and treated all of the girls and fellows in our office on the night watch. We had fun, for everyone likes Geri. She gets the biggest kick out of the least little thing you do for her.

We all wanted to do a lot for her, especially because the night before her birthday she received a telegram saying her fiancé in the Navy had been injured pretty badly and they didn't know whether he'd live. She nearly went crazy. However, she realized she'd have to concentrate on something else so she acted crazy all day. She put on an admirable act, I must say. Sally and I bought her a white wool scarf and most of the other girls in our wing went together and bought her a box of candy and perfume.

Patricia Spellman, the girl from California who lives on one side of me, gave us a surprise the other night when she revealed an ability to tell character from one's handwriting. We've tested her out and have discovered she's really good. I even had her look at your handwriting Mother and Daddy. She told me your characteristics and they were exactly right. Also, she said both of you had great minds! Give yourself a pat on the back. Mother, she said you were calm and even-tempered, and Daddy, you know how to make decisions and stick to them. She said Eleanor was a good student, had a good disposition, and was interested in nursing. She said Richard had the ambition to become a doctor and something had hindered it. Also, Richard would make a nice husband. She said David couldn't decide just what he wanted to do yet, was spiritual underneath, and kept things to himself. As for myself, she said too many things that were true, such as my thinking about myself too much, etc., interested in art, should concentrate on one goal, and that a lady with gray hair and green eyes was interested in me and would influence me a great deal. That last part was the only thing that sounded silly as usually it's all very good and very logical. Well, it's fun anyhow. Pat is a very nice person. In this wing we have two Pats, two Glorias, one Hermione, one Butch whose real name is Rose, Ruth, Grace, Jean, Anne, Helen, Sylvia, Judy, Geri, Sally, Peggy, Olive, Regina, Ann, Hilda, Frieda, Marion, Eleanor, Georgeanne, and Henrietta! All a swell bunch of girls despite various differences and backgrounds.

About pictures—I will try to have mine taken one of these days. I look positively terrible in the hats, but the suit isn't so bad. As soon as mine are altered, I think I'll love wearing them because they're cut well and feel good. The nicest thing is navy blue always looks neat.

One of these Sundays I do want to go sightseeing in Washington—see Mount Vernon and the Washington Monument. Today would have been perfect to see them in the warm sunshine. I've seen the Capitol many times as I passed by on the bus, but I really want to see it up close.

I got my *Leader* Friday and was so amazed to read that Paul Hinds and Howard Moore met in the Pacific![58] Probably was in Australia since that's where Paul has been.

Today I've been thinking about you all eating a good birthday dinner and enjoying yourselves. I'm glad Aunt Fannie could come down.[59] It seems funny that Mildred [McBride Berkey] is teaching again. I hope she likes it better than I did. But even I could stand it for $200 per month! Well, bye now. I must write to some of my poor neglected friends.

All my love,

Lucy

November 15, 1943

Dearest Folks,

Here it is Monday again, and it seems as if it were just Monday yesterday. Time has a way of seeming slow and fast at the same time. For instance, it seems as if I've been a WAVE for ages, yet it's only been two months. Being a civilian now would seem queer, but if I were, the WAVE experience would be like a dream. That's the way life it is, and it's really a good thing—helps us to stay happy.

Georgeanne Turner is playing the violin and it sounds so beautiful! She has such good expression in her playing. She lives across the hall from me. I want to tell you about her because she is the finest example of a lady I have ever met. Georgeanne's home is in San Francisco, California, and she comes from a wealthy family. She is not snobbish

---

58   *The Salem Leader*—Lucy's hometown newspaper.
59   November 7, 1943 was Aunt Fannie's 45th birthday.

or affected in any way because of that money, but is very sweet and human. Her mother died when she was just out of high school and she's had quite a time recovering from that. She is now 23, just my age. Some of her ancestors were Spanish, and so she has very deep-set gray blue eyes with dark brows, and her hair is naturally curly. She just misses being beautiful, is about 5'5", and has a rather slender figure. She is unofficially engaged to fellow from a prominent family at home. He was in the Philippines working as a civilian when war broke out and is now in a Jap prison camp. She was working at the Navy base when she decided to join the WAVES. She has one sister who is married. To be with Georgeanne is very soothing because she is so calm and collected, and yet she's so much fun! She used to be a regular tomboy and described her tree house equipped with a hoist to bring up food, etc.! At our church here at 9:00 a.m. on Sunday mornings, she plays the violin so sweetly that it brings tears to your eyes.

Saturday night we went over to the recreation hall and banged on the piano, ate sandwiches and apples, and gabbed. Sunday we went to National City Christian Church and Georgeanne saw the sister of the fellow she's engaged to. She'd seen her when she first came to Washington, but this meeting was so very unexpected. She was thrilled, and the boy's sister, Frances, is a lovely girl. Also, I saw Josephine at church and we talked a while. Cecil wants me to come to eat Thanksgiving dinner with them, but I'll have to work all day. Christmas is the *only* holiday, according to the Navy. After church we ate at a pretty Mayflower restaurant and I met a Marine girl from South Bend, Indiana. She was sitting across from us and called me over. She asked where I was from and when I said Indiana, she just about had a spasm! "Where?" she asked, and when I said, "Salem," she told me I wasn't the same person, but I certainly resembled a friend of hers. She and her friend were in the first class of Marines and they just love it. *Tartu* with Robert Donat was on at the theater, so we went to see it and it was quite thrilling.[60] This theater always has a stage show and it was good. There was an orchestra, two good

---

60   *Tartu* plot: A British soldier goes undercover to sabotage a German poison gas factory.

roller skaters, two crazy guys, a flat-noted singer, and Jean Parker, a movie actress. There were such good shows on that we decided to go to another since it was too windy and cold to go sightseeing. *Princess O'Rourke* was on with Olivia de Havilland, but the waiting line was so discouraging. So we went to see *Sweet Rosie O'Grady* with Betty Grable and it was very good—music and craziness all mixed up and Technicolor to boot.[61] Since we're service people, we get into shows very cheaply, so we enjoyed ourselves. At one of the theaters, a man played the organ for singing. There was the cutest song about *Pistol Packin' Mama* joining the WAACs and how she dropped a bomb and sank the whole Jap fleet. Another song was a tongue twister, Mother—you'd have liked that. Georgeanne and I nearly fell off our seats laughing. When we got back home, there was a birthday party for one of the girls in our wing and we ate cake and sang. We have a birthday fund so we can make girls feel good on birthdays. We buy a cake, decorate it, write a cute verse for her, and get very simple refreshments. It's so nice.

Last Monday I received the box of cookies and stuff and it was so wonderful coming from home. Those flowers! Mother, they were so sweet and made me feel so good. I was so surprised to see cookies and flowers and bittersweet! The flowers were so fresh it was as if they had just been picked, and they're still nice. I put them in Jean Heath's cast off olive bottle and they make the room so cheerful. Thanks so much for all of it! The bittersweet is lovely, too. All the girls want me to thank you for the cookies. Geri thought your letter was so wonderful. She really appreciates things and laughed over that letter until I thought the fat was going to shake off her sides.

At last I have permission from my boss to tell you a bit more about my work. However, don't tell too many people—just for safety. I'm a lithographic draftsman and work on zinc plates that are sensitized

---

61   *Princess O'Rourke* plot: A pilot falls in love with a princess posing as a traveler crossing the country to become a maid. *Sweet Rosie O'Grady* plot: An American music hall star leaves London engaged to a duke. Back in the United States, a journalist exposes her as a burlesque queen and threatens her engagement.

for our work. We use ordinary ruling pens and a regular pen and pen points. We do a lot of lettering and it's so small I have to use a magnifying glass in order to train my pen on the right place. We do various things and I wish I could explain them all, for it's all very interesting. I don't do any original drawing because I'm not good enough. None of the WAVES are. All the people in our office are so good to help us in learning this type of work, and we do appreciate it. Mac, our assistant boss, says I'm doing fine, though I do get discouraged at times. Now that I'm on days again, I'm doing much better work. Sally and I sit side by side and we can talk if we wish, and that makes work comforting. There are scads of tilted drawing tables in our enormous room, and we all cut up and have fun. It's such intricate work that they expect you to relax as much as you wish, for it'd get the best of you otherwise!

Saturday afternoon I went downtown with Jean Heath and Pat Hollingsworth, and we bought new hats for winter because today we had to go into winter uniforms. That is, we change to blue hats and black gloves. My hat has a snap on the top or crown, and two white crowns came with it, so it's really three hats. None of us love the hat so much for we look rather stinko in them, especially the blue ones. Also, marvel of marvels, I had my suit fitted at a department store. I'm so proud of myself for getting that done at last, for maybe I'll look human again! I'll get the suit on Thursday night, when the stores are open.

I'm sending a picture of myself walking down F Street in Washington. It's a horrid picture of my face but will give you an idea of me in my uniform. I'll have pictures taken one of these days. I want this picture back someday for my photo album.

Jean Heath had a date the other night, came home and told me I knew him and he knew me! His name is Scotty McIntosh, from Hardinsburg. He went to IU last year and is now a Marine in training at Quantico. After she told me about him, I read about him in the *IU Alumni Magazine*. Then Saturday, when he came for her I talked with him for a while. He's tall and dark haired and very nice looking. Said he'd gone to IU one year, last year. It was Virginia he knew instead of me. He knew Richard from basketball games. He played on the Hardinsburg team. Jean really likes him. He's leaving this week for Marine paratroop training.

Have you heard from Jonie lately? He owes me a letter. Some sailors in our office told me David was plenty lucky to be at the University of Chicago. Eleanor, your letter was so funny—I read it to several girls, and we all died laughing. Your picture of me was about right—maybe a bit more sloppy! I'm sleepy, so I think I'll get a good rest tonight. Hope everyone's well.

Much love,

Lucy

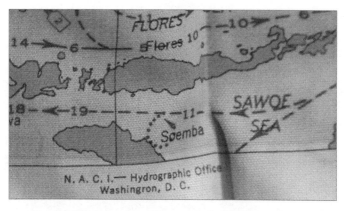

Detail of Hydrographic Office map saved by Howard Miner
PBY Pilot, U.S. Navy, South Pacific Theater, WWII
Courtesy of Ron Miner

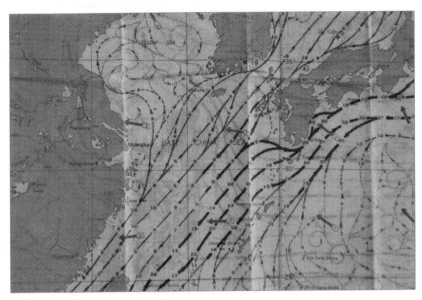

Detail of Hydrographic Office map saved by Howard Miner
PBY Pilot, U.S. Navy, South Pacific Theater, WWII
Courtesy of Ron Miner

November 29, 1943

Dear Folks,

Tonight I decided that no matter what I have to do, I'd write this letter instead. Last week on Thanksgiving I thought I'd write, but then decided it would make me more homesick. It hardly seemed like Thanksgiving because I had to work all day long, as usual. Josephine and Cecil had asked me for dinner at noon, but of course that was impossible. That night Jimmy Arneson, a sailor, took me out to turkey dinner and a show. The dinner was nice, but when I thought of our wonderful meals at home, it seemed rather pathetic. I'm so glad Marilyn could be there with you since so many of us couldn't get home. Some of the girls got off, but only because their homes were near, or because their brothers in the service are home. It's like Ensign Wilson said today, it's up to us to stay happy because no one is going to be around to help us personally. Now I know definitely I won't be home for Christmas. That really will hurt, but I can try to get used to the idea. We have to be in six months before we can get a leave, so it will be March before I can come home. The girls who'll get Christmas leaves are those who've been in long enough, those who live near enough to go home on a 48-hour pass, and those whose husbands are home on furlough. I won't be able to send you much for Christmas, but I'll send something.

Speaking of packages reminded me that I haven't ever thanked you for the lovely box of candy, the beautiful card, map, and apples—yum! I did so enjoy it all! The candy was delicious and so fresh. The apples were just what I needed. There's something so nice about receiving a package. I have some things I want you to send me if you have them and don't think it's too much to send. It's so terribly cold in this hall because of its poor construction. I'm afraid to think about really cold weather. So I need a blanket, because we only have two thin wool ones on the bed. Even now I freeze at night. Also, I need my housecoat since that thin silk one is so cold. For sports, we can wear any civilian clothes we wish and I'd like to have my slacks and several sweaters. My poetry book would be nice to have, too. Of course, I don't need the poetry, but I truly do need the other things. If I can save enough money, I'm going to try to buy an overcoat. Yesterday I was out all afternoon, and I nearly froze in my thin raincoat, even with the lining. The coat is $33.50 and that's pretty stiff. I'll see how my purse holds out. I had to buy a new hat for $5.95 last week when we went into winter uniform. Also, I'm going to buy fur-lined kid gloves because those thin ones are freezing.

Jimmy and I went sightseeing yesterday afternoon. We first went to the Washington Monument and took pictures around there. We had to wait so awfully long to get in the monument and it was horribly cold with the wind rushing around the base. It was worth it, though, because that view makes Washington so much clearer to me. It was pure luck to find Jimmy to take me because he lives in Washington and could point out everything, with names included. We had to leave his camera downstairs because they won't allow anyone to take pictures from the top of the monument since the war began. After that we took pictures with the Capitol in the background. It was loads of fun, even if it was freezing. We stopped a couple and had them take several pictures of us together. I do hope they turn out well so you can see me in full uniform. I met Jimmy at Riverside Stadium when I was rollerskating last week. He's home on a 30-day furlough, the first in four years. He's a boilermaker on a destroyer, and he's been in several major battles. He has a red hash mark on his sleeve for four years of service with good conduct. He is one month older than I am and is like a big brother, very nice and lots of fun. He invited me to his home for Thanksgiving dinner when he heard I couldn't be home, and I thought that was swell. Of course, I couldn't go, so we went out that night instead. He left at 5:00 on Sunday for Virginia to spend a few days hunting with his cousins. He's leaving Friday for duty—where, he doesn't know.

Perhaps I should explain my roller skating. I better tell you I've taken it up so if I'm injured, you'll know what caused such an untimely accident! I started because of Justine Love. She works in the same room I do at Hydro. I met her when I was first here, but didn't really talk with her until two weeks ago. We went to town together to go shopping one night and she asked me if I'd go roller skating with her the next night. I said I couldn't skate, so she said she'd teach me. Later I discovered she is a champion roller skater! What a lucky break—a champion for my teacher. She's from Dearborn, Michigan, and worked doing drafting at General Motors in Detroit. By the way, today she received a Christmas present from the plant—a $16 check, plus a blueprint Christmas page with signatures of all plant employees. She's engaged to a fellow from Detroit who's in Army air cadet school down in Miami, Florida. I'm so glad I met her because she made me branch out and do a few new things and not worry about them. The first time that I got on skates was pathetic. Eleanor, you really would've laughed at me. I grabbed hold of everything in sight—people, too! There are three rinks in the place—a small one for beginners with bars on the sides, the main large one, and another rather small one for figure skaters. The place is usually pretty crowded, and everyone has so much fun. There are loads of service girls there. Last Friday

I went for the third time and did much better. I even skated on the big rink once, with Justine to help me along. You should see that girl skate. She can jump, spin, waltz, etc.! I'm getting so enthused over the sport I can hardly wait to go. I think it won't be long until I'm flying around with the rest. Sunday before last I went to the Uline Arena with Justine to watch her ice skate. It was the third time she'd ever tried, and you would have been amazed at how well she did. By the end of two hours, she was jumping and waltzing on ice. She bought her own skates and is going every Sunday afternoon. One soldier I watched that day couldn't stand on blades when he came in and, believe it or not, by the end of those two hours he was flying around pretty nicely. It was loads of fun just watching. So I decided if he could learn, so could I. The reason I haven't tried is because I haven't the right clothes and I wouldn't want to tear my uniform. On roller skates, it isn't too bad. Best of all, I feel so much better since I started skating. I really need to exercise after sitting cramped over a drawing board all day. Surprised at my courage, yes?

My work has been pretty much the same. However, my lettering is definitely improving and my boss, Mac, complimented me today. He said he'd take my work for granted from now on and wouldn't worry about my doing it right anymore. Also, a fellow who's been in lithography work for 30 years told me I did nicer work than any of the WAVES in our room. Though I hardly believe him, it made me feel good—very good in fact! Friday night Sally and I leave for her home for the weekend—I'm looking forward to it. Things have been so nice for me lately. Monday I go back on the night shift for two weeks. Will Richard be home for Christmas? Hope you're all okay!

All my love,

Lucy

Lucy with Jimmy Arneson near the Smithsonian Castle
Washington, D.C. November 28, 1943
Photographer unknown

December 8, 1943

Dear Folks,

Now that I'm on the night shift again, I'm sleeping myself to death. This morning I wanted to get up and go to town to buy my exchange gift for the hall. Even though I put a note on my door, no one called me until 11:30, so I didn't go to town. Guess I'll go tomorrow, since we don't have drill. There's a flu epidemic and the infirmary is filled, so they are afraid drill and inspection would cause a few more to become chilled and take the flu.

Last Friday was quite a thrilling day because Captain McAfee visited us. About 11:00 in the morning, she made a tour of the office and saw what we were doing. Then at noon we passed in review before her and all the naval big shots. I didn't think our marching was so hot, but Ensign Strang seemed to think it was fine. Miss McAfee is so gracious and sweet and has the nicest smile. And neat, whew, she put us all to shame! I certainly would be proud to point her out to anyone as my Cominch![62] There's a write up of her visit in the latest *Scuttlebutt* and I'll send it if I can locate a paper.[63]

Well I didn't go home with Sally after all because I just decided it was too expensive a trip just before Christmas. Train fare to New York is $5.60 round trip. Then we would have to take another train to her home in Rye, which is about 30 minutes from New York. Besides, Sally caught a terrible cold and I thought it'd be better if she rested. I'll go sometime the first of the year. I've been thinking, even if I don't get a leave until March, I'll need to start saving money for it soon because leaves are expensive. For a round-trip ticket we have to pay one dollar more than a civilian does for a one-way ticket. Geri Knight is leaving tonight for Kansas for a 14-day furlough—four days traveling time are included, and she has been saving money for ages. The reason she's getting a leave so soon is because she has a sister in the WAVES who's on leave now. When they went into the WAVES they were promised their first leave together. Poor Geri has such a bad cold she's afraid she'll spend her first day at home in bed with one of her mom's plasters on her chest.

Today I got another photo of myself walking down the streets of Washington. This was taken the first day I came to town. Ruth Wickersham, the girl from Indianapolis, is with me. It's a horrid picture of her since she is very attractive. As usual I have my eyes closed and my mouth open! Thought you might like it anyway. Don't worry about sending any of these back because, as you might know, I haven't started my snapshot book yet. Justine and Geri and I took pictures in her room last week and they came out very good. And as soon as I get some made, I'll send them. Justine has a wonderful camera! We also took some color pictures the

---

62   Cominch—Commander-in-Chief.
63   *Scuttlebutt*—newspaper published by and for the employees of the Hydrographic Office.

same night on a roll her father sent. We haven't seen those yet because the film has to be sent to the Eastman Company and back.

The boxes came Tuesday and I was so glad to get them. The housecoat is too small since you washed it, and I don't quite know what to do about it. Maybe if I washed it or wet it again and stretched it, it would be okay. Let Virginia have the sweater, or Eleanor. I really don't need more than one, although it's all right to have more. This week it's turned warmer so I don't need the comfort, but wait till cold weather and it'll be swell. The apples were really appreciated, too! The girl next door, Pat Spillman, has been giving me so much stuff—cookies, fig and date bars—that her mother and aunt sent. I gave her some apples to sort of make up for it. As for Christmas presents, I won't send much but a few things for you. Think how awful it would be to not be able to buy anything to send. That's the fun of Christmas giving. As for the coat, I think I'll decide later and try to make up my mind if I have to have it before I go ahead. That's a lot of money for a coat.

I'm glad Josephine is going home for Christmas. I don't think she's too satisfied in Washington. As every week draws closer to Christmas, I want more and more to go home. However, most of us will be here and they've planned some nice things for us. I should be glad I have a home I can go to when I get time off. So many girls here are alone in the world. The reason Jo didn't find me at church was because I've been going to church out here, with the Navy chaplain in charge. When it's cold and I'm tired it seems such an effort to go clear into town, take a bus ride and then catch a streetcar.

The worst thing now about this night shift is that I'm not able to continue my roller skating. Just when I was getting good, too! Saturday night I went skating with three other girls and I met a sailor from Bloomington, Indiana, and another from Dayton, Ohio. Both of them helped me skate around the big rink and that was thrilling, and dangerous. After skating, the four of us girls were coming down F Street and were headed for the Mayflower shop for waffles and coffee. We stopped for a streetlight, and someone spoke my name.

I turned around and there was Clair McKinney.[64] He was with two other Marines, and they're all in officer candidate school at Quantico, Virginia. He looks perfectly wonderful as if he's in the best of health. One of the girls went on home and another met her boyfriend and we were still standing on the corner talking. Finally, Clair suggested eating, so we went to a restaurant and ate and gabbed. One of the Marines left and so there was only Sylvia and me, and Clair, and Lou. This Lou is a swell person, and so full of life he almost wears you out. Anyway, it was getting late so the fellows took us all the way home in a taxi. Clair said he wanted to see the place where I live. It was so good to talk over things and people at home. He'll be here until April. At times he gets such a blank, faraway look in his eyes. I imagine he's not over his wife by any means.[65] This Lou liked Sylvia so much, and vice versa, that they had a date Sunday and have another for next Sunday!

Gloria Hackney, a red-haired beauty in our wing, wanted me to double date with her. She had a date with a civilian at Hydro, and he had a sailor friend who also works at Hydro. He's very nice, a blond from North Carolina. We went to the zoo, and I was so glad, for it's beautiful there. All we did was cut up and laugh all day. Coming back to town on the bus, the bus collided with a station wagon and turned it over. The station wagon driver was in the wrong. Mr. Kingsmith, 61 years old, was the driver of the car. He was lying on the ground when we got out. His ear was bloody and they said he had brain concussion. He kept asking about his dogs, two beautiful dogs in the back seat. They were okay. He's very wealthy, an owner of an art school. I didn't even know what was happening. I just thought we were stopping quickly. Gloria and Herb were sitting in the back where there was no seat in front to stop them and they went sailing down the aisle in front of me. Next thing I knew I was standing on her hat! We died laughing about it all, later. Quite thrilling—ha ha ha—as Richard would

---

64   Clair McKinney was from Lucy's hometown.
65   *Editor's note*: Despite considerable research, I cannot determine what happened with Clair's wife. He did marry again on December 1, 1945, had two daughters, and worked as an optometrist.

say. Well, I must get ready for work or I'll be late to muster. Hope you're all fine.

All my love,

Lucy

Hydrographic Office WAVES Review December 3, 1943—Suitland, Maryland
Lucy is in second row of WAVES—second from right
Captain McAfee—front, third from left. Courtesy of Eleanor Guza

Lucy with Ruth Wickersham (on right)—October 8, 1943. Photographer unknown

I'll Be Seeing You 109

December 17, 1943

Dear Mother & Daddy,

At last, I managed to wrap my meager little packages of Christmas cheer and send them off. I won't apologize for going ahead and sending things when you said not to, because I wanted to and it was fun, and besides, who else have I to buy for? Christmas isn't any fun when there's no one to surprise or make a bit happier. I'm as slow as you, Mother, about Christmas cards. I just started writing mine today. Maybe they'll get there around Christmas, at least. I got the sweetest card from Olive yesterday, which reminded me of the letter I owe her. Already I've gotten so many cards it's wonderful. Maybe my friends do remember me even if I am in the Navy and owe them letters.

Mother, I decided to send a few of the things back that you sent. Not that I don't appreciate your sending them, but I really don't need the pink sweater and thought Eleanor could get more good out of it than I would. You see, it's more of a dress sweater and I only need sweaters for skating and sports and keeping warm here in the hall. The blue and red are plenty and are fine. As far as the slacks, I can't wear them at all because they're too small. Last fall they were tight, but now I can't even get them around me. I hope Eleanor can wear them—I'll get some later. I've gained so much weight it's pathetic. One of the suits I had taken up is too tight now. I sent some pictures in which you can see how fat I am. One picture I've had for ages is my section picture at Hunter. It was such a horrid snap of me I hated to send it, but I decided you'd like to see it anyway. Miss Booth, on the left, was our company commander. On the right is sweet Miss Wilson, our platoon commander, and Miss Kellison is holding the flag. (see page 88) She was our section leader. Miss Kellison is a crack tennis player and lots of fun. The other pictures are ones Justine and I took in her room. My room is just like the one in the photograph, except my chair is different. I think they turned out wonderfully for indoor pictures. I'm having some others made up for my photo book.

I meant to tell you about sending those gym shoes. They were issued to us at Hunter, but they're so large for me, and I never will need them here. Maybe Eleanor can wear them. Also, I sent that brush that won't brush well. I really don't need it. Boy, was I ever glad to get your blanket last week. It was absolutely freezing and I do mean freezing. It was only a little above zero and I don't think I could've stood the nights without the blanket. There has been a flu epidemic here and the infirmary is full. So far I haven't taken cold, and I believe it's because I take a vitamin B pill every night. About a month ago I discovered I could work much longer and better with extra energy, so I got some vitamins. They really help, and I expect that's why I've gained weight.

Just now Sally brought up my mail and I had a letter from you, Mama. The most wonderful thing was hearing from you about Jonie being better. Somehow I'll enjoy Christmas more knowing he's okay. It's been a year now since I've seen him. About Richard saying I asked for this—I'm not sorry and never will be—I enjoy my work and love being in the Navy. However, one can want to visit home once in a while anyway. As you were saying once, I've lots of opportunities here, and I realize that.

Sunday, I was asked to dinner by Cecil, and little did I think you'd hear about it before I told you. Gene Rodman was there when I arrived, and my mouth fell open when I saw him.[66] He is stationed close to Baltimore, Maryland. We had a delicious meal, prepared by Margaret Ann, and then Rodman, Kathryn, Margaret, and I went to the cathedral again so Gene could see it. I did see the Bishop's Garden for the first time and it's beautiful. We all had such a wonderful time. Gene had to go back early, but I stayed on and talked and ate candy. I left about 5:00 p.m. Margaret Ann and Kathryn will be alone because Cecil and Warren are going to New York for Christmas. Mr. Crim is coming and they invited me to spend the day with them.[67] However, I feel as

---

66   Gene Rodman was from Salem and one of the best friends of Lucy's brother Richard.

67   Mr. Crim—Margaret Ann and Kathryn's father, from Salem, Indiana.

if their family circle would be better without me, so I'll stay here. They have a nice program planned at church with a children's party on Wednesday, hanging of greens, a Christmas Eve party with fellows invited, caroling, refreshments etc., and a Christmas dinner. I think it will be nice. On the 23rd our wing is having an exchange party. We drew names about a month ago. They really do try to make us happy here, and I'm beginning to like the officers more all the time.

I'm so glad Grandmother is with you now. Wish I could see you all at Christmas, having a good time as always. I'll be thinking about all of you. Monday I go on days again, and am I glad. Besides I can go skating again! I must get ready for work.

Love,

Lucy

With Justine Love—December 1943
Courtesy of Justine Love

I'll Be Seeing You   113

CHAPTER EIGHT
A NEW YEAR BEGINS

January 2, 1944

Dear Folks,

This is the first time I've written 1944 and it seems so funny. Time just flies anymore. My Christmas was very unusual but very nice. Daddy, I even hung up that sweet little sock you sent, just for fun! Thank you so much for the money and the card. Christmas Eve afternoon, we had a party at Hydro and had cake and ice cream. It was fair. Then that night, Grace Loveless and I went to the show *Lassie Come Home* and it was very good.[68] Then we tried to go to Mass, but the church was too crowded. Christmas morning, I got up at 9:30 and opened my gifts. It seemed funny to not run downstairs and have everyone yelling! I was so proud of everything. And Mother, I'm so glad you sent some fruitcake—I sort of hoped you would. The pictures were so unexpected, and so good of all of you. It almost made me cry when I saw all of you before me. All the girls have seen the pictures and raved about my good-looking family and I agree! You couldn't have sent me anything I wanted more. Virginia's gift, the slip, was so lovely and just what I needed. Sally also gave me a beautiful slip. Eleanor, you rat, I thought I'd never finish unwrapping that box! Whew! It was fun, though. I almost fell off the bed, I laughed so hard! Thanks so much for the cards—they're so pretty. And the peanuts, too, were appreciated. Mother, you do know what I need—I was practically desperate for soap and I'm glad to get it. The food was certainly delved into in a hurry. The other girls around enjoyed it all with me. Most everyone left though, because we had weekend liberty. The worst tragedy—the oranges were spoiled! The tangerines were okay though,

---

68 *Lassie Come Home* plot: A destitute family is forced to sell their beloved Lassie, a collie dog. Lassie escapes from her new home in Scotland and makes her way back to her family in Yorkshire.

and they really smelled and tasted Christmasy! Those cookies were delicious, and the fruitcake—yum! Thanks for the stockings, Mother. Of course, for dress we wear rayon, but those will be wonderful for work. After opening my presents, I went back to bed till 2:00 p.m.

Christmas afternoon about 4:30, I went out to Margaret Ann's and on the way it started snowing and sleeting. It was so good to see Heber Crim and hear more news from home. He eats at Mrs. Shanks, and she sent a lovely fruitcake and other food, even wonderful homemade butter. Rodman's mother sent a chicken and more stuff and presents for Eugene. About 5:30, Gene came and brought with him a fellow from Fort Wayne who'd graduated from IU. He and Eugene have been together since they went into the Army and knew each other when they majored in chemistry at IU. His name was White and he seemed very nice. Kathryn's boyfriend, Don, a sailor, yeoman, was there too, and is he ever nice and good looking! He brought her a gorgeous orchid and also gave her a fountain pen for Christmas. He's from Pittsburgh. We had a wonderful meal with plenty of seconds. Then we all went to a formal dance put on by the Christian Endeavor of the church where the girls go. The admission was the purchase of a 25¢ war stamp. The dance was small, but extremely nice, and we had loads of fun. I was the only service woman there, for all the other girls wore formals. It was nice to be the only WAVE around for once. I took a taxi back to town to make my bus. It had gotten so slippery and the car slid around. The driver told me 101 accidents had been reported during the last hour! Sand was being put on all the main drags, but the weather was awful—so terribly damp and cold. When I finally got to the bus stop, there were tons of people waiting for buses. Well, I stood and froze from 1:00 to 2:00 a.m. and still no buses. I called the hall and the ensign said okay, and that lots of others had called, too. She said to get a bus when I could and if not get a room in town. Finally, a bus came at 2:15 a.m. and I struggled on. Boy, what a mess! The ride back wasn't bad. The next day it was worse, and fog added to the dreariness. I slept most of the day. At 4:00 I dressed and went outside to see if it was fit to venture out. It was dark and rainy and puddly and grayish. I came back and told the girls it looked like the movie *The Hound of the Baskervilles*—all fog and ghastliness and mud![69] So I stayed in and washed and ironed, played records, gabbed, and ate! Somehow I couldn't settle down to writing letters. Quite a Christmas!

This past week has been a busy one. I had a rush job at the office, floating letters on a Duco zinc plate. My former job (a matching one) was printed and I was proud of it. I think it's the best I've done. Just now I heard through scuttlebutt that Mr. Baker thought I did fine work. I am amazed, for he never says a word to me! Working is nice, and yet it's like any job—some days I'm so discouraged and can't seem to letter at all, and other days the outlook's bright. Working hours seem longer because the work is close and you have so much time to think. It is nicer than any other job I can think of at present, though.

About two weeks ago Clair McKinney called on Sunday and wanted me to meet him downtown, so I did. We went to the Treasure Island Club and ate, and the food was wonderful. I had the most delicious ice cream cake. The music was good, too! He had invited me out to Quantico for Christmas, but I told him I was going to visit the Crims. He still broods about his wife. They took a picture of us and I cut it down so I could send it, since there were people nearby I didn't know anyway. I want it back for my book. I think it's one of the best pictures I've ever taken. Earlier in the afternoon of the same day, Jimmy Arneson appeared very unexpectedly and brought the pictures we'd taken that Sunday. I think they're pretty good, too. Jimmy's at Norfolk, Virginia, in school now, before he ships out again. I meant to have my picture taken before Christmas, but studios were so busy I decided to wait. Besides, prices are simply sky high for even a couple of good pictures.

I haven't been skating the past week because I've been too busy. The week before I fell on the big rink and bruised my knee—also tore my hose! My knee was stiff for a while, but it's okay now. I'm going again Tuesday. I've decided to buy a winter coat if I can. Saw another good

---

69   *The Hound of the Baskervilles* plot: A legendary, supernatural hound stalks the estate of a young heir, prompting an investigation by Sherlock Holmes and Dr. Watson.

show on New Year's Eve—*Jack London*.[70] Georgeanne and I were in the theater when the clock struck 12! Somehow I got to thinking of that New Year's Eve I went to Louisville with Mr. Dexter. He kept worrying because you had told me I should be in by 1:00! New Year's Day, I worked my usual half-day, and then washed and ironed clothes all afternoon.

Friday I got a letter from Olive Minniear, saying Betty Patty was stationed in Washington and giving me the address of Martha Ellen Bales, who works for the FBI. Martha lived in our wing at Forest Hall and graduated from IU one year before I did. She's very sweet—tall, has red hair, and majored in business. Tonight I went out to see her at Harvard Hall, where she shares an apartment with three other girls who work at the FBI. She wasn't home, but a Corveta Livingston was, and she was so sweet to me. They have a lovely apartment and keep it so spotless. She gave me some cookies she'd just made, and were they good! I visited a while and left my address and phone for Martha. Hopefully, we can get together soon. I haven't located Betty, though I know she's with the 2nd Signal Service Battalion. The holidays have made me rather homesick and discovering friends here has made me feel better today.

All my love,

Lucy

P.S. I'm so glad you had such a lovely Christmas. I got a Christmas card and letter from Jonie on Friday. Said he'd had malaria and was sending me a present at home, that it wasn't much, but I'd know it hadn't been made in Brooklyn. He said he would like a picture of me. It was a wonderful letter, for him, and I was so happy to get it. His buddies made the card and it had a verse typed on it and was very clever.

---

70 *Jack London* plot: Episodes in the life of the famous American novelist.

With Clair McKinney—December 1943
Photographer unknown

Lucy and coworkers at Hydrographic Office
Lucy is seated in center with head turned to the left
Photographer unknown

January 18, 1944

Dear Daddy,

Finally getting around to writing you a letter in answer to all of your sweet letters. We can't even relax in our rooms—they always have to be just-so for inspection. I put all my letters away, and then it's easy to forget about answering them—some excuse!

I was supposed to meet the Souders at church Sunday, but decided not to go because of the deep snow. I don't have galoshes, and thought I'd get too wet going out. I called them, and Mr. Souder said they weren't going either because of the icy streets. So next Sunday I will try to see them.

It started snowing Saturday morning and turned to hail and sleet. Then by Saturday about 6:00 p.m., it began snowing steadily and was so beautiful. Saturday night I went with two WAVES on a blind date—my date was a naval air lieutenant from New York. He'd gone to college at Iowa State, was awfully nice and intelligent—truly! Sunday I stayed home and slept and mended. I wanted to go out and have a snow fight but didn't have shoes or slacks. Some of the girls made a beautiful snow lady out in front, and she's still standing today though it's pretty warm. Sunday night I went to see *Madame Curie* starring Greer Garson and Walter Pidgeon. It is a really grand picture![71] You know we read that book, by Eve Curie, in French during my sophomore year. That made the picture so much more interesting. Every day I'm more than thankful for my college education, Daddy. It means so much more than you realize while you're actually in school.

This last week of work made me feel pretty good, because I did the best job I've done so far. Usually after we finish with a piece of work, something is wrong—it comes up scummy or dirty, etc. The fellow in the transfer room called me in to see my zinc plate after it was worked up and congratulated me on doing a good job. He said, "Now do all of them like that!" Would that I could! Mac, the assistant boss, told me it was the best lettering I'd ever done, and some of the fellows who are really good thought it was swell, and kept calling others over to see it. Mac told me he was promoting me to harder jobs, so now I do work more like the men do. It's really intricate and takes more brainwork, too! Then later, one of the girls in the section next to mine said she heard Mac telling her boss I was the best draftsman among the WAVES in Damage Control, and was the envy of a lot of WAVES. He said I was a perfect example—stuck to my desk, worked, and didn't give up. I really put on a halo when I heard that. I actually couldn't believe it!! I'm telling you, it's pretty unglamorous work—it's tedious, tiresome as far as backache is concerned, and hard on the eyes and nerves. So when you get a compliment like that—it really helps. I do like it and think that's why I do so well. However, I'm

---

71   *Madame Curie* plot: biographical depiction of the romance between Marie and Pierre Curie and their discovery of radium.

working harder than ever, simply because I know my own mistakes and know it'll be a long time before I'm halfway satisfied with my own work. Even the men say they always feel a job could be improved, and they're as good as they come!

Monday I started on nights again. Somehow I don't mind night work as much as I used to—it's much more quiet to work because not many people are there.

Yesterday I went into town to try and get my pen fixed. I can't even write with it. There's only one place where they fix Parker pens, and they won't take it until February 1st. So I've borrowed a pen to write this letter. It's much better than mine. I hate pencil, and that pen has to be dipped in ink every two minutes. Besides, the point is sprung and won't slide smoothly. Maybe they can fix it up.

Daddy, I want to thank you again for the Christmas gift. I still get out that little sock and look at it. It is so cute. I'm saving the money and I'll get something I can keep, something I like very much—sometime.

Georgeanne Turner got a book of poems and a leather picture frame with the money her father sent. She is still my favorite WAVE friend, because she's always the same. We have it all planned that I'm to visit her in San Francisco after the war is over.

The pictures are wonderful of all of you! Eleanor is getting so tall and glamorous, I'm going to be afraid to stand beside her. Richard looks as if he's gained more weight—whew—what a man! And you and Mother look so sweet together. I'm glad to have a picture of Mildred, although I've seen better ones of her. Jonie's picture was one I really appreciated since it's the first I've seen since he left. It's a little hard to see his face, but you sure know it's Jonie! I'm going to keep it a while longer to show some more of the kids.

Sally is on special leave because her father came back from his survey tour Thursday. Last week he was reported missing, and then it was confirmed. Poor Sally nearly went out of her mind. Then Wednesday she got a wire from him saying he was in California and coming to Washington to report to his chief. She's a different girl now. She got seven days leave so she could be at home while he had leave, too. He'd been in Burma, Australia—in fact all over—and was in action. He's a naval air lieutenant, as is her fiancé, Bud Hammel. She's to be married in September. This week she's having her gown fitted. For Christmas she got quite a bit of silver.

We only get 10 days leave per year and can take that altogether or in parts. I wonder if you'd rather I came home five days in March and five days another time, or 10 days in March? If I take five days, a lot of that time will be taken up with traveling, since they give extra travel time only west of the Mississippi. Of course, as yet I don't know when I can get home, but it won't be too far away.

Here's a funny little poem I heard the other day:

> *I think that I shall never rave,*
> *About another Navy WAVE,*
> *A WAVE whose appetite's no fake,*
> *Who orders caviar and steak.*
>
> *A WAVE who looks at me with stars,*
> *Then turns her head for silver bars,*
> *A WAVE who must forever wear,*
> *Six inches cropped from off her hair.*
>
> *A WAVE who loves to stay out late,*
> *But can't be kissed at her front gate,*
> *God, give me strength my soul to save*
> *And never date another WAVE!*

While Captain MacAfee was here, one of the girls took quite a few pictures. They're very good, and I got several. I'll send some home and you can return them later.

Well, I must hurry and finish this, clean up my room for inspection at 3:00, and off to work at 4:30. I'm really tired today. Went to bed at 2:00 a.m., was up at 7:00 a.m. for inspection, back to bed, up at 11:00 for muster meeting, and now inspection at 3:00 again!

Well, Daddy, I hope you're well. Write me again and I'll try not to neglect you for so long this time.

All my love,

Lucy

January 24, 1944

Dear Mother,

Everyone has been writing me about Wayne's death.[72] Virginia, Geneva, and other kids too. Geneva told me about Daddy giving money for flowers from our class—I'm so glad. Somehow it won't seem the same at home without Wayne—he was always so full of life. Even yet I can't believe he is gone. Every time I look at his picture in the paper I can't quite stand it. His wife is through school, which is lucky. She can work and go ahead somehow. Virginia said Cookie was so worried now about Louie and Harold. After all, they were in as much danger a month ago as now, so it's no worse. Anyone in the service is in danger, and when they go, it's really brought home to their loved ones. All we can do is have a lot of faith—our worrying won't do them any good.

Today it's so beautiful out, so I slept to almost 1:00. I meant to go to town and get some shoes—and I was so dead I couldn't seem to move. I'm on the night shift this week and time seems to drag as it always does when I work at night. Sally is back from her leave and sorta hates to begin working again. However, her dad works here in Washington, so she can see him often.

Saturday I bought a book—*The Robe* by Lloyd C. Douglas. If you haven't read it, I'll send it when I'm through. It's *very* good. Also, I saw a good show, *Flesh and Fantasy*—very weird in spots and yet, interesting. It was about dreams—and had a good moral.[73]

---

72   Wayne Simpson, one of Lucy's high school classmates, died in a plane crash January 14, 1944, near Santa Ana, California, where he was in bomber pilot training.

73   *Flesh and Fantasy* plot: Three somewhat connected occult tales with romantic and ironic twists.

I think I told you Betty Patty is here in Washington. Olive M. wrote me right after Christmas that was she was here working with the 2nd Signal Service Battalion. I called her, and we found every time she was on nights I was on days, and vice versa. Besides, she works Sundays! Then today she called and said she had the day off on Thursday, so we're going to meet in town then. It'll be good to see her, even if we did have a time last spring. Betty is always lots of fun. It's funny—we were in college together, then Columbus, and now Washington! She says she thinks she'll go home next week on a five-day leave. Incidentally, I learned we're the only WAVES, or service women, in Washington who don't have to work on Sunday. Really, I guess we're the only service women in Washington who have a great many privileges. There are a few important ones—no work on Sunday; every other half day off on Saturday; our own rooms; very nice, lenient officers; a lovely place in which to live; a nice recreation hall of our own; we work right beside our hall; and very nice bosses to work for, in general. I am a lucky girl!

I got a nice card from Aunt Belle and Aunt Fannie, and I must write them. Every time I look in my pathetic drawer and see those ripped seams and socks that need mending, I know how much I'd like to have you around, Mother!

Today I have to laugh—I got a card from the IU Bureau of Teacher Recommendation asking me to fill it out and send it in, since there was a scarcity of teachers. I just wrote my name and rating on it and sent it in. Ha!

About my picture—I still haven't had any taken, but as you need one, I'll have one taken this next week. Can't think of any more news. Hope you're all fine.

All my love,

Lucy

February 6, 1944

Dearest Mother & Daddy,

Sunday once again, as time really flies. This week has been extra full with an extra large washing and ironing, meetings, etc. Last week I was sick with a terrible cold, my first since being in the Navy. I'm okay now.

Last Sunday, I finally met Mr. and Mrs. Souder and Martha at church. They were so nice to me and took me out to dinner at the Ivy Terrace, where I had the best food I've had since I left Salem and home. Martha is tall and slender, blonde, and very pretty. We had such a nice time together. Martha is a sophomore at the University of Maryland and is all wrapped up in college and such. She had to go back to school in the afternoon. At 6:00 p.m. that same day, I went to the church annex and attended the Young People's supper and meeting. Everyone was so nice to me, and I met several WAVES and Marines. The main feature of the program was a talk by Mrs. Hastings, wife of the minister. She's an ordained minister herself and gave one of the finest talks I have ever heard. Everyone seems to love her. All the young people are so nice. There are a great many 4-Fs among the boys, I daresay.[74] But we'll have to expect that now. Tuesday night I went to a church banquet at the annex. It was just like Conference.[75] We used our Conference clap, sang, and had an excellent meal. Afterwards we played games and had fun. Kathryn Crim was there with her sailor boyfriend, Don.

Personal inspection has got to be the most important thing in our lives. My platoon has inspection at 7:45 a.m. on Tuesday mornings. Every Monday I kill myself pressing clothes and putting up my hair real tight. If you're placed on the inspection tree for too long hair, an un-pressed suit, dirty anchors, rating badge on wrong, etc., you're deprived of a week of liberty for one or more weekends according

---

74   A selective service rating of 4-F meant a man was not qualified for military service often due to a vision, hearing, or other medical problem.

75   The summer church camp Lucy attended as a teen was called Conference.

to the type of thing wrong. Then you have to stand Anchor Watch, 2:00-4:00 a.m., for so many weeks. I hold my breath every time the ensign passes me. So far, under this new system, I have passed. Some of the girls are just killed when they have planned to go home for the weekend and have to stay here because they have a dirty anchor on their collars. I think it's the worst thing yet, and certainly lowers morale. Just because a few girls are sloppy, the rest of us have to suffer for it. I guess I ought not to complain since we have so many privileges, especially the single rooms, which are so wonderful.

Last Saturday Martha Hilton and Clair McKinney called me and wanted me to meet them in town. They have gotten together, and Martha was thrilled to death since Clair was the first person from home she'd seen since she left. I couldn't go in because I just got off work and was in the midst of washing and ironing. So I've never seen Martha but will try to soon. She said she just loves the Marines—I'm so glad!

Best news of all—I'm coming home on leave! I asked for a pass before my time was really up, and got it, since no others were leaving from our office. I'll be starting on the B&O about 6:45 on the evening of February 22nd. I'll be home sometime on the 23rd. I'll have to look up exact schedules. Leave has been changed now to 14 days with no travel time. So I'll really be home on leave seven days now and take seven more later. I'm already so excited it's terrible! I wanted to leave at that time so I'd see Richard in case he is moved rather soon. After all, I do want to see as many of you as I can. I'll remember to eat very little before my train ride this time and maybe I won't get sick.

Another very important thing is I'm now a S1C, Seaman 1st Class. I was promoted today! It doesn't mean just I was promoted, for it goes according to length of WAVE service, conduct, etc., and a whole bunch of us were promoted at once. I'm quite proud, even if still a seaman.

This letter has been written in installments—it's now Tuesday. I'm so glad grandmother liked her gift. How is she anyway?

All my love,

Lucy

A valentine Lucy sent home

Lucy's insignia—an anchor was worn on each lapel and one on the hat

INSTRUCTIONS FOR ENLISTED PERSONNEL ON LEAVE

1. Leave is granted subject to immediate recall; therefore, maintain communication with your leave address. Keep papers in your possession at all times.

2. It is understood you have sufficient funds to defray your expenses on leave, including round-trip transportation or necessary funds therefor. Each case of transportation obtained from recruiting stations, or other naval activities, by personnel on leave, will be investigated, and where no urgent necessity was apparent in applying for transportation request, disciplinary action will be taken.

3. You are directed not to participate in press conferences, talk to reporters, or other individuals, or talk over the radio, on matters pertaining to the naval service, except after consultation with, and clearance by, a Naval Public Relations Officer. You are accountable for censorable information which you may communicate in any form. Do not talk to anyone concerning the questioning of prisoners of war, ship movements, or other vital information pertaining to the naval or military services.

4. Inform yourself of train schedules and make allowances for delays. Missing train connections is not an excuse for overleave. Train and bus schedules and connections are frequently unreliable. DO NOT BE A.O.L.

5. Cooperate with Shore Patrol and Military Police at all times, particularly on trains. Misconduct will be cause for disciplinary action. You are subject to orders of your superior officers in all branches of the armed services.

6. Requests for extension of leave will be granted only for emergency reasons. If necessary to request an extension, communicate with your commanding officer by telegram or letter. IF NO REPLY IS RECEIVED, YOU WILL CONSIDER YOUR REQUEST NOT GRANTED.

7. In case of serious illness or injury incurred while on leave, requiring medical attention or hospitalization, report facts to your commanding officer, by telegram, and request instructions.

8. Correct telegraphic address of your ship or station is:

> COMMANDING OFFICER,
> U. S. NAVAL BARRACKS,
> WEST POTOMAC PARK,
> WASHINGTON 4, D. C.

I have read and understand the foregoing instructions.

Lucy M. Berkey Sp(x)3/c
(Name)   (Rate)

Courtesy of the National Archives

Miss Lucy Berkey, S1/c, who is a lithographic draftsman in the hydrographic office at Suitland, Maryland, a suburb of Washington, D. C., plans to arrive today to spend 5 of her 7-day leave with her parents the J. G. Berkeys. Pvt. Richard Berkey, who is completing his basic course in engineering at the University of Cincinnati and Miss Virginia Berkey, a senior at Indiana University, plan to join their sister Seaman Berkey, in the visit home.

February 23, 1944
Courtesy of The Salem Leader

Top row: Martha Neal Huffman, Eleanor Berkey
Bottom row: Jean Berkey (cousin), Lucy, Richard, Virginia, Mildred Berkey
February 28, 1944
Courtesy of Geneva Head

I'll Be Seeing You   129

Lucy and Richard with their parents, Jim and Lennie
February 28, 1944
Courtesy of Geneva Head

130 Karen Berkey Huntsberger

Lucy and Richard
February 28, 1944
Courtesy of Geneva Head

I'll Be Seeing You 131

February 29, 1944

Dear Folks,

Got back here at the hall at 9:00 a.m. The train was late, so it's certainly lucky I took the early train instead of waiting. From West Virginia on there was snow, and in Washington practically a *snowstorm!* I took a taxi out here from Union Station because it was so bad out. What a difference in weather! I slept most all day and went to a show tonight with my sailor. Such a wonderful leave! I've never had such a swell vacation—or maybe I appreciated it more. News—I rode all the way with a soldier from Madison, Indiana, who played on the basketball team when they went to state in '39. Also, we do get 14 days, so I'll get my other seven days and may not have to wait six months either. Also, we now can apply for a 62-hour leave over the weekend, so I may be able to come home on such. Wonderful news! I must get to bed for I'm very tired. Have to report in the morning at 0830. Will write more later.

Love,

Lucy

March 14, 1944

Dearest Mother & Daddy,

After ironing and washing all evening, I feel like sitting down, and for a long time. So I'll write a letter while I'm sitting. I've been so busy since I've been back from leave. Work at the office is stacked up. Everything is pretty dreary right now—one day it snows, then rains for two days, and is freezing cold the next.

Mother, you feel just the way I do when you say my visit home seems like a dream now. However, it was so wonderful and I keep thinking about it all the time. I was so glad Richard could hitchhike home to see me, at least for a little while. Anyway, I don't have that "want to go home" feeling I did have for a while before my leave. Leaves really do help!

Things have been rather humdrum here, the only excitement being Maxine Fisher's wedding Sunday at 1:00 at the Nazarene Church. She married Benjamin Kean, who's a CPO and stationed in Virginia.[76] They are both swell kids and Maxine is loved by everyone. I was one of twelve girls who formed a color guard and saluted as they came out of the church. We had rice in our left hands and it kept dripping on the walk as we stood there waiting. Boy, did we ever plaster them with rice! Her father came from Arkansas to give her away. Her mother is dead and Maxine said she so wished her mother could have seen her married. There's a fellow, Mr. Feris, in our office who has been so wonderful to Maxine. He and his wife became acquainted with her right after Christmas and had her out at their home. Since then she's practically one of the family. They have two small children. Mrs. Feris made Maxine's satin wedding gown and it was so beautiful. The reception was held at the Feris home and Maxine's roommate, Helen Pagones, helped supervise things. Helen is our mustering petty officer and a grand girl. She's from Missouri. Saturday was sunny and so lovely and then Sunday just before the ceremony it began to sprinkle. It wasn't too bad to stand outside and the couple made a dash for the car as soon as they passed the color guard. Eleanor Guza, who took some of those pictures of Miss MacAfee's visit, took pictures during and after the ceremony, so I'll have a few more pictures for my collection. Eleanor is a professional photographer.

The pictures from my visit home in February were swell and turned out better than I had expected. Your description of Richard and me was good. We do look funny in those pictures. I'm on tiptoe, too! The one of Richard and the girls is good and the one of you, Daddy, Richard, and me is very nice.

You remember my speaking of Georgeanne so much. She did live across from me, but has moved into another wing so she can have a corner room with two windows and a nice view. She wanted the

---

76   CPO: Chief Petty Officer.

room, but hated to move. I really miss her for I had more fun with her than anyone here. She comes down quite often, though.

I still haven't seen Betty Patty and I believe Martha Hilton's home now. After the wedding Virginia Hill and I went to town. It began pouring and continued to pour all night. We went to a show and ate. She told me her fiancé, a CPO, is on a sub chaser in the Pacific. She saw him in December when he was docked in California, and he took her all over the ship. She's going to tell me all about the sub chaser when we have time. She's one of the nicest girls I've met here.

Not much news, so I'll stop. Maybe I'll write to David tonight. Do you know when he'll be home again? I might make it.

Much love,

Lucy

CHAPTER NINE
TEA WITH
MRS. ROOSEVELT

April 16, 1944

Dear Mother & Daddy,

Whew! I really felt ashamed when your letter came, telling me I'd written only once since I was home in February. I knew it'd been a long time, but goodness. I haven't written anyone, not even sweet little David while he was in California. I could hardly stand it when I read he was out at sea—if I could only have seen him first. I'm glad Jonie is so well and has received mail at last. Mildred [McBride Berkey] wrote me a very nice, long letter.

To go way back, right after I returned from leave I went to two good dances with about 40 girls from here. The first one was at Solomon's Base, and it was fairly nice. Then we had a marvelous time at Stump Neck Base down across the river from Quantico. They fed us as soon as we arrived, after a two-hour drive, and what a meal! Heaps of fried chicken, peas, mashed potatoes, hot rolls, olives, celery, tomatoes, cookies, and ice cream! There was so much fried chicken left over, they gave each of us a sack of it to take home, and we ate royally for days.

We've all been having quite a time getting our summer uniforms. I now have my two seersucker work uniforms. The dress fits me just perfect, but the jacket is so messy looking. Of course, we won't have to wear a jacket here at Suitland, just when we go into town. I still have to buy a white uniform and a lightweight dark blue one when I get the money. I also need white shoes, a white bag cover, and I should get a summer raincoat. It's terrible downtown since warm weather arrived—all the stores are mobbed and the people practically kill you as they push and shove. Now I know Washington is crowded, and how! This summer it'll be worse, too.

Eloise Park Kinney came to see me one day, and they told her I was too busy at work to see her. I was so mad when I read her note, for I could easily have seen her. She asked me to come see her, as she was leaving in three days. I was too busy to go see her, though, because of other appointments, and couldn't get through on the phone. I hope she doesn't think I didn't want to see her, for I did. Also, I got a letter from Mary Louise Ford, a WAVE ensign I knew at IU. So far, we haven't gotten together yet.

I saw the movie *The Song of Bernadette*, and it is absolutely the best motion picture I've ever seen.[77] Thank goodness I saw it before my eyes went phooey, for it is a three-hour film. You must see it.

This will amaze you! I visited the White House on 4/4/44—and it was just one of the nicest things in which I've ever been included. One of the girls here has "pull" through a lady who is a friend of Eleanor Roosevelt. She arranged for 25 of us from here and 25 from another barracks, including officers, to be presented at tea at 5:00 p.m. We stood in a circle in the blue room and Mrs. Roosevelt shook hands with each of us. She was such a surprise to me, for she's much nicer looking than her pictures show her, and also, more slender. And charming—well, you can't help liking her. Then we went into the formal dining room and had punch and cookies. The plates were lovely and fragile, with a gold band around the rim and the gold seal. I was scared I'd drop my plate! The room was paneled in wood, and is one of the most beautiful of all, I think. Mrs. Roosevelt talked to us very informally and we had fun. Then they brought in Fala, the dog, and some of the girls played with him. Not me, of course. I was afraid he'd want to play with me! Soon Eleanor went upstairs, for the president was ill with a cold. One of the guards showed us through the rest of the main floor and the basement. As we were going through the front hall, it began snowing, and I shall never forget how beautiful it was to look out between those magnificent columns and see enormous snowflakes floating down. That trip is something I won't soon forget!

---

77   *The Song of Bernadette* plot: A teenage French girl attracts a following when she reports having seen "a beautiful lady" at the city dump. Rumors follow that the "lady" is the Virgin Mary. The government and the church attempt to suppress Bernadette and her followers.

On Easter, I submitted my membership at church. It is a special thing for service people. You don't really take it from your home church, or I would not have done it. But I wanted so much to have it in here, because I've enjoyed the church and young people so much. After church I went home with Jo for dinner, and Margaret Ann had a lovely meal prepared for us. Cecil was gone and so was Kathryn. We saw the cherry blossoms in the afternoon, and what beautiful things they are! It's like looking at a pink mist. Across the water they make a beautiful picture with the Jefferson Memorial in the background. It was terribly hot, though, and we were glad to get out of the crowd and back to town.

That night I went to Young People's meeting and we had a play that was wonderful. Some of those kids are really talented. That same evening there was a sailor there from Indianapolis, and I've been going out with him ever since. He's undoubtedly the nicest fellow I've ever dated or ever will. I'm afraid he'll be leaving soon for preflight training, though. He's in VR8 at Patuxent River, Maryland. Today he's in New York seeing a buddy of his but will be back this evening. I hope, because we have a date at 8:00.

So, IU is out already! It doesn't seem possible. It will seem peculiar to not come to the end of the school year as I've been doing since I was six years old.

It's so beautiful today that all the girls are taking sunbaths out back. Georgeanne and I took a walk after lunch and it was so hot we almost died in our winter jackets. We go into summer uniforms May 15.

I received a short note from Richard yesterday saying he's been moved to Camp Campbell and assigned to the 84th Medical Battalion, 14th Armored Division. He was so happy because Buster is there, too! And he's a cook! They're in the same division, it seems, but different companies. I do hope they can be together when they go overseas. Richard heard from Jonie, who has been promoted to lieutenant! You probably already know all this, but in case you don't, now you do! Ha!

Love,

Lucy

EDITOR'S NOTE:

I felt sure there had to be photos of the WAVES tea at the White House. I first contacted the National Archives who referred me to the FDR Presidential Library. I learned that there was not an official White House photographer until the Kennedy Administration, and there are no known photos of this event. The staff there provided me with copies of the three documents below.

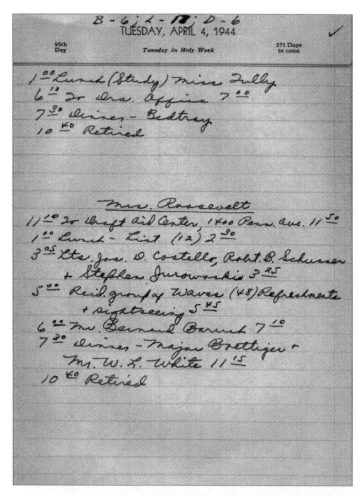

*Daily calendar page of President and Mrs. Roosevelt's Appointments
Courtesy of the Franklin Delano Roosevelt Library*

Congress of the United States
House of Representatives
Washington, D. C. Feb. 18, 1944.

FEB 22 REC'D

Mrs. Franklin D. Roosevelt,
The White House.

My dear Mrs. Roosevelt:

A group of approximately twenty-five
WAVES stationed in my district, at Suitland,
Maryland, are anxious to have an appointment
with you. I understand they do not wish to
take up any problem and that there is merely a
personal desire to meet you. I am informed
they represent twenty-three different States.

If it is in order to fit this request
into your busy life, I would appreciate your
advising me as to the details as to how they
may realize their desire.

Very sincerely yours,

Lansdale G. Sasscer

Letter from Representative Sasscer to Eleanor Roosevelt
Courtesy of the Franklin Delano Roosevelt Library

WAVE QUARTERS "H"
4400 SILVER HILL RD. S.E.
WASHINGTON 20, D. C.

April 4th at 5

Cards sent out 4/3/44

Lt. (jg) Julia W. Wilson
Tennessee   E 201

Ensign Helen Joan Schutz
California   HH 256

Norma Jean Ford   S 2/c
Illinois   D 213

Constance Bambeneck   S 2/c
Minnesota   E 217

Patricia Spillman   S 2/c
California   C 108

Shirley Weik   S 1/c
Connecticut   D 213

Eileen Barker   S 2/c
Michigan   E 101

Betty Jean Buel   S 2/c
Iowa   E 216

Elizabeth Tuckwood   Sp(P) 3/c
Florida   B 119

Patrician Hollingsworth
Colorado   C 107

Betty Bower   Sp(P) 3/c
Ohio   C 109

Evelyn Anderson   S 2/c
Connecticut   E 101

Hermione Jacobson   S 2/c
Pennsylvania   C 121

Judith Underdahl   S 1/c
New York   C 120

Olive Pullen   S 2/c
Maine   C 114

Mary Lundquist   S 2/c
Idaho   D 105

Mary MacGowan   Sp(S) 3/c
Montana   D 225

Ensign Myrtie Glasser
Minnesota   C 201

Margaret Wilson   S 2/c
Florida   HH 223

Elizabeth A. Beddow   Sp(S) 3/c
West Virginia   HH 121

Rita Harvey   S 1/c
New Jersey   E 213

June Tuchman   S 2/c
Colorado   E 205

Georgean Turner   S 2/c
California   -B 126

Lucy Berkey   S 2/c
Indianna   C 101

Beulah Haynes   S 2/c
Vermont   E 204

Ruth Kolwitz   S 2/c
Ohio   D 101

Jean Heath   S 2/c
Missouri   C 101

Rose Dean   S 1/c
Pennsylvania   C 123

Ida Mae Rolls   Y 3/c
California   E 203

Ellen Coyne   S 2/c
Illinois   E 218

Jayne Munson   S 1/c
New York   E 212

Bette Lovelace   Sp P(3/c)
California   B122

(Accompanied by
  Mrs. H. B. Mayhew
  5812 44th Avenue
  Hyattsville, Md.)

List of Suitland WAVES invited to White House tea with Eleanor Roosevelt
Courtesy of the Franklin Delano Roosevelt Library

MRS. ROOSEVELT AT HOME

On the unusual date 4/4/44 a group of Suitland WAVES had the pleasure of meeting Mrs. Roosevelt in the White House.

The WAVES were greeted in the Blue Room by Mrs. Roosevelt. She was very gracious and soft-spoken and personally welcomed each girl. From the Blue Room she led the girls into the formal Dining Room for punch and cakes. There she told them a few of the interesting facts about the White House.

Then one of the most popular residents of the White House was called forth to meet the girls.

The President's scotty, Fala, seemed to be accustomed to welcoming people in the same gracious manner as his charming mistress. Mrs. Roosevelt put Fala through his various capers, and, being a very well-mannered dog, he obeyed her commands.

Before Mrs. Roosevelt took leave, the WAVES presented her with an orchid, and to Fala (in keeping with the time) they gave a live Easter rabbit.

The girls were then conducted by a guide through the formal rooms of the White House.

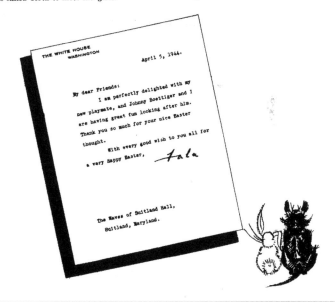

From WAVES Hydrographic Office Book published July 1944[78]

---

78   Johnny Boettiger was the son of Franklin and Eleanor Roosevelt's daughter, Anna. He and his mother lived at the White House during World War II.

Seaman Lucy Berkey Attends White House Tea

Lucy M. Berkey, S1/c, who is stationed with the WAVES at Suitland Hall, Maryland writes an interesting letter to her parents Mr. and Mrs. J. G. Berkey of her recent visit to the White House in company with forty-nine other WAVES and officers from their barracks, when they were presented to The First Lady at a five o'clock tea.

Seaman Berkey writes: "It was one of the nicest things in which I have ever been included. We stood in a circle in the Blue Room and Mrs. Roosevelt shook hands with each one of us. She is so much nicer looking than pictures show her and also more slender. And charming—well, you cannot help liking her. Then we went into the formal dining room and had punch and cookies. The plates were lovely and fragile, with a gold band around the rim and the gold seal. This room is paneled in wood and is one of the most beautiful of all, I think. Mrs. Roosevelt talked to us very informally here and we had fun. Then they brought in Fala the dog. Some of the girls played with him. Soon Eleanor went upstairs where the President was ill of a cold and one of the guards showed us through the rest of the main floor and the basement. As we were going through the front hall it began snowing and I shall never forget how beautiful it was to look out between those beautiful columns and see those enormous snowflakes floating down! That trip is something I will not soon forget!"

April 26, 1944
Courtesy of The Salem Leader

May 15, 1944

Dear Mother & Daddy,

Today is so beautiful, I decided to go for a hike, so I'm waiting now for Mildred Pittala to get ready to go with me. I guess I'll leave my laundry for Wednesday night. Tomorrow night is the last church Young People's social for the winter and spring. Two weeks from now we go to Rock Creek Park for the social, and I'm really looking forward to that.

Yesterday I had such fun and such a nice day, probably because it wasn't planned. I started to church, and on the bus met Judy Underdahl. Halfway to town she asked me how to get to a certain Lutheran church, and it happens to be on Thomas Circle right beside the National City Christian. So each of us went to our own church and met afterwards for dinner. We had a lovely meal in a Childs restaurant and then decided to spend the beautiful afternoon at Oak Park Northwest at the zoo. We met two sailors who'd been in Bermuda, and they told us so many interesting things about the place. They were especially impressed with the gorgeous blue color of the water and the various colored houses made of coral. It was funny—we were all looking at the peacock and trying to coax it (by mental telepathy!) to spread its tail. Somehow the bright colors seem to remind the sailors of their Bermuda sojourn, so they told us a bit about it. We saw so much our eyes about popped out, but we had fun. Judy is always fun. Sometimes she reminds me of Virginia. Finally we became so tired, mainly foot tired, we flopped into the restaurant there in the park and had strawberry sundaes and iced tea of all combinations! We sat down with a sailor and a WAVE (you usually sit with people anywhere in this crowded city) from South Carolina and had a nice conversation with them. Judy kept giggling because the sailor was so flirty and the girl was so obviously annoyed by it all. There's a nice little pond by the restaurant so we sat on a bench by the pool and gabbed and rested in general. Then at 6:00, Judy went with me to Young People's meeting at church. We're having a series of lectures and discussion groups called the School of Christian Living. We went to the marriage group, which was led by Kippy (Mrs. Hastings) and she was, as usual, quite inspiring. Judy really enjoyed everything and I was so glad. Then one of the fellows went to town with us and bought us something to eat and put us on our bus. Quite a day, but would there were more of them! I forgot—Judy and I had the most fun deciding which animal looked like which acquaintance of ours and it was a scream. One of the owls looked like Mr. Burke!

I heard from Donovan quite some time ago. He's at Pasco, Washington, close to Seattle. The address you gave me is the same one on his letter, although he's in Washington. Crazy, isn't it? He said his work was light so he was getting a much-needed rest. He said, "Have gained 15 pounds since leaving the South Pacific. With this good chow we eat I should develop a Navy Chest before too long!" He's a screwball!

As for the photo, it was horrible. It's the worst picture I've ever had taken, and all my friends agreed. So I'm having another taken at a different studio. Bob is also about to kill me for a photo, so I better come through. It's awfully hard to break even on money now, what with summer uniform expenses. Do you think I should get a white suit? I'm not too sold on the idea since they get so filthy in such a short time, but still—they're smart looking. I asked, because I think I'll take my seven days leave in July and a white suit would be nice to wear at home. I've had so much trouble with my seersuckers because they came too small and I have to exchange one of them. I wore one before I realized how short-waisted they were. It's not bad to stand in, but when working at the drafting table, it's bad! Since I wore it once I have to keep it anyway. Last week we had gear inspection, and I had a time, since I didn't know we'd have it here. Remember those nametags from New Albany that didn't come? Well, I had to put adhesive on everything and promise that as soon as I got nametags I'd have another inspection. The ones I ordered at Palais Royal came yesterday and are very nice with U.S.N.R. after my name. Now for the fun of sewing them on!

May 31, 1944

I started in on this letter where I left off on the 15th and forgot to tell you I was beginning again quite a bit later. You'd think I ran Washington myself, I'm so terribly busy! Now that we either wear a white skirt and blue shirt or seersucker for work or dress, it's washing and ironing practically every day. White shirts are so hard to keep clean, especially when you know your jacket won't be there to cover up wrinkles. This last week I've been getting together some winter things to send home. I have a closet that's running over.

Good news! At last I have my Saturdays changed so I can get off now every other Saturday. I work this coming Saturday and get the next one off. My Saturday off will probably be spent getting a permanent, since my hair is dragging the ground now. Besides, it's so hot it falls constantly and is a mess, especially with the uniform. If Richard gets another weekend off and you know it a week ahead of time, write me and maybe I can come home on the weekend. Of course, if I have the money and it's my Saturday off.

It seemed to me I told you I was still in Damage Control, but maybe not. However I don't letter on zinc plates anymore, but work on regular architect's linen tracing paper, which is terrifically expensive, so I heard. I do tracings of ships, using India ink, and it's loads of fun and not so hard on the eyes.

The letter about Jonie and David meeting made me the happiest WAVE in the Navy, *undoubtedly!!* It seems almost impossible that such a wonderful thing could happen, but I'm happy it did, and how! Then the letter today made things nicer than ever, learning about all the details.[79] Does David have an address yet? I'm glad

---

79   On May 12, 1944 Lucy's brothers, Jonas and David, met each other by accident on the island of Espiritu Santo. After receiving a letter from David with the postmark of Espiritu Santo, Jonas immediately went to the receiving station and found David had been assigned to spend the day unloading ammunition. Due to his rank of captain, Jonas was able to request that David come aboard his ship, where they spent the day together.

Richard transferred, if it makes him more satisfied. David just slays me—volunteering for KP! What a sailor! I'll bet it's beautiful in the South Pacific this time of year, in spite of armaments, etc.

It's getting so unbearably hot in my room I feel as if I'm smothering. This is the stickiest hot weather I've ever known and I can't say I love it—no energy. You know—ha! ha! as Richard says.

A week ago Monday night, I went to a banquet at the church. It was one of the night sessions of the Conference they're having. They had a lovely chicken dinner, no dry speakers, and a pageant describing the history of National City Church. It was really fine, too. The young people put it on. I discovered the other night one of the sailors there is from Indiana and went to Hanover. His wife said she used to come to Salem on Saturday night, when they'd go fishing at the Muscatatuck River. They're both grand kids, but at the moment I can't think of their names.

Saw a good show—*The Story of Dr. Wassell* with Gary Cooper and Laraine Day—excellent Technicolor and a nice story.[80]

My best news you may have noticed—ahem! I hope! I'm now, as of 16 May, SP (specialist)(X)3/C E.D. (engineering draftsman). It really makes me happy to be able to wear my eagle at last. The pitiful thing is—I haven't strutted around yet because they're out of X badges in town, wouldn't you know!

I went to a dance Saturday night at Patuxent Naval Air Station in Maryland, where Bob used to be, and it was very nice. It was still light out when our bus arrived, and I got to see their huge hangars and glimpse some of the planes in the distance. It's beautiful out there. Bob's now at Colgate University in Hamilton, New York, and says the training is plenty stiff. I won't see him for about 12 weeks.

---

80 *The Story of Dr. Wassell* plot: As Japanese soldiers attack during World War II, Dr. Wassell plans an escape from Java with a dozen wounded sailors left behind when their crewmates were evacuated to Australia. Based on a true story.

Keep *The Robe*—it's for you. The church group will go on a moonlight boat ride on the Potomac Monday night. It ought to be nice.

Love always to all,

Lucy

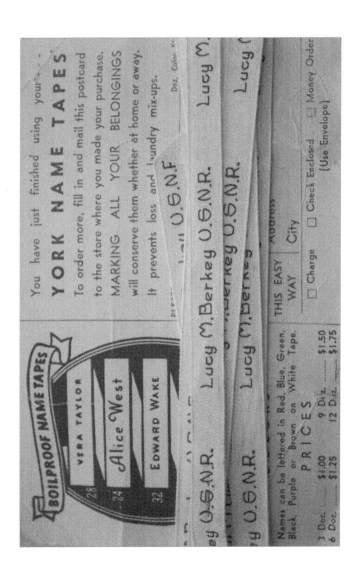

Studio photos of Lucy taken in Washington, D.C.
Photographer unknown

CHAPTER TEN
D-DAY

June 6, 1944

Dear Mother & Daddy,

Today seemed longer than usual, as we've been glued to the radio all day listening to D-Day news. I had chills listening to the actual battle and wondered if anyone I knew was landing on those beaches. Girls with brothers and fiancés in Europe were desperately trying to find out if their divisions were in the attack. We all did our best, but it seems like we hardly got any work done today, and it was so quiet without the usual chatter. The officers were listening, too, and as anxious as anyone else for the war to be over. The mood was very somber with some girls crying from time to time. We all hope this invasion will make a difference in the fight against Hitler. They don't usually allow the radio on, but Admiral Bryan said it was okay due to the circumstances.

Tonight I'm washing and ironing as usual. There isn't much new to tell except the D-Day news. After supper tonight, Janet and Justine came to my room to listen to more news on the radio. I'm sure tomorrow's papers will tell us more about what's happening. Of course, I know my brothers aren't there, but there are still so many to worry about. I hope I can sleep! Off to bed now.

All my love,

Lucy

June 26, 1944

Dear Daddy,

I'm getting awfully anxious to come home again. At this time, I'm not certain whether it will be July or August. We have a birthday celebration of the WAVES July 30th and are now having drill in order to get ready for it. It will be quite a spectacular affair with many thousands of WAVES participating.

Thank you so much for the bond, Daddy—that's fine and comes at such a nice time, too. Also, it's sweet of you to send the other money. I'm putting it with the Christmas money you gave me and will buy something extra special one of these days.

Everyone was so nice to me on my birthday—Mother with those delicious cookies, and they were extra good—birthday kisses mixed in, I'll bet. I received cards from Aunt Fannie, Richard, Bethany Circle, and the girls here. That night I went to a ballgame with a soldier from Camp Springs Army Air Base, and he brought along two friends. We had a nice time and the evening was just perfectly beautiful. It was my first big league baseball game—Washington Nationals versus the New York Yankees. Everyone said it was the most exciting game they'd ever seen. There was a fight on the diamond and then later, they carried the fight into the pit and also into the grandstand. One time the ball cracked into the bat and it splintered into a thousand pieces scattered everywhere. Also, the fellow up at bat threw the bat instead of a ball to the catcher, and broke the bat. Plus, it was an overtime game. Whew! Everyone was on fire and was yelling like mad. I kept wishing you were there, Daddy. I told Jack I knew you'd have really enjoyed that game.

Happy Father's Day—better late than never. I was so broke last week before payday it was pathetic. I thought of you all day and wished I could see you. We had a nice program at Young People's meeting at church that night, and afterwards a crippled fellow asked me to go to the Watergate concert out by the Lincoln Memorial. He's such a nice guy—has something wrong with his legs and uses a cane—so I went and we enjoyed it so much. Just as it got a little bit dark, a tiny sailboat glided by, and it was the most beautiful thing. Sometime I want to ride on a sailboat. Johnny used to tell me what a wonderful free feeling a sailboat gave you. Anne Marshall, my Atlanta, Georgia, friend here, says her boyfriend feels the same way. He was based in

New Guinea for a long while and had time to build a tiny sailboat model. He named it the "Anne L." for her. It's a beautiful thing—so delicately made—you can see how much he loves boats. He lives in San Francisco.

I'm writing out here on the sundeck behind the hall and it's beginning to get pretty dark. The moon is out, and it's a new one. I can barely see the face. Oops—the fire bell! Well, I'm out here, so I might as well stay. It's a fire drill, I hope. We haven't had one for a long time.

Daddy, do send me David's address so I can write him. I heard from Jonie on Wednesday, and he said he was fine and that his ship was the best looking sub chaser anywhere. How nice—he's a good officer—I have no doubt of that.

On Father's Day, I always feel good because I know I have the best daddy anywhere!

All my love,

Lucy

July 23, 1944

Dear Folks,

You remember Bob, the sailor I have gone with since Easter? He's from Indianapolis and is in school at Colgate. I've been so worried about him lately. He's a naval air cadet and his course is really tough! They're kicking them out right and left because there aren't enough pilot casualties overseas to necessitate training so many new pilots. All grades must be in the upper third. Even one grade can mean doom. Bob didn't write for two weeks, and I felt sure he'd flunked out and was afraid to write me, but Friday I got a letter. He said he'd been so busy with tests, since preflight is almost over, that he had to put off anything else, but he is doing fine in his work. What a relief! He probably won't get a 72-hour pass to come here until the last of August.

The news about Richard was astounding. I'd really planned on seeing him at home on my leave.[81] However, if I can see him here that will be wonderful! I had awfully nice letters from David and Jonie the other week. David told me about making his own furniture. Funniest thing—last night I had a dream that Jonie came home on leave. I was just starting to talk to him when Georgeanne came in and threw a pillow at my head! I sure wish I could have talked to him longer—he looked wonderful!

Well, Virginia's birthday and, as usual, I'm going to be sending her gift late because the stores were closed the other day when I went to town. I think it's so nice Virginia and Mildred could teach together at Conference. I really would like to go myself. National City Christian doesn't seem to be much on Conferences, I'm sorry to say. I'm not surprised at Eleanor—some girl! I'm so glad she went to Conference. Every young person should go at least once.

Four weeks ago, I went home with Mildred Pittala to Long Island in New York. Her family is large—seven girls and five boys! Six girls were home and we had loads of fun. The father is dead and from what I can gather, they have quite a hard time. Of course, all the boys were gone, but the girls made up for them. They're all lovely—so nice looking and so nice. Mama is so pretty and cheerful. I've never been anywhere in my life where I've been treated so nice and made to feel so much at home. I had loads of Italian spaghetti that was *really Italian* and enough food all weekend to last for a week. Mildred's older married sister has a cottage at Long Beach, so we went down Saturday evening and had all day Sunday at the beach. That night they took me down to the boardwalk and I *saw the ocean for the first time!!* It was really breathtaking, especially at night. The amazing thing was watching those white-capped waves emerge out of the blackness, get higher and higher and then roll over and crash on the beach. Gee, the water is powerful! They had a storm last winter that swept away several houses next to the beach, so they built a bulkhead underneath

---

81   Richard had received word that his division, the 14th Armored, would soon be moved for transport to the European Theater of Operations.

the boardwalk and even out in the shallow water at the worst places. When that water came crashing up to that bulkhead it simply roared. I could watch the ocean all day, as it changes constantly and is so beautiful and even *frightening* at times. On Sunday morning, we went out to swim and had to wait until the tide went out enough to leave a decent beach. The sand was wonderful, as it was soft, white, and packed nice and hard. Boy, I was really scared the first time a wave crashed over my head, but I got used to it and learned to "jump" a wave. Salt water is so different from fresh—it holds you up. It's too hard to swim in, though, and I didn't dare try until I really knew how for sure. Anyway, as soon as I'd been in the water for an hour, I was exhausted, so I decided to go back to the cottage. Everyone lounged around all afternoon and then decided to go ride on a double bicycle. I tried, but had to give up as the seats were so high I could hardly reach the pedals. At 9:00 p.m. we walked for at least two miles down the boardwalk, and it was freezing. I was amazed to see how dressed up everyone was—all the "big shots" from New York City in furs and veils, heels, etc. We got a delicious frosted malt and walked back dragging our tails behind us. By the time we got to the cottage, my skin was burning like fire from sunburn and windburn. For the next week I could hardly stand to wear clothes. Now I'm peeling like mad. Anyway, I had a wonderful time and could take a sunburn anytime for that.

Myrtle Esther and Mary had me out to lunch week before last. They live in one of the loveliest parts of the city, Foxhall Village. Their home is so sweet and they're having more fun keeping house for Kennard.[82] We had a perfectly beautiful luncheon prepared by Mary and talked ourselves into a lather. They laughed about their "garden" that consists of one lone tomato plant with one lone tomato on it! They said Kennard came home one night and said, "Well, I must water the tomatoes!"

---

82 Siblings Myrtle Esther, Mary, and Kennard Bush were from Lucy's hometown. Colonel Kennard Bush was a career officer military serving with the Army in Washington, D.C., during World War II. He had served in the Philippines from 1924–1926 and in the South Pacific during World War II. Myrtle Esther had been Lucy's high school English teacher.

This week has been a little cooler. I hope you can read this—my pen is broken and I'm using one at the Pepsi-Cola Center while knocking off a couple of hours before Young People's meeting.

All my love,

Lucy

July 31, 1944

Dear Folks,

It was good to hear from you and know you were having a nice time at the farm. I'll bet it's nice there now. I really need some sun for other than the time I was at the seashore, I've been indoors, working or washing clothes. That sunburn all peeled off and I'm almost as white as ever.

So, Richard is still in Kentucky! I'm so thrilled to know he may make it home when I do. I have seven days leave starting August 10th. I'll get to Mitchell about 9:45 a.m. on August 10th. That's because I can travel on my liberty that begins at 5:00 p.m. on the 9th. Boy, I'm really looking forward to this leave. I'm bringing home a publication that I worked on and am really proud of. Lieutenant Jones had the idea that we should put together a kind of yearbook to show what WAVES have been doing at Hydro this past year. After all, Hydro was always "men only" until a year ago. The book describes all the divisions here and has photos of us at work. I was asked to write a couple of sections of the book and help with layout. I can't wait to show you the parts I worked on!

Yesterday the WAVES celebrated their second birthday, and the program was impressive. The ten thousand WAVES here marched up the hill on one side of the Washington Monument and down to the Sylvan Theater on the other side. Many naval dignitaries were seated there. Captain McAfee was so gracious, and Admiral King spoke a few words. A message from Admiral Nimitz in the South Pacific was broadcast and overhead planes were circling taking pictures. Lieutenant Rich, the one I saw in Indianapolis, planned this affair and spoke a few words in her strikingly deep voice. There's something magnetic about her, as well as our captain. A choir from WAVE Quarters "D" sang some Navy songs, and they were plenty good. We of WAVE quarters "H" didn't do so well on our singing because they gave us a song we didn't even know. Just as we started marching, it started to rain, lightning flashed, the wind blew, and spectators began leaving. We had to sit on the damp grass all through the program. It never did rain terribly hard, though. Captain McAfee said it demonstrated the often-questioned fact that the WAVES could stand water! I wish you could've seen those WAVES marching! We turned and watched them, since we were the first company to leave. As they came down the hill they looked perfect, even if we knew they were a bit sloppy in places. It was really a thrill! Afterwards we had a party here with two beautiful cakes and tea. Later there were "Photo Fantasies," with some gorgeous slides, all nature pictures. Soft music was played as the pictures were flashed on the screen as suitable poetry was read. I loved this, especially the poetry.

All my love,

Lucy

Lucy Berkey, who is stationed with the Waves at Washington, D. C. as a Specialist 3/c in the hydrographic office, arrived Aug. 8 to spend her leave with her parents the J. G. Berkeys. En route to Washington Monday, Miss Berkey was accompanied to Mitchell by her parents and her younger sister Miss Eleanor Berkey.

August 16, 1944
Courtesy of The Salem Leader

August 23, 1944

Dear Folks,

Things have been buzzing since I got back from leave—work aplenty and, of course, washing and ironing. We're having a wing meeting soon.

So glad I wasn't sick on the train on the way back, but it was dreadfully tiring. I sat with a very sweet girl from Illinois who was joining her husband who's in Connecticut in a Navy hospital. We had a nice time talking, which made the time pass faster. I tried to get a Pullman, but no luck. That sweet little blonde stewardess who took care of me on my way to Hunter recognized me again, and brought me ammonia in case I was sick. She said, "Well, look who's here! And you have a stripe now, too! I was so amazed that she noticed my rating I almost fell over dead. The train pulled in on time so I had plenty of time to get to work.

Last Thursday, I was getting ready to go downtown to shop when I got a call from Gerald Nicholson, a corporal from Fort Belvoir, Maryland. He's from Little York and called because Geneva had written to tell him he should look me up. I met him about 9:00 and we went to see the movie *Mrs. Miniver*, as neither of us had seen it before.[83] It was a marvelous picture. Of course, Gerald and I didn't know each other, but we had a nice time anyway. He's a very nice looking, very clean, neat sort of person—rather small and has a sweet expression, perhaps a bit on the bashful side.

On Sunday, I attended a wedding at the Foundry Methodist Church, located only a few blocks from National City Christian. The church is beautiful inside and out and the service was especially nice. Our own Captain Jacobs gave Ginger away since her folks couldn't come from Florida. Even our Admiral Bryan was there with his wife.[84] Ginger was absolutely beautiful. She has golden hair, blue eyes, pink

83   *Mrs. Minver* plot: The story follows a British family struggling to survive the first months of World War II.
84   Rear Admiral George Sloan Bryan was the Hydrographer of the Navy. Captain Walter Jacobs was the Assistant Hydrographer.

and white skin, and is very slender. Jim was handsome in his captain's uniform. His brother was best man and just back from overseas. A captain, too, he is handsome and was decorated with scads of medals!

After the wedding I went to church and we went out to Rock Creek Park for our service. It was so cool and pleasant out there. We had punch and cookies and then went up on a high hill for vesper service. We had Dr. Ray Hunt for our guest speaker. He's very well known and has just been married to Laura Aspinwall. She is the sweetest thing! Dr. Hunt struck me as being especially interesting because he spoke of things as an artist would—in terms of line, color, pattern, beauty, etc.

After the service, Mr. Hanan, the assistant minister, took three other girls and me to the Watergate Concert, given this time by the Army Air Corps. It was very fine. That Ben Hanan is a screwball and we all laughed until we couldn't breathe.

Mother, the ration books were misplaced because Jean and Anne were moving. They live beside and across from me now. The books were discovered at last and I'll send them. Thanks for the Kleenex—it was a miracle to get that gold!

Lots of love,

Lucy

Cover of WAVES Hydrographic Office Book—pub. July 1944

Staff

ADVISOR
Lt. (jg) Margaret Jones

EDITOR
Olive Pullen Sp(P)3-c

LAY-OUT
Carolyn Chadwick Sp(X)3-c
Kathryn Howard S2-c

PHOTOGRAPHERS
Patricia Embshoff Sp(X)3-c
Dale Ward Sp(P)3-c
Alice Minard Sp(X)3-c

ART-EDITOR
Patrician Hollingsworth Sp(X)3-c

COVER
Virginia Holdsworth S1-c

ADVERTISING MANAGER
Gloria Luers Sp(X)3-c

CONTRIBUTORS
Lt. (jg) Boner
Ensign Muriel Braeutigam
Ensign Doris Finney
Lucy Berkey Sp(X)3-c
Zelda Carmine S1-c
Arlene Garber Y2-c
Frieda Hanna Sp(X)3-c
Virginia Holdsworth S1-c
Patrician Hollingsworth Sp(X)3-c
Janet Knight Sp(X)3-c
Eleanor Kordecka Sp(I)3-c

ARTISTS
Elinor Ball Sp(X)3-c
Betty Bower Sp(X)3-c
Henrietta Carter Sp(P)3-c
Marjorie Heath S1-c
Virginia Holdsworth S1-c
Margaret Lunger Sp(P)3-c
Anna Marshall Sp(X)3-c
Alberta Ridge Sp(X)3-c
Carmen Spiers S2-c
Judith Underahl Sp(X)3-c

Table of Contents

From WAVES Hydrographic Office Book—pub. July 1944
Index showing Lucy as a contributor

The large Lithographic Division, in one year and approximately six months, has increased its WAVE personnel from two to sixty-five. WAVES working in Lithography are doing everything from making corrections on plates to operating the multilith machines which print 8″ by 8″ approach, landing, and target charts used in aviation. They are trained right on the job in this section and have quickly adapted themselves to a great variety of tasks. Lt. H. T. Birgel is in charge of the Lithographic Division.

Control Office. This office employs four WAVES. The chief function of the office is the control of the flow of work in the Lithographic Division. A reporting and scheduling system is maintained; statistical data is compiled; time studies regarding status of the progress of the Division's work program are prepared, and surveys are made regarding the effectiveness of operations and procedures of the various sections (six in all) of the Lithographic Division.

All four WAVES display Y3c ratings on their sleeves, performing clerical work in the collection, compilation, verification, computation,

continued . . .

From WAVES Hydrographic Office Book—pub. July 1944
Lucy is in bottom picture, third from left, back table, seated

analysis and presentation of statistical data regarding production and work of the Lithographic Division.

Composition. The duties of the Composition Section are numerous : One of the main features of the work is the keeping of a record of all jobs coming into the office. On each record must be the date the order is received, the amount of material and time spent on each, the name of the workman, and the date of delivery. The jobs must also be delivered to the various sections of the building. A WAVE is multigraph operator for the Hydrographic Office and sets up her own type and prints all jobs calling for multigraph printing.

Lithodrafting. The WAVES in the drafting section have the all-important responsibility of making chart corrections on existing zinc plates, as well as preparation of new ones. To complete this work on both the old and new plates they must have a working knowledge of Surface Navigation Charts, Air Navigation Charts, and Miscellaneous Strategic Diagrams.

continued . . .

From WAVES Hydrographic Office Book—pub. July 1944

ALABAMA
Knight, Janet Sp(X)3-e
Riggs, Agnes Y3-e
Rogers, Claude M. Sp(P)3-e

ARKANSAS
Boatright, Alice S1-e
Kean, Maxine Sp(X)2-e
Routh, Mary S2-e

CALIFORNIA
Allen, Dorothy S2-e
Anger, Adelon K. Sp(P)3-e
Baker, Patricia S1-e
Bruhn, Phyllis S2-e
Campfield, Doris Y3-e
Cone, Mollie S1-e
Cosentino, Louise Sp(P)3-e
Dodds, Jean S2-e
Frank, June Y2-e
Friis, Catherine Sk3-e
Harris, Cassie Sp(X)2-e

Lima, Alice Sp(X)3-e
Schena, Florence Y3-e
Walsh, Dorothy Sp (I)3-e
Weik, Shirley S1-e

DELAWARE
Wright, Eleanor S2-e

FLORIDA
Hannaway, Mildred Sp(X) 3-e
Hillemann, Florence Y2-e
Langlois, Doris Sp(P)3-e
Lunger, Margaret Sp(P)3-e
Rogers, Marjorie Sp(X)3-e
Thompson, Anita S2-e
Tuckwood, Elizabeth Sp(X)3-e
Ware, Mary Lou Sp(X)3-e

GEORGIA
Butts, Mildred Prtr 3-e
Fulton, Sarah S2-e
Marshall, Anne Sp(X)3-e

Ford, Norma Jean S1-e
Hansen, Helen Y3-e
Havens, Bertha S1-e
Hayes, Ellen S2-e
Hull, Marion Sp(I)2-e
Kulisek, Emily Sp(I)3-e
Lawson, Alice S1-e
Lewis, Louise Y2-e
Luers, Gloria Sp(X)3-e
Lyons, Ethel Y2-e
Maxwell, Ida Fae S2-e
McKerman, Kathryn Y3-e
Philippon, Elnora S2-e
Sennott, Gloria S1-e
Svendson, Sylvia Sp(X)3-e
Tucker, Patricia S2-e
VonBehren, Ruth Sp(I)3-e
Wolleson, Lillian S2-e

INDIANA

Friis, Catherine Sk3-c
Harris, Cassie Sp(X)2-c
Hill, Virginia Y2-c
Hirshon, Florence Sp(P)3-c
Hostutler, Virginia Y2-c
Johnson, Dorothy S1-c
Lovelace, Bette Sp(X)2-c
Miller, Dorothy S2-c
O'Guinn, Helen S1-c
Palmquist, Mary Sp(X)3-c
Payne, Edith S2-c
Postel, Katherine S2-c
Ridgway, Grace S1-c
Robins, Lorraine Sp(X)3-c
Seyfarth, Constance S2-c
Taylor, Gloria Sp(X)3-c
Turner, Georgean S1-c
Walker, Margaret S1-c
Ward, Dale Sp(P)3-c
Wheaton, Winifred Sp(X)3-c

COLORADO
Cannon, Jane Sp(X)3-c
Donovan, Dorothy Sp(P)3-c
Ellwanger, Mary Y3-c
Hollingsworth, Patrician Sp(X)3-c
Thornton, Virginia Y2-c
Tuchman, June S1-c

CONNECTICUT
Anderson, Evelyn S1-c
Barton, Avis L. Y2-c
Eselby, Mary Sp(X)3-c
Holdsworth, Virginia S1-c
Jones, Beatrice Y2-c

Fulton, Sarah S2-c
Marshall, Anna Sp(X)3-c

IDAHO
Allis, Fay S2-c·

ILLINOIS
Atkins, Gara Y-2c
Blackwood, Laura Y-2c
Blankenship, Kathryn Y2-c
Campbell, Tennys Sp(X)3-c
Coyne, Ellen S1-c
Crites, Mary Jane Y3-c
Davidson, Peggy S1-c
Edwards, Pauline S2-c
Embshoff, Patricia Sp (X)3-c

INDIANA
Berkey, Lucy Sp(X)3-c
DeVaux, Gloria Sp(X)3-c
Garber, Arlene Y2-c
Pest, Alyce Y3-c
Ray, Lorena Maxine Sp(X)2-c
Ridge, Alberta Sp(X)3-c
Skurka, Betty S2-c
Tezak, Mary D. Y3-c
Thomas, Betty S2-c

IOWA
Bell, Geneva Y2-c
Buel, Betty S1-c
Campbell, Marilyn S1-c
Martin, Ruth Y3-c
Seerist, Evelyn Y3-c

KANSAS
Black, Esther S1-c
Knight, Geraldine Sp(X)3-c
McKee, Florence S2-c
Radocaj, Rosemary S2-c
Swanson, Isabel Y2-c

KENTUCKY
Austin, Marguerite Sp(X)3-c
Hetsch, Jean Y3-c
Judson, Evelyn S2-c
Karem, Elizabeth Sk3-c
Penzello, Katherine S1-c

LOUISIANA
Tidmore, Ruth S2-c
continued . . .

From WAVES Hydrographic Office Book—pub. July 1944
Lucy is listed under Indiana

MAINE

Chadwick, Carolyn Sp(X)3-e
Chagnon, Hortense Y3-e
Coltart, Helen S2-e
Goodsoe, Margery S2-e
Hamilton, Barbara Sk3-e
McCarthy, Frances S2-e
Potenzo, Anna S1-e
Pullen, Olive Sp(P)3-e

MARYLAND

Hanna, Frieda Sp(X)3-e
Kordecka, Eleanor Sp(I)3-e
Outland, Isabelle Sp(X)2-e

MASSACHUSETTS

Aylward, Aileen Sp(X)3-e
Barnes, Cora Y2-e
Carver, Eleanor Sp(X)2-e
Donnelly, Jane S2-e
Dunbar, Eleanor Sp (X)3-e
Estabrook, Sally S2-e
Farrell, Marion Sp(X)3-e
Ferguson, Edith Y2-e
Forni, Mary Sp(X)3-e
Loveless, Grace Sp(X)3-e
McCluskey, Mary S2-e
Morse, June S2-e
Munyan, Edith Sp(X)3-e
Pidgeon, Elsie S2-e
Porter, Jean Y3-e
Rising, Dorothy Sp(X)2-e
Rollins, Natalie Sp(X)3-e
Serpa, Mary S1-e
Sherman, Phyllis S1-e
Stock, Pauline Y2-e

MISSOURI—Continued

Heath, Marjorie S1-e
Kirlin, Blanche Y2-e
Pagones, Helen Sp(X)2-e
Reynolds, Kathryn S1-e
Semon, Rose Y2-e
Spiers, Carmen S2-e

MONTANA

Holmes, Frances Sp(I)2-e
Lindsay, Geraldine S2-e

NEBRASKA

Carmine, Zelda S1-e
Cerovac, Rose Sp(X)3-e
Steffen, Dorthy S2-e

NEW HAMPSHIRE

Howard, Kathryn E. S2-e
Trudeau, Rita S2-e

NEW JERSEY

Boehner, Frances Sp(P)3-e
Bofird, Ann Sp(P)3-e
Brown, Dolores S2-e
Brown, Doris Y1-e
Friedman, Mildred S2-e
Gallagher, Mildred Y2-e
Garvey, Gertrude S2-e
Gelernter, Frances S2-e
Harvey, Barbara S1-e
Harvey, Rita S1-e
Hubert, Rosanna Y2-e
Keefe, Anita Sp(X)3-e
Kotler, Arline S1-e
Laedeke, Gloria Sp(X)2-e

NEW YORK—Continued

Pittala, Mildred Y3-e
Platt, Eleanor S2-e
Ports, Mavis S2-e
Schafer, Norma S2-e
Schneider, Freda S2-e
Slemschek, Helen S2-e
Smith, Frances Y2-e
Stephens, Lillian S2-e
Swartz, Selma S2-e
Trachtman, Blanche S2-e
Underdahl, Judith Sp(X)3-e
Vought, Hannah Y2-e
Walker, Mary D. Sp(X)3-e
Unger, Arline F. Sp(X)3-e

NORTH CAROLINA

Boschen, Lillian Sp(P)2-e
Gorham, Sarah Y2-e
Hales, Marjorie Y2-e
Harris, Evelyn S2-e
Jordan, Dorothy Y3-e
Winston, Mary Y2-e

NORTH DAKOTA

Dieskow, Agnes S2-e

OHIO

Anderle, Frances Y2-e
Bower, Betty Sp(X)3-e
Brown, Pauline Y3-e
Citron, Bernice S1-e
Davis, Ruth Y3-e
Elliot, Audrey S1-e
Filimon, Sylvia Sp(X)3-e
Fladung, Vida Y3-e

Serpa, Mary S1-e
Sherman, Phyllis S1-e
Stock, Pauline Y2-e
Sullivan, Constance S2-e
Ward, Irene Y1-e

MICHIGAN
Barker, Eileen S1-e
Billig, Elizabeth Sp(I)3-e
Carlisle, Jayne S2-e
Collier, Henrietta S2-e
Hammer, Ruth S1-e
Heise, Berwyn S1-e
Johnson, Barbara S1-e
Nampa, Justine Sp(X)3-e
Philips, Patricia Sp(X)2-e
Schott, Mary Y2-e
Waterman, Joyce S2-e
Wilson, Irene Y2-e

MINNESOTA
Carlson, Anna Jean Y2-e
Chier, Idell Sp(P)3-e
Goehrig, Priscilla Sp(P)3-e
Hackney, Gloria Sp(X)3-e
Kuslich, Mary Y3-e
Mach, Alma Sp(X)3-e
Protzeller, Betty Sp(X)2-e
Stewart, Mary Y2-e
Zieman, Lois S1-e

MISSISSIPPI
Worthington, Florence Y2-e

MISSOURI
Blumberg, Thelma Sp(X)3-e
Elfgen, Ruth S2-e

Kotler, Arline S1-e
Lueddeke, Gloria Sp(X)2-e
Manners, Dorothy Sp(X)3-e
Manning, Kathleen Y2-e
Roper, Jacqueline Y3-e
Walkinshaw, Helen Y3-e
Zarling, Beverly Y3-e

NEW MEXICO
Hartnitt, Joan Sp(X)3-e

NEW YORK
Battiste, Jayne S1-e
Borger, Audrey S2-e
Brown, Jessie Sp(P)3-e
Carter, Henrietta Sp(P)3-e
Champlin, Eleanor Sp(X)3-e
Crandell, Bernice S2-e
Crusade, Sadie S2-e
Devlin, Norma S2-e
Driscoll, Evelyn S2-e
Durrence, Pauline S1-e
Dwyer, Margaret S2-e
Fraser, Edith S2-e
Geoly, Angelina S2-e
Gomez, Maria Prtr(M)3-e
Grimaldi, Evelyn S2-e
Habes, Rita Sp(X)3-e
Hannis, Marilyn Y3-e
Heron, Marjorie S2-e
Hill, Joan Terry Sp(X)2-e
Koch, Helen Y2-e
Koenig, Helen Sp(X)3-e
Mattonen, Marion Sp(P)3-e
Minard, Alice Sp(X)3-e
Motz, Winifred S2-e

Filimon, Sylvia Sp(X)3-e
Fladung, Vida Y3-e
Josephs, Dora S2-e
Klein, Ruth Y3-e
Kolwitz, Ruth S1-e
Lajcak, Helen Sp(X)3-e
Logan, Harriet S1-e
Marquardt, Doris Y3-e
McCoy, Betty Y2-e
Mitchell, Mary Y3-e
Montrose, Joan S2-e
Pry, Evelyn Y3-e
Radick, Helen Y3-e
Schackmann, Mary Y2-e
Shaffer, Jean I. Sp(I)2-e
White, Martha S2-e
Wiener, Sarah Sp(I)2-e
Wright, Norma Sp(X)3-e

OKLAHOMA
Adams, Sylvia Sp(P)2-e
Beard, Daisy M. Y3-e
Miner, Claire Y2-e

OREGON
Ball, Elinor M. Sp(X)3-e
Conley, Elizabeth Sp(X)3-e
Timmons, Adelaide Y3-e

PENNSYLVANIA
Balt, Frances S2-e
Black, Margaret Sp(X)3-e
Browning, Martha Sp(P)3-e
Buchina, Irene S3-e
Dean, Rose S1-e

continued . . .

From WAVES Hydrographic Office Book—pub. July 1944

PENNSYLVANIA—Continued

Deveney, Winifred S2-c
Firstin, Mitzi Sp(X)3-c
Goetz, Dorothy S2-c
Haddad, Adele S1-c
Hallas, Evelyn S1-c
Herr, Murial S2-c
Hogan, Sidney Sp(X)3-c
Januskevicius, Regina Prtr(M)3-c
Kelley, Viona Sp(X)3-c
Kostak, Julia S2-c
McGinnis, Marie S1-c
Pasley, Lois Sp(X)3-c
Rosell, Helen S2-c
Rowland, Louise S1-c
Vedor, Gloria S2-c

RHODE ISLAND

Bergquist, Hope S2-c
Mottram, Elaine Sp(I)2-c
Procter, Alice Y3-c
Tully, Mary S2-c
Varone, Francesca S2-c

SOUTH DAKOTA

Jackson, Lillian Sp(X)3-c

TENNESSEE

Craighead, Doris Y-c

TEXAS

Boman, Thelma S2-c
Faubian, Nora Sp(I)3-c
Hamm, Imogene S2-c
Lanham, Stella S2-c

Officers

LIEUTENANTS:

Lois Stidham .... Arizona
Mary Sears .... Massachusetts

LIEUTENANTS (jg.):

Edith R. Montgomery .... Florida
Frances A. Clark .... Ohio
Helen E. Peck .... West Virginia
Margaret Jones .... Washington
Bernice A. Boner .... Indiana
Elizabeth A. Bogert .... Virginia
Henrietta Bonaviez .... Nebraska
Wilma F. Geer .... California
Evelyn Marie Dutra .... California

ENSIGNS:

Jean Combrinck Graham .... New York
Amy L. Turner .... Texas
Helen Banta .... Iowa
May Elizabeth Bradfield .... Texas

Hamm, Imogene S2-c
Lanham, Stella S2-c
Sheridan, Genevieve S2-c
Smith, Irma W. Sp(X)3-c
Stark, Marion S1-c
Stumberg, Marie S2-c

UTAH
Sidwell, Betty S1-c

VERMONT
Haynes, Beulah S1-c

VIRGINIA
Allison, Leola Y3-c
Edwards, Gwendolyn Sp(X)3-c
George, Sarah S2-c
Guza, Elinor Sp(X)3-c

WASHINGTON
Cose, Chyrl E. Y2-c

WEST VIRGINIA
Eckley, Elizabeth Sp(P)3-c

WISCONSIN
Brasch, Florence S2-c
Friedeck, Mary Y3-c
Gagnelius, Rita Y3-c
Hubbes, Helen Y3-c
Kitoha, Anna Sp(X)3-c
Lampson, Avalon Y3-c
Scott, Helen Y2-c

Helen Bantz	Iowa
May Elizabeth Bradfield	Texas
Dorothy Hagen	Missouri
Dorothy G. Lloyd	Florida
Betty Shaper	California
Ardel C. Thompson	California
Muriel F. Hazard	Maryland
Ruth I. M. Laatsch	Wisconsin
Effie Virginia Edwards	Missouri
Doris J. Finney	California
Margaret Marston	Pennsylvania
Georgia S. Geer	California
Madge Penton	New Jersey
Margery Duff Howarth	Michigan
Phyllis Winter	Illinois
Muriel Helen Braeutigam	Missouri
Evelyn B. Bandy	Connecticut
Mary E. Fairman	Pennsylvania

WAVE OFFICERS
at
WAVE Quarters "H"

LIEUTENANT (jg.):
Julia W. Wilson .... Tennessee

ENSIGNS:
Elizabeth E. Thorn .... Tennessee
Cecil F. Royalty .... Illinois
Doris M. Acker .... New Jersey
Myrtle Glasser .... Minnesota
Helen Farley .... Illinois

From WAVES Hydrographic Office Book—pub. July 1944

I'll Be Seeing You   167

CHAPTER ELEVEN
THE WAR ESCALATES

September 24, 1944

Dearest Folks,

I've just gotten home from Young People's meeting, and I'm rather tired. It's so wonderful about Jonas, I can hardly think of anything else. Saturday was my Saturday to work, and I came home at noon to get my mail. When I found out Jonas was coming home, I was so excited I could hardly work all afternoon, but then no one works very hard on Saturday, not even the boss. I do hope Richard won't be leaving before Jonas gets here. I can imagine how excited Mildred must be—gee, it's really wonderful! I guess the fortune-teller was right in saying he'd be here in October.

Bob was here for one whole week of his leave. All the naval air cadets at Colgate got 25-day leaves following completion of flight prep. He came here August 24th and left on the 31st for Indianapolis. He came back past here on September 15th and left Sunday night the 17th. So I really have seen a lot of him lately. And he's just as nice as ever, in spite of being a bit younger than I am. Bob finally took me to visit Mount Vernon. We took the boat trip about 1:30 p.m. on Saturday, August 26th, and what a beautiful day it was! The sun was so lovely shining on the water. We sat on the boat deck in deck chairs and the sun felt so good on our backs. I was surprised to discover Mount Vernon was so high up above the Potomac River. I always pictured the front lawn sloping down to the water's edge. We went through the house and were both amazed at the smallness of the rooms. I think our rooms of today are much more cozy and comfortable. There was an artist drawing the utensils in the queer old kitchen. I very subtly leaned over his shoulder to see and found they were very fine pencil sketches. By the time Bob and I came to the display of articles, we were so tired we were hysterical, and laughed ourselves sick over the funny dental instruments and some of the queer clothing. George's shoe buckles looked as if they would have made corns on top of his toes—they were so heavy. Some of the silver and china was lovely. Pictures of Mount Vernon really make the house appear huge and long across the front, when actually it's very ordinary looking. I was glad to see so many lovely paintings and etchings in the rooms, though most were by artists I did not recognize. George's bed made me feel more "awed" than anything else. I couldn't help feeling it was a good thing there was no footboard since the bed was so short. George's feet would have banged against it. The gardens were just lovely, and everything had an air of peacefulness about it. It made me feel as if I'd like to just stay and lie on one of the huge lawns and forget about time, just like Rip Van Winkle. But, the boat was blowing its horn and we had to scramble down the rocky, rough steps and get aboard. It was an unusual trip and even nicer than I had anticipated.

All the time that Bob was here, except the weekend, I was on the night shift, so it was hard to do much of anything except eat, go to the show, and walk around someplace close so I could get to work on time. Wednesday I got a special delivery letter and two telegrams from Bob. The letter told me he had a stopover on his way to Chapel Hill, North Carolina, to preflight school. The first telegram said to meet him at Union Station at 9:00. The second telegram said their plans had changed and that he wouldn't get to see me after all! However, since North Carolina is not so far away, I may be able to go down and see him on a weekend off. He has to stay there until preflight is over and that's December 4th.

Went to a wedding this afternoon—Martha Ellen Bales, my old Forest Hall friend, who works for the FBI. She married a very tall civilian who looks very nice, though I don't know his name. Martha looked lovely in a white satin gown. She is tall and slender and has long soft auburn hair and blue gray-green eyes. The wedding was in a sweet little chapel in the Mount Vernon Methodist Church.

We had a candlelight tea at church tonight and I helped serve and worked in the kitchen. We had a good time. I'm to lead the program three weeks from today on religious poetry, "Singing Verse." Mother, if you have any ideas please let me know. Next weekend I'm going home with Mildred Pittala to New York and we're going to see the Rockettes, we hope.

We go into semi-winter uniform October 1st and I'll need my blue shirts, so could you please send them as soon as possible?

Love,

Lucy

October 9, 1944

Dear Folks,

What wonderful and sad news in your letter today, Mother. I'm so sorry that Richard will ship out before Jonie gets home.[85] At the same time, I'm so thrilled Jonie is coming home—it seems like a dream. I'm so anxious to see him!

This coming weekend is my weekend off, but Sunday night is my Young People's meeting and as leader I can hardly step out at the last moment. Besides, there's so much to be done. Tonight I am over at Hydro—Geri is typing about 25 poems for me, and I'm correcting them and trying to think of some new ideas for introductions. We're going over to her apartment later to cut out pictures for the slides. It will be an all night job. Then, tomorrow night, we have a smorgasbord dinner at the church, the beginning of our Youth Fellowship week. Afterwards there is a social hour with square dancing, and after that a meeting with four girls and two fellows who are going to do some choral reading for us Sunday night. Wednesday night there is another practice, and a speaker, Thursday night a dinner, social, and the Fellowship. Probably Saturday will be taken up by getting the place decorated and Sunday another short practice plus church

---

85   Jonas and Richard missed each other by a couple of days. Richard's division was stationed at Camp Campbell, Kentucky, and departed on October 6, 1944.

in the morning and evening. Mildred [McBride Berkey] wrote me about several helps that have been very fine. I do hope the program turns out all right.

Last weekend I didn't do much as I had to work on Saturday. The weekend before that, I went home with Mildred Pittala to New York, and we had a nice time in spite of my getting a terrible cold and blowing my nose every two seconds. The whole family was wonderful to me as well. We went to Macy's on Saturday, and it was really a thrill seeing that huge place. We could shop for everything from a needle to a car. I wanted to go to Saks but Mildred didn't especially want to. Since she's always lived there, she can't see anything thrilling about department stores. We went to Schrafft's at Fifth Avenue and 13th Street for lunch and had wonderful food and delicious ice cream. At 4:00 we went to a tea dance at the Women's Service Center and met two Merchant Marine midshipmen from the Academy at Kings Point. They invited us to come and visit the Academy the next day so Mildred's sister and brother-in-law drove us out. It was simply beautiful out there, all new, only a year old. It used to be an estate. They told us some of the nicest trees had been uprooted by a hurricane. I've never seen so many good-looking fellows in all my life. They were so neat and had such perfect manners.

Mother, the box came through fine—thanks a million for the lovely housecoat. It fits beautifully and all the girls are crazy about it. The fruit tasted so good and just like home. Georgeanne said that apple was the best one she tasted since she's been in Washington.

Bob is fine, though run to death in his new course—preflight. He's at Chapel Hill, North Carolina, and likes the place immensely. Says they have lovely quarters and equipment to use in the gym and game rooms. The gym has four huge basketball floors plus many swimming pools, etc.

I have four days emergency leave starting next Wednesday, October 18th, at 5:00 p.m., so I'll be home Thursday morning and will have to leave Sunday noon. I'm so anxious to see Jonie and so happy he's home at last.[86]

Loads of love,

Lucy

Mildred Pittala is second from left and Lucy is on far right
Washington, D.C.—restaurant unknown
Photographer unknown

October 24, 1944

Dear Mother & Daddy,

Got here safely at 7:40 Monday morning. The train was on time but the lousy taxi driver almost made me and another WAVE late. He

---

86   Jonas was transferred back to the U.S. after 18 months at sea. During this time, he had been hospitalized for malaria three times: two weeks in May 1943 in Panama, two weeks in November 1943 in Espiritu Santo, and a week in February 1944 in Fiji. After several subsequent attacks, his medical condition finally necessitated transfer to a temperate climate. Between malaria and seasickness, Jonas weighed only 137 pounds by the time he left the South Pacific. Jonas was 6'1" and weighed around 170 pounds when he enlisted in the Navy.

insisted on taking a Marine out to the Naval Air Station first because it was on his way. That girl wouldn't have been able to catch a plane anyway, it was so foggy. We finally got here with five minutes to spare, thank goodness.

I had a nice trip until we came through the mountains in West Virginia and everyone almost froze to death. It was so horribly cold, I wrapped my coat around me and put a pillow between my feet and the crack in the side of the car where cold kept seeping in. I think the air conditioning was on, too. Anyway, back in Washington the weather was decidedly colder than at home. Today it has warmed up, and it's really a beautiful day. Most of the way I rode with a soldier from Pennsylvania, and he told me all about his wonderful wife and beautiful little two-year-old daughter. He'd only been in three months and could hardly stand being away from his family. He really was a nice fellow. He and some sailors and WAVES on the train really enjoyed the candy, Daddy. I've been passing the rest of the candy around our wing since I got back. Seems as if there's an extra lot in that box. At any rate, it's certainly been enjoyed.

This morning was inspection, and we had it outside in back of the rec hall. I noticed, as we were standing there, how colorless the trees are. A lot of them have turned, but they're such a muddy color. Indiana beats all the states as far as autumn color goes. Even in Ohio, the trees weren't as beautiful.

I've just sorted out my duty clothes and I certainly have a stack of them to wash. Guess I'll get that done today since I have to go into town tomorrow.

Last night I talked to Junior and he said my radio hadn't been fixed yet. They're trying to find out what causes so much noise in the set. Also, he's going to get several maps for me from Hydro so I can send you one, Daddy. I'd like one for my room to cover up the bare wall. So many girls have maps from there already, so they had to smuggle them out. Officers can just walk out with maps, darn it!

I guess Jonie is about ready to shove off. I've been entertaining the night shift with his experiences. Sure wish he could come here. Must get back to my washing!

Love,

Lucy

November 30, 1944

Dear Folks,

I was so thrilled to hear about your letter from Richard! I confess, I was very sorry to hear he was seasick going over. But, I had to laugh a little picturing his big hulk leaning over the side with his face pea-green. "4 eye" must have been a beautiful sight.[87] What I wouldn't have given to be there with a paintbrush and paper!

It was nice to hear about how you spent Thanksgiving. I could just see all of you sitting around playing pounce.[88] My Thanksgiving was very nice. Of course, we worked all day then I went to a dinner at church. The tables were decorated with green strips of paper down the center of each table and big bowls of fruit with a paper turkey atop each one. Green candles in red holders lined the strips, and the light from them shining through the tomato juice glasses was beautiful. Boy, what a smell met my nose when I entered the room. They passed down huge platters of turkey, broccoli, potatoes, dressing, gravy, and cranberry salad. Also, there were salad plates of crisp carrot strips, celery, olives, and radishes. The hot rolls were really hot, too. Pumpkin pie for dessert! We all had a wonderful time eating and laughing at the same time. Jim Wickman, a crazy guy but very nice, really made things go around. He's tall, and thin, and blond, and terribly intelligent. He works at the Navy Building and is one of the backbones of our Christian Youth Fellow-

---

87   Richard wore glasses.
88   Pounce: card game like solitaire where each player has a deck of cards, but building piles are shared between players. When a player has removed the final card from their pounce pile they yell "pounce" and that round ends.

ship here at church. He's been one of my best friends at church during these past months, mainly because I'm the third Lucy he has known, but now he considers the name a jinx for him! He goes with the second Lucy, off and on, and she has red hair. Boy, I really take the teasing from that fellow. There were 179 of us at the dinner. After the meal, we all participated in singing a round in which we had to jump up and throw our arms above our heads and shout out the words "jumma ja." Some of the older people couldn't take it and had to keep their seats, for it really did stretch that turkey. There was a special song by one of the girls, a Thanksgiving reading, several other songs, and that was it. Everyone had a grand time. Outside, I discovered it was raining and had to run to catch my streetcar.

Tonight I went over to Mildred Pittala's apartment at Suitland Manor. We had dinner, and then I came home early. It is really getting cold, and I was shivering my way along in back of the Census Building when I noticed ice on the puddles left by this morning's downpour. I tested it—just couldn't help it—crazy, as always! I stepped out on the edge of a puddle and it crackled under my shoe. That was a nice sound—the first ice of winter, and yet that means more wraps and icy winds to stand. My cheeks were red as apples by the time I reached my little room and I suddenly realized how much better I felt for the walk in the crisp air. The sunset this evening was perfectly breathtaking—lavender, pink, and white clouds topped by golden strips of light. Then tonight, to top it all off, a gorgeous very, very round moon winking across the sky to a huge star, by far the largest star I've ever seen.

I've taken up roller skating again, and I'm progressing faster this time. Now I have hopes of graduating from the lowly beginner's rink. At least I give the spectators a laugh now and then!

It's so nice to feel that Christmas is in the air again with its usual expectancy. What about sending Richard Christmas gifts? How can we?

Love always,

Lucy

December 15, 1944

Dear Folks,

Can't wait to tell you the good news—I'll be home for Christmas!!! Only on liberty, though. Later I'll write and tell you the exact time to meet me, for I'm not sure whether it will be Saturday night or Sunday morning. Only 10% of enlisted personnel can be off at Christmas in each department. We drew slips of paper, and I was lucky to get liberty and a 64-hour pass. I have Saturday, Sunday, and Monday off. However, I'm on the night shift and won't be able to start out until Saturday morning. The catch is, the train doesn't leave till 6:30 Saturday night. I may be able to get a different train, so I can be home by Saturday night. I'm so glad I won't have to be here again on Christmas, for it's the hardest time of the year to be away from home.

Last week I received a box from the church and yesterday the one from you. Now I really feel silly, as I'm coming home!! I must get busy with my Christmas shopping now.

If Bob gets through preflight okay, he'll be here Saturday and Sunday before going on to Indianapolis on leave. Wish I knew what to get him. I shudder when I even think of shopping, for the stores are jam-packed! This Christmas it's much worse than last, as everyone pushes and shoves until you give up in despair and go home.

I've spent a lot of time roller skating in the last month and have had so much fun! I'm getting better every week and you should see me!

Richard will get socks from me, and that'll be about all! I haven't heard from him and can't send things very well without a request letter.[89]

---

89 Without a specific request letter, families at home in the U.S. could only send limited quantities to soldiers. The soldier's request letter had to be taken to the post office to verify that the request had actually come from the soldier. Some of the things Richard requested: cookies, cake, candy, peanuts, candy bars, buckwheat pancake flour, baking soda, an American flag, toothpaste, toothbrush, airmail stamps, double edged razor blades, and soap.

Hope the trains aren't too horribly crowded on the way home.[90] It would be tragic if I couldn't get on. However, I've developed a good right shoulder and will battle with the best of them just to get home. See you Christmas!

Love,

Lucy

December 19, 1944

Dear Folks,

Gee, it's been good to feel ice crack under my feet. It made me remember going down to the creek and testing ice to see if it was hard enough to stand on or to run the sled across. Mother, I remember you getting furious with me for sliding on the school grounds with all the boys! I'd usually be the only girl, and once had the record for going the farthest—to the railroad track and over!

The work at Hydro has been speeding up so's to get our charts to the ships faster, and scuttlebutt was that we'd have our usual privilege of every other Saturday off taken away from us. There are two hundred charts that need to get finished immediately, or sooner!! Therefore, I decided to hurry and catch up on my sightseeing. I visited the Capitol, the Smithsonian Institute, at least part of it, and Arlington Cemetery, where I saw the Tomb of the Unknown Soldier. One of the most beautiful places, tho', is the Lincoln Memorial and the Reflecting Pool!

Guess I'll have to go to that stinky Navy dentist soon, as I broke two pieces out of one of my good teeth. Thankfully not in front! What's more, I was eating a cracker. Gee, these bakeries are lousy since the war!

90　By this time, 100,000 passengers a day traveled through the organized chaos of Union Station in Washington, D.C. Extra ticket windows had been added, platforms had been lengthened to accommodate war time travelers, women's voices now announced arriving and departing trains, and the long benches in the massive waiting area were always full. Lucy's journey from D.C. to Mitchell, Indiana, was approximately 15 hours by train.

Madly trying to get all the last minute things done to get ready to leave Friday. Talked to Josephine on the phone tonight and she has decided to stay here over Christmas and not brave the crowds. However, she was anxious to go on home, I think. She said there was no school today because of the snow. We had six inches starting in the night and continuing until late this afternoon. Most snow I've ever seen here!

I'm going to try to make the 6:30 p.m. train Friday evening. If I can't get on, I'll get the 8:30 one. I'll be in Mitchell at 9:30 a.m., as usual, unless I miss the 6:30. Then it'll be about 11:30 when I get in. Several girls are going to Louisville, so I'll have company this time. I'll have to tell you about my nice weekend in New York the 7th and 8th. Jean Hamm was with me. See you Saturday morning!

Lots of love,

Lucy

CHAPTER TWELVE
WAITING FOR NEWS

January 2, 1945

Dear Mother & Daddy,

I had such a good time at home this Christmas, even though I had to go back on Christmas night. But, at least I got to be there. The tree was so beautiful, and tall, and everything was so cozy and Christmasy. All that was missing was the three boys and Mildred. Getting Richard's letter on Christmas was the best gift of all. I'm so glad we all wrote him a reply letter together. With the war news so bad, though, it is hard to not be anxious about him.

The train ride back was okay, but I almost got smashed by crowds at times. The whole trip was such a rush that I just tried to sleep this time, and did manage to at times. The train was late getting into Washington due to the mobs of people, but I was on night shift so didn't have to go in till 4:00.

Thanks for letting me know about Dale Huckleberry being killed, Mother. It's so very sad. I hope Maxine's husband can recover from his wounds and that Pauline will hear from Mancil soon. The mail situation seems to get worse all the time. If only there were a faster way to get news.

There's not much to report, as it seems as if all I do is work, wash, and iron. I did attend the New Year's Eve church service and heard a good sermon about hope for the New Year. I saw Josephine for a few minutes afterwards and heard about her Christmas. We had a small party here at the hall in the evening. With New Year's Day on a Monday, we couldn't stay up too late. But we did have a good time and, of course, feel more like a family than we did last year. I've made some really good friends here and I hope to keep in touch with them after the war is over. If it's ever over...

Love,

Lucy

January 27, 1945

Dear Folks,

I was so upset over the news of Richard being wounded, I couldn't seem to feel like myself until I heard he was getting along okay.[91] What a wonderful relief! I'm hoping he'll send more details soon about what actually happened. Wish we'd hear from Jonas about his assignment.

This work seems to be getting the best of me lately, and I've had to take it easy. Every time I even looked at anything for two weeks, my eyes swam and I was so dizzy. I couldn't work for a while—just sat at my table and tried to look halfway intelligent—even that was an effort. Consequently, I haven't written letters, read, or done anything to strain my eyes, and now they're much better. Every time I would sit down to write, I gave up because of dizziness.

Lately I've done a lot of roller skating because I don't dare wear my glasses for that anyway. Then, two weeks ago, Hydro had an ice skating party and I went and skated and liked it and didn't fall down! I was held up all the time—ha! Of course, I had no intention of going, and then one of the nicest sailors at Hydro, Owen Holland, asked me to go with a friend of his friend who had come down from the New London Submarine Base for the weekend. Owen and his sweet wife, Shirley, Bill and Ruth, a graduate of American University and a lovely girl, and Donald Seel and I went to the party and had a marvelous time. From there we went to a basketball game at the YMCA boy's gym where Bill's brother Elihu was playing on a Baptist Church team.

---

91   Lucy's parents received a telegram at 10:00 p.m. on the night of January 6, 1945, saying that Richard had been wounded. He was a front line infantry combat medic. Wounded by shrapnel in the upper right arm on the morning of December 18, 1944, at Oberotterbach, Germany, he stayed on the battlefield helping others until late afternoon. After his arm hurt too badly to continue, Richard turned himself into the aid station and was transported to a hospital in Epinal, France, and later to a hospital in Dijon, France. He was operated on three times and was away from his unit until February 22, 1945. He received the Bronze Star for valor on the battlefield. On January 7, 1945, Richard's mother phoned Lucy and Virginia to give them the news and sent a telegram to Jonas, who was stationed in Miami, Florida.

Another Baptist team was playing them and it was a good game. Elihu drove us out to his home and we met his wife, who's so pretty and very charming. We had sandwiches, potato chips, frozen custard, cake, cookies, and ate ourselves to death. They have a rec room in the basement and we played ping-pong and danced. By that time it was after 12:30 and Bill and Don collapsed on the living room couch and went dead asleep. Since they live out in Silver Springs, Maryland, clear across the district from Suitland, Elihu and his wife asked—or rather, insisted—we stay there, so finally we did. Ruth and I shared a wonderful bedroom with a bed that was divinely comfortable. I slept like a log! Elihu and his wife and their two babies had their own bedroom, and Holland and his wife had the back bedroom. The boys they left on the couch, and Elihu dragged out a sleeping bag for one of them. Elihu is a lawyer and as nice as he can be. Sunday morning, we had a huge breakfast and went to a little country Methodist Church nearby. The sermon was really good. Then we went to Shirley's mother's and met her uncle and his family who were over there for dinner. From there we went on to a Hot Shoppes restaurant and had a fine meal, then downtown to meet Ruth and Bill, who'd had dinner at her home. We took Don to see the White House, the outside. He'd been sightseeing Saturday afternoon but missed the White House. Then to Bill's home, where we met his very lovely parents, his aunt, niece, and nephew. The two kids are children of Charlie Frick who works in our office and is Bill's brother. Bill worked at Hydro when I first came there but I barely remembered him. They had a fireplace, and it just seemed so homey to sit there and toast my feet and relax. We rolled back the rug and danced and then had cake and ice cream and just talked and had a wonderful time. Finally at 10:00, we took Bill and Don down to Union Station to catch the train. I had more fun than I've had since I've been here, because they were all such fine, Christian people—no smoking, drinking, swearing—just good clean fun. Don is 26 and was in the lithographic business before the war and is quite an artist, too. He is from St. Paul, Minnesota, and attended art school there. He was a super date and a wonderful skater.

I received my *IU Alumni Magazine* and was so happy to see our smiling faces there! It was so nice of the Alumni Association to ask you for our pictures. I'll be home February 10th—I hope you can meet me. I have a couple of days of liberty, so can stay until Monday evening. I'll be on nights and will have to be back by 4:30 p.m. on Tuesday.

Love always,

Lucy

Lucy is second from left, others unknown
Photographer unknown

A University Family . . .

Lt. JONAS M. BERKEY, AB'40, Sp. (X) 3/c LUCY M. BERKEY, AB'42, and Pvt. RICHARD J. BERKEY, '44, children of Attorney and Mrs. James G. Berkey (LENNIE R. MARTIN, AB'17), of Salem, comprise another University trio in service. Mr. and Mrs. Berkey have another son, David, a radioman on Bougainville, called to service just after he finished high school, one daughter still in high school, and another, VIRGINIA, a senior at I.U.

Lt. Berkey was in I.U. Law School when he enlisted in the Navy in January, 1942. After training at Notre Dame and Columbia University, he was commissioned an ensign on December 2, 1942, and two days later married MILDRED McBRIDE, AB'41. Subchaser training at Miami was followed by 18 months' service in the South Pacific from which he returned as skipper of his own subchaser and a promotion in rank. After a furlough last October, he reported at Miami for a refresher course. His

LUCY M. BERKEY
. . . a draftsman

MILDRED McBRIDE BERKEY
. . . former teacher

wife, who taught at Kewanna, Jeffersonville, and Martinsville since her graduation, is with him at Miami.

Specialist Berkey, assistant supervisor of art in the Columbus schools for a year after leaving I.U., enlisted in the WAVES in August of 1943 and took her boot training at Hunter College, N.Y. She was assigned to the Hydrographic Office in Washington, D.C., where she works on ship diagrams as an engineering draftsman. She lives in Snitland Hall.

Pvt. Berkey was a junior pre-med at I.U. when taken into the Army in January, 1943. He was assigned first to a medical detachment at Darnall General Hospital, Danville, Ky. Entering the ASTP, he completed three terms at the University of Cincinnati as an engineering student. After the breakdown of ASTP, he went into another medical detachment and was stationed at Camp Campbell, Ky., until October, when his group went overseas with an armored infantry battalion from New York.

RICHARD J. BERKEY
. . . in infantry

JONAS M. BERKEY
. . . subchaser skipper

Indiana University Alumni Magazine, January 1945
Courtesy of the Indiana University Alumni Magazine

February 3, 1945

Dear Folks,

My plans have been changed—no more liberty that includes Saturday, Sunday, and Monday. Those days will be counted as leave from now on. Instead I have Friday, Saturday, and Sunday, so I'll be at Mitchell Friday morning, February 9th, at the usual time, I hope.

The weather here has been bitter cold and I'm suffering with a chest cold. My eyes are much better this week and I'm so encouraged.

I'll Be Seeing You   183

However, I have 10 fillings to look forward to—my mouth is taking primary place now. Ugh!

Glad to hear they're going to check up on Jonie's health—it's about time. Wish I could get a request letter from Richard. I have three packages ready to send him—already wrapped and ready. I've scads of work to do tonight, so I'll stop. Will see you next Friday!

Loads of love,

Lucy

February 14, 1945

Dear Folks,

We have a lull in work now and I can use a few minutes to write a letter. Got here safely Monday morning. The train was so hot this time.

My new job is very nice. I do hand collating. That means picking up sheets in order and making stacks to be used for books. Then several girls punch holes along the sides of the sheets so they can be put in a loose-leaf notebook, then we put them in envelopes or book covers. So far, it's been very interesting because there's always something different to do each time. The girls I work with are all civilians and are very nice. I can't tell any difference in my eyes so far, but this work is certainly less of a strain.

This afternoon I went to the dentist. He filled one tooth and ground out another and put in a temporary filling until tomorrow. Said he might have to pull it, for it was so bad, the nerve is exposed. He's very jolly and reminds me of Dr. Claude in the way he acts. I'm glad to be getting my teeth fixed. I certainly did enjoy being home. I hope Grandmother is better.

Love to all,

Lucy

February 27, 1945

Dear Folks,

Here I am writing again while at the office, as there isn't any work at present. I certainly was happy to hear more about Richard, though I wasn't surprised to hear about his good work—that's just the way he is! Guess I'm used to being the sister of a hero, so used to it I have to tell everyone about it! There're probably a thousand heroic deeds per day if we only could hear the stories. One good thing about it is those boys are certainly learning about cooperation—so maybe there's some good coming out of all this mess.

The same day I received a letter from home, one came from Richard—the first I've received from him since he's been overseas. I was so excited I could hardly open it! It was such a nice letter. He told me that he ate Christmas dinner in the hospital and said, "if you can imagine that!" He probably was annoyed because he couldn't run around the house two or three times and come in for seconds and thirds. He said the fellows found some rook cards and they've been playing rook for a week or so. He said it reminded him of times we played it at home. The most amazing thing was—Richard was here in Washington for a couple of hours while I was home on leave seeing Jonie last October. He said, "We might have done the town up together!" He said he had enough time to do a little bit of sightseeing in New York before he went across. I'm really sick about not being here to see him, but then I'd have missed Jonie, and I'd seen Richard since I had seen Jonie, so there it goes. It seems so queer to me that I've never seen David in uniform. Wonder where he is now? I was just getting ready to send him a box with books, figs, pears, etc., but now he's a saltwater sailor all of a sudden. So I won't send it now. I did send Richard socks and some other things. They let me send it without a request letter—I sort of played dumb—didn't have to try very hard! Some fun!

Do you believe that I am almost 25? Even Eleanor says I'm the silliest thing! Ha! Virginia sent me the cutest valentine. I didn't send any this year, being as I'm not too filthy with money at the moment. My winter coat finally came, and it's too small. I ordered an 8 because

Irene's coat fit me perfectly and it's an 8. However, this is a different style, and that accounts for it. I'd been counting on getting last year's model, as they're much nicer, and here I get this year's. That's why I ordered it in the first place, to get a nicer one. Well, it serves me right. Now it will be another month before I get it, I expect.

Virginia's Ensign Phil called me the other night. He said he was going to school at night this week but will be able to see me next week. He seems very nice and has a nice voice over the phone. I got to thinking about how funny it was when we met at IU and I started giggling. Now he probably thinks I'm nuttier than ever! Ha!

Janet and I went to the Ice Capades at Uline Arena last week, and the show was marvelous—the first ice show I'd ever seen. We also heard Mrs. Roosevelt speak at our church on "Youth's Stake in Tomorrow's World." She was very, very good, as expected.

Love always,

Lucy

Lucy with unknown officer outside Hydrographic Building
Photographer unknown

March 21, 1945

Dear Folks,

A letter, at last! I've had another bad cold. I'm much better today, though Sunday I stayed in bed and even missed a wedding. One of the fellows in the transfer room got hitched to a gorgeous creature. Janet said she was one of the best looking brides she'd ever seen.

It was as hot this last Friday and Saturday as any summer day here in Washington—the hottest, most humid spot there is. I went to town Friday night, and even the sidewalks burned my feet. The cherry blossoms are out, and seem even more beautiful than last year, though it's always that way with spring—it's so breathtaking, you seem to forget about last year. The forsythia is everywhere on the Capitol grounds and around the Washington Monument. It is so bright and cheerful. Magnolia blossoms seem more profuse than last year. Everyone is so afraid that all the flowers will be killed because of this early warm spell, and I wouldn't doubt if we have another snow again in a couple of weeks. I still say there's nothing like Indiana in the springtime. Here, it comes so suddenly, and it's usually a jump from freezing weather to boiling.

A couple of weeks ago, I got to visit Annapolis and it was a real thrill. I've told you about Mr. Earle Mauck who I met in Hecht's department store. His son, Buck Mauck, was President of the Senior Class of '40, Jonie's class, at IU. Anyway, he invited me to go to Annapolis. He had to go out to get his daughter, Virginia, who had been at the Saturday night hop. She's engaged to a midshipman, Richard Savage. We left here about 1:00, and on the way we killed a dog. Just as we passed two cars parked by the side of the road, a dog jumped from the car window right in front of our car. Mr. Mauck swerved over toward the other side of the road, but the back wheel hit the dog and fractured his neck. The owner was very nice about it and realized it was an accident, for we weren't going very fast. It was a shame though—so very sad.

Annapolis is very quaint and not quite what I expected it to be. The town is small, with a great many old red brick, low houses, and courts. There is a distinct atmosphere about the whole place. It's as if the military figures everywhere make the whole town hold their heads a little higher. We looked around several halls and saw plenty of naval equipment and souvenirs from various wars. I even saw the American flag that was first flown at Bougainville. Everything was right up to date. It was one of the most interesting museum displays I've ever seen—count on the Navy, ya know!

We passed by the statue of Tecumseh, the Indian chief. He's the one who gets all the money thrown his way in exchange for some good luck on exams. There's something about that statue that makes you stand in awe before it. The court out in front of the dormitory was one of the most interesting things to me. Here they assemble for inspection and various ceremonies. The bricks are ivory and are very small and close together. There are two ramps leading up to the main door and they are paved, also. This dormitory is the largest in the world—houses three thousand midshipmen! Boy, and are those fellows good-looking, whew! This Richard Savage is a handsome one, too! Nice healthy pink cheeks and a nice build. He's only 21 and so is Virginia. Virginia is a very sweet girl and quite pretty. The dormitory is gorgeous and so is the chapel. I was so sorry I didn't get to go to chapel, and I'm determined to go back some Sunday. The chapel is beautiful and quite unusual. In the basement is the tomb of John Paul Jones, rather eerie and interesting at the same time.

We had Mr. Mauck's two younger daughters along, so we started back early. Virginia made grilled cheese sandwiches and got out ginger ale, so we had a nice time eating and talking after we got back. It was a lovely day and I enjoyed it all so much. The Maucks treated me just like one of the family.

At long last I went to the eye specialist—Dr. Frances Marshall. She is one of the nicest persons I've ever met, so sincere and genuine, besides being a wonderful doctor. She has prescribed bifocals for me. She has studied myopia for 10 years and knows what she's talking about. She says every nearsighted person should wear bifocals because one lens only helps distant vision—is too strong—too powerful for close work and thus strains the eyes.

I'm still working down in the bindery and will be until after I get my new glasses and get used to them. I'll have two pairs, one for reading only, so I can see a large area comfortably like my whole tracing close-up. It's terribly expensive, but I'm certain it will be worth it. Dr. Marshall gave me tests for three hours and will see me again after I've worn the glasses for 10 days. She says my basal metabolism is surely below normal, for I focus my eyes too slowly, so I'm going to find out what that is. She says the glasses I'm wearing are much too strong, especially for close work, and that after I wear more restful glasses I'll be able to see better even without glasses. Isn't that wonderful?

Will see Phil Ferguson tomorrow night. Virginia will be anxious to hear about that—ahem!

It's so tragic about Dee.[92] I must send his parents a card. I keep thinking about how many times Dee was at our house. I heard from Richard—he's fine but should be back in combat now. He will be so sad to hear this news.

Love,

Lucy

---

92   Sergeant Harold Dee Bush, 23 years old, one of Richard's best friends, was killed March 3, 1945, in a plane crash during Army training near Alexandria, Louisiana. Dee was a radio operator. All eleven members of the Flying Fortress crew were killed in the crash.

Lucy with unknown WAVES
Photographer unknown

March 24, 1945

Dear Daddy,

By this time, you're probably thinking I am a very forgetful daughter. Here I sent your birthday gift so late and didn't even put in a card. Well, I was going to buy you something that I couldn't get after all. I thought it would be here in time, and then when it wasn't, I sent candy and kept the card for the nice gift to send in a couple of days. Now I'm still waiting, so I think I better send the card. Daddy, you should be here in Washington, for you'd really love this hot 86° weather. I don't like it very well, but you'd be right at home. All you'd need would be the farm!! Boy, I sure wish the war would be over so we could just relax down at the farm like we used to. Ah me—I sound like a schoolteacher, ahem!

My eye doctor is really fine and her fee isn't bad at all for a specialist. It was $15 for the first two exams and after that will only be $3 each time I see her. It's the glasses that are so expensive, especially the bifocals—$45 for the two pairs. I'm getting new gold frames—that's why they're so expensive. She said the ones I had were always crooked and kept my eyes out of focus. So far, I think maybe I'll be able to get along without any extra money, but if not, I'll have to write for a bonus—ahem!

I've just been looking out the window and the clouds are moving so fast and are so black, I think they're going to surprise us with a bit of rain.

Daddy, I'm awfully sorry about the birthday gift. I was thinking about you, as I always am, even if I'm not too prompt about doing things. Just so you're okay and had a nice day—that's what counts. Be good, and don't forget to have Eleanor remind you of your vitamin pills!

Much love,

Lucy

March 30, 1945

Dear Folks,

Easter again! It just doesn't seem possible, for it was on Easter I met Bob, and that doesn't seem a year ago. Also, I remember I was so sick with a cold I decided to not go to the sunrise service at Arlington Cemetery. This year I hope to be able to make it. It's been so beautiful these last few days, actually hot in the afternoon about 4:30. There hasn't been much work here in the bindery section for the last week, so we've been getting off at 4:30. I've been able to get some shopping done.

Tuesday I got my new glasses, and I'm struggling to adjust to them. My eyes are better now that I've been away from drafting for about a month. The jerking and turning out of my left eye has disappeared and I can enjoy seeing movies again.

Haven't been going out much lately because of financial reasons, ahem! A couple of weeks ago I met a Marine at a dance and so that helps my finances. I'm not really a gold digger, ahem, but well! He's just a marvelous person, 5'11" with blond hair, blue eyes, and a ghastly name—Donald Curl. I laughed when he told me his name, though I'm more used to it now! He's from Orange, California, and is in OCS at Quantico. He graduates in two weeks and has invited me to his graduation, which I daresay, I will be really excited to attend. I've always wanted to see what it looks like at Quantico. It takes about an hour to get there on the bus from here. Harriet Johnson, one of the WAVES here, was with me when I met Don. She's been going out with Don's buddy, T.L. Davis, Jr., from Oklahoma. We've had so much fun together. Last Sunday we went to see the cherry blossoms, which incidentally, aren't half as beautiful as they were last year. There was so much pink to them last year—they're more whitish now. We walked till we almost collapsed! We went to the National Art Gallery, Smithsonian Institute, Washington Monument, and Jefferson Memorial. This Sunday, Don is platoon commander and has to stay at Quantico, so I guess it'll be another week before I see him again.

The dentist and I have been very chummy lately. I've had five teeth filled—seven fillings in an hour and a half. He's a wonderful dentist and hardly hurt me at all. I also had my teeth cleaned, so now I'm all fixed up for a while and very thankful I didn't have to have those two bad teeth pulled.

I saw Phil last week. We went to a show, had something to eat, and that was all. I'm so sorry I got a bad impression of him at first, for I like him very much. He's really brilliant and Virginia should be proud of him. He left last Saturday and didn't know where he'd be sent. Hoped he could go through Indianapolis and see Virginia as he had called her. She needn't worry about me—he talked about her all evening! Besides, he's about Bob's age.

Happy Easter to all of my nice family. Wish I could be with you. I think we'll have a beautiful day.

All my love,

Lucy

CHAPTER THIRTEEN
THE PRESIDENT HAS DIED

April 15, 1945

Dear Folks,

All of Washington is so upset over the president's death that things are very glum this weekend. None of the shows are open, and radio programs are canceled—just organ music—oh well, you know about that. We got yesterday, Saturday, afternoon off and some of the kids went down to see what they could see at the White House. Janet Knight said she saw Stettinius and Morgenthau come out of the White House and drive away in a car.[93] Their eyes were red and swollen. It seems so hard for everyone to believe—that Roosevelt is dead. It all happened so suddenly.

Friday, I had the day off and went over to the Naval Air Station to get a permanent. I got a cold wave, and the smell of the ammonia solution made me a little dizzy. Then afterwards, I went downtown to have my shoes fixed and then to a restaurant to eat. You should see my hair. It's about 1½" long all over my head! At least I'll pass inspection now.

Well, it won't be long until Virginia graduates. Wish I could get home, but right now it doesn't seem like that will be possible. Ah, dear Navy! I was so glad to hear that all the boys are okay. I must write to them today and answer some of their questions.

Boy, am I sleepy. The more I sleep, the more I want to. Bye now—more later. Hope everyone is okay.

Lots of love,

Lucy

---

93   Edward Stettinius was Secretary of State and Henry Morgenthau was Secretary of the Treasury during the administration of Franklin D. Roosevelt.

MEMORANDUM FOR AVIATORS

18 April 1945

Dear Folks,

Hope you like my stationery - best
I could do here at work. Didn't know
I'd become a pilot, did you? Join the
Navy & they're liable to make most
anything out of you!

Thought I'd better write real
soon like as I forgot several things
I wanted to tell you in my letter
Sunday. The main thing is that I'll
need my summer uniforms by May 1,
so send them as soon as possible,
Mother. I just want the seersucker, of
course, as we don't wear those blue
gabardine "gremlins" anymore. I had thought
I'd be home on leave & bring the dresses
back with me, but it seems as if
I'm not going to get there for awhile.
Besides, I have to pay for my watch
on the 27th & see the eye specialist
next week again. Everything comes at

First page of Lucy's letter—April 18, 1945

I'll Be Seeing You   195

April 18, 1945

Dear Folks,

Hope you like my stationery—best I could do here at work. Didn't know I'd become a pilot, did you? Join the Navy and they're liable to make most anything out of you!

I thought I should write again soon, as I forgot to ask several things in my last letter. The main thing is that I'll need my summer uniforms by May 1, so please send them as soon as possible, Mother. I just want the seersucker, of course, as we don't wear those blue gabardine "gremlins" anymore. I had thought I'd be home on leave and bring the dresses back with me, but it seems as if I'm not going to get there for a while. Besides, I have to pay for my watch on the 27th and see the eye specialist next week again. Everything comes at once, it seems.

The other thing I forgot was that one of the girls wants me to get her six yards of material just like my housecoat. She wants that same color. She'll give me the money if you can get it. I've certainly had more compliments on that one thing.

News at present—and I mean news! We're moving. We're to be out of the hall by June 1st, but no one knows yet exactly when we'll actually move out, maybe in a couple of weeks. I'll be sending my radio and a lot of other junk home. We'll move either to Anacostia, which isn't far, or clear across town to Barracks K. Anyway, it'll be a barracks and I won't be able to have anything but essentials. We're all wailing and bemoaning our fate. We'll be brought to work by bus, I guess. They won't renew the lease for the Navy, as they need that room for civilian girls. They're getting so many new civilian girls at the Census Building. So we'll get kicked out!

Rained all day yesterday, but today is sunny and beautiful and invigorating. I'm going to see a show tonight with Janet—*A Song to Remember.*[94]

Lots of love,

Lucy

---

94   *A Song to Remember* plot: biography of Frederic Chopin.

KAREN BERKEY HUNTSBERGER

April 30, 1945

Dear Mother & Daddy,

I was thrilled to receive a wonderful letter from Richard this afternoon, dated April 11th. I saw it in my mailbox as I was going through the lobby on my way in from work. Boy, I was really excited because it was the first time I'd heard from him in ages—it made me feel 100% better. Best I've felt since they denied the surrender story Saturday night. Jeepers, it was good to hear from that brother of mine! He sent me a ritzy Nazi emblem, and I was glad to have it even if it is a Nazi one! The emblem is really a beautiful thing—black and gold. It evidently was an officer's sleeve insignia. Janet was having more fun with that badge, going around with it pinned over her rating and getting everyone in the place as curious as could be! They all thought she was crazy—and she is, that's why we all get along so well! Really, she's as fine a friend as I've met since I've been in the WAVES! Richard also wrote that he had finally received my packages. Gee, I'm so glad he got them at last! Now I won't be afraid to send things. After he didn't receive those things you sent, I felt sure my packages would be lost, too. He didn't say how the fruitcake came through—I hope it wasn't awfully stale. I tried wrapping wax paper all around it, but sometimes moisture gets in anyway. He was glad to get the socks, and they fit just right. I told Richard to please ask me if he wanted anything special, for I can get things here in Washington easier than you can at home. He said he was sending you a flag and a string of beads to Julia Thixton and that he must send something in the way of a graduation gift to Virginia. That's about all he said. I haven't heard from David.

I wrote Richard back right away and congratulated him on his two medals. Last week, when you wrote me about him receiving his Bronze Star, I almost fell over dead, rushed down to Janet to tell her there was a medal in my family and, well gee, I was some proud specimen! After all it's not every day a G.I. Joe gets such an honor bestowed upon him. I received a church newsletter from home that told of two medals, and so I found out about the Purple Heart that way!

Of course, I knew he would get one, but seeing it in print really felt great! After that, well, bragging must be in my blood, for the more I rave the better I get—what an explosion!

Virginia has graduated, and I wasn't there to see it all. I had hoped to get home on leave, but can't get away now till September, it seems. I'm so glad for Virginia, for she's safely graduated, which is something in wartime. And I'm so glad to hear her application to Yale School of Nursing has been accepted for the fall term. She's as goodhearted a kid as you can find, and I know she'll make a terrific nurse. It probably bothers her as much as it does me to go home and find so many women, as if I hadn't seen enough of them since I've been in the WAVES. Yes, men are welcome creatures, especially nowadays, and especially some brothers I know! Here's hoping this mess will be over soon and Richard and David can come home.

Saturday night I was sitting here in my room calmly reading a good book when the radio announcer seemed so excited, I stopped my reading to listen more closely. He said Himmler had said Germany would surrender unconditionally to all three great powers, and the only thing they were waiting for now was for Eisenhower to make a final, definite statement, and for that to be confirmed by President Truman. Honestly, I was so excited I could hardly sit still enough to listen! I heard girls everywhere, in all the wings, yelling and telling their neighbors the wonderful news. Every few minutes, announcers on the Blue Network would interrupt programs to tell us a statement was expected momentarily.[95] This kept up for an hour, with announcers and commentators wondering why they hadn't seen any celebrating in the streets yet. Then, suddenly, it was stated that President Truman had cut short the bright hopes going around, by saying the former statement was only a rumor, and that there was no real basis for it. He said he had called an official in Europe, and that it was not true. This was really a sad place after that, long faces and plenty of the silence that gets you, the kind we felt around here just after we

---

95   The Blue Network was the second radio network of the National Broadcasting Company (NBC).

heard of President Roosevelt's death. However, things certainly can't last much longer, and the paper today feels that they are holding off VE Day until after Russia declares war on Japan.[96] Sometimes I think these papers are crazy. I must sign off and do a washing and ironing.

Loads of love,

Lucy

---

96   Victory in Europe Day was commonly referred to as VE Day or V-E day.

CHAPTER FOURTEEN
VICTORY IN EUROPE

May 8, 1945

Dear Mother & Daddy,

At long last, the war in Europe is over!!! We were glued to the radio at Hydro this morning listening to the reports. Of course, everyone was overcome with joy and ran around cheering and hugging each other. We listened to President Truman's speech, then King George and Winston Churchill. It was thrilling to hear all the people cheering in celebrations in Europe! I'm so relieved that Richard won't be in the thick of things any longer, but I'd imagine it will be a long time before he comes home. I hope he is not sent to Japan.

Such a bittersweet day to come home to a letter from you, Mother, and learn that Glen Huckleberry, Maurice Lloyd, and Paul Tackett had all died in the Philippines. Such fine boys, and it's so hard to accept that they are gone now. I'm so hopeful that it won't be long before the war in the South Pacific is over. We believe our work here at Hydro has been really critical for our fighting forces in the Pacific. I'll be anxious to hear how dear old Salem celebrated today's news!

All my love,

Lucy

May 27, 1945

Dear Folks,

I finally have my boxes packed to send home. Yesterday I had the day off and spent the whole time going through junk and trying to decide to throw things away. I usually ended up putting them back—the old efficient housekeeper, as usual. I think I'm more of a collector than I used to be.

Well, the suspense about moving has gotten us all on edge. At the moment, we're not sure of anything, just a little bit more certain than we've been for the last month. Wednesday I'm moving to E wing, and just what room I'm not sure. That same day, 30 girls will move to the New Colonial Hotel downtown. In a couple of weeks, 70 more will move to a different hotel so that a hundred rooms will be available for civilians. This weekend most of the girls moved from my wing to upstairs, as they're putting WAVES upstairs and civilians downstairs, except for lower E, where I'll be moving. They needed so many more civil service workers over at the Census Building and the government had to promise those girls a place to live, so they're kicking us out. The Navy was lax in renewing their lease here, and the government was happy to take advantage of it. I'll probably move in the next group. I'm not going to send my radio until I leave here, since I can hardly get along without it. I'm so used to listening to the news every night and morning. Since I seldom get to read a paper, that radio news is about I all get.

Well, the bindery business is lousy as usual. I must say, I'll be thrilled to get out of that place. It's really hard work. All day I pack skids with stacks of paper, help on a machine—keeping paper straight, any number of things—but most of the time I walk around the table, pick up paper, and then jog it. That jogging just cuts my hands to shreds sometimes and paper cuts are hard to heal. Every night I'm dead tired, but then it is helping my eyes, so I guess I should be thankful. The atmosphere is pretty bad down there because I work with all civilian women and some of them are really nasty about anything that concerns WAVES. They make some pretty sad remarks—jealousy, I guess.

I saw the eye doctor on Wednesday, and she's pleased with the improvement in my eyes. She wanted me to have a basal metabolism test taken, for she felt my eyes focused too slowly, and so I did. The test was normal, thank goodness, and I'll take the results to her and get her verdict in June. She says my whole system works too slowly—as if I and everyone else didn't know that already.

When I try to think of what I've done lately, my mind seems a perfect blank. I've just hurried through the last month. Janet Knight, my dear schoolteacher friend, left two weeks ago for overseas, and all of us are really broken up about it. Her orders came quite suddenly, after she'd given up hope months ago. She was so thrilled to be going. We had a party for her down at the Madrillon Restaurant and had a picture taken that was very good. We gave her stationery and a beautiful green leather writing portfolio, and she was so pleased. But then, Janet always appreciates any little thing you do for her. I miss her so much, it's pathetic. Then, just after Janet left, Jean Hamm left for Texas on leave and will be gone 21 days. So that took my two best friends in a big hurry.

Janet and I saw the Skating Vanities the Sunday before she left and we enjoyed it even more than we did the ice show. They really had some marvelous roller skaters. One trick artist stood on his head on a platform, juggled balls on the floor, and turned around slowly all at the same time. I certainly enjoyed it, as I'm really a roller skating fan now and go to the class every Tuesday night.

My financial situation is lousy at present. So many kids have had birthdays around here; I've had eye doctor bills; I still have Virginia's gift to buy; there was the party and gift for Janet; plus my own gift of the Chambray set for her; I've had to buy new seersucker dresses as I only have one; seersucker hat; needed new slips; had to buy a new purse as my old one was falling apart; new white gloves; shoes; hose—well, it's a great life—in the Navy, I mean!

I decided to wait until I knew more about Richard before I took my leave, in case he gets a break and gets to go through the States. I'm so glad Jonas is so well and that he'll be near home. Well, I must get to bed or be dead tomorrow. I've just found out my new room number is E-115.

Lots of love,

Lucy

my room

2 July 1945

Dear Mother & Daddy,

At last I am settled in my hotel room & life is progressing in a rather slow sort of way in this heat. It has been unbearably hot for the last week, & yesterday the temp. rose to 99°. I got up from my seat in church & boy! my back was soaked clear through. Dr. Hastings told all the men they could re- move their coats, & it reminded me of Mr. Mace doing the same thing in our church! It got even hotter last night & we almost passed out at Young Peoples meeting. However, afterwards there was plenty of watermelon, & that did help! I've just come from work, & there's a nice breeze now, for it started raining about 4:00 this afternoon. My room is still hot, for all our windows were closed, but it probably won't take long to

COFFEE SHOP AND DINING ROOM
Radio Loud Speaker in each Room

First page of Lucy's letter—July 2, 1945

July 2, 1945

Dear Mother & Daddy,

At last I am settled in my hotel room and life is progressing in a rather slow sort of way in this heat. It has been unbearably hot for the last week, and yesterday the temperature rose to 99°. I got up from my seat in church and my back was soaked clear through. Dr. Hastings told all the men they could remove their coats, and it reminded me of Mr. Mace doing the same thing in our church. It got even hotter last night, and we almost passed out at Young People's meeting. However, afterwards there was plenty of watermelon, and that did help.

I just came from work, and there's a nice breeze now, for it started raining about 4:00 this afternoon. My room is still hot, for all our windows were closed, but it probably won't take long to cool off. This is a nice room, one of the nicest the WAVES have in the hotel. Of course, civilians have the nicest rooms! My room has six windows where most of the rooms have only two. At first Mary Palmquist and Ann Kitcha asked me to room with them. I accepted, as they're lovely girls and very intelligent. Just after we moved, Betty McCoy got transferred from the Martinique Hotel. The rest of the WAVES had moved to the Martinique Hotel—it's only a block away on 16th St. Mary got moved to the New Colonial and wanted to live with Mary and Ann, so I moved out. They had originally planned to live together so I didn't mind too much.

However, by that time all my friends had their rooms filled so I had to move in with two girls I didn't know at all. Edith Mulholland is a seaman who just came from Hunter. She's from Yonkers, New York. Frances, also a SP (X) 3/c is from Richmond, Indiana—another Hoosier! Frances works here in town and Edith works at Hydro. They both seem very nice and are cooperative except for being a bit messy, but I guess anyone would seem messy to old straightener-upper me! So, I guess we'll get along.

Hotel life seems to be agreeing with me beautifully, for I already feel better than I ever felt at Suitland. I think the main thing is because I'm eating better food. I get up at 6:00 a.m. and I'm ready to go down at 6:45. We have to get up early to avoid one another. Oh yes, we have a private bathroom, too, and most of the girls have to share theirs with another room. At 6:45 I go down to the lobby and buy a paper, then get a seat in the coffee shop where they start serving at 7:00 a.m. Then I have a big breakfast of orange juice, bacon and eggs, toast with butter and jelly, and coffee. Other mornings I have cantaloupe or hot cereal, or French toast, wheat cakes, prunes—in fact—most anything I want! Then we leave by Navy bus at 7:30 and get to Hydro at 8:00. So I have plenty of time to relax before work at 8:30. I usually have time to see kids I never see any other time or go over to the hall for soap flakes and stuff we can't get in town. The coffee shop at the hotel serves wonderful meals and they're very reasonable. You can get an appetizer, main meal with two veggies, dessert, and drinks for 85¢. It's wonderful to be able to eat right again!

Honestly, I'm so ashamed of not thanking you for my birthday gifts over the phone. That was one of the main reasons why I called. Thanks a million for everything! The savings bond is the most wonderful thing I could receive, and the extra cash will be wonderful. Mother, the card had the sweetest watercolor picture on it—such clear color. Getting Richard's picture was almost like seeing him! I had a nice letter from him this week that he wrote on my birthday. Of course, he was kidding me about getting so old! He didn't say much except that he had visited Paris and that there were "quantities of beautiful women!" He also told me about his first aid room—his "quack" business. I sent two boxes recently, one to Richard and one to David. I hope they get there okay. Both of the boxes were too heavy, and I had to untie them and take out things I wanted to send.

Mother, that letter all about Richard was really wonderful. I read it to several kids and they enjoyed it, too. You know, he surprises me by being such an interesting writer! I never did know he was that good.

I almost forgot to tell you about the beautiful roses Bob sent for my birthday. There were a dozen red roses, with ferns and baby's breath included. They made a gorgeous bouquet. I let the officers use them for a centerpiece at the dinner in honor of the WAVE officer who was being transferred. Of course, now all Navy personnel have been removed from Suitland Hall.

An amazing thing—I received your latest letter a day after it was mailed in Salem, Mother. It was mailed the 27th and I got it on the 28th! The difference is that it always took a day or more to get out to Suitland from the main post office here. You would laugh at my essentials—three suitcases and two huge boxes—that's all! You forget I've been here almost two years and being a famous collector and all—I honestly don't know how I possibly collected it all!

The weather is getting nicer all the time, much cooler—I can breathe again. It's so good to be close to church. It's only one block away. I must go eat, as I'm starving as usual.

Lots of love,

Lucy

July 23, 1945

Letter from Frances Hyatt

Dear Mrs. Berkey,

By now, you probably have received a card from Bethesda Naval Hospital telling you that Lucy is a patient there. I do hope this didn't scare you. As far as we know, all Lucy had was a bad case of food poisoning and, of course, that isn't any fun. Since the hotel did not have the proper facilities to handle her case, it was thought best to send her right out to Bethesda.

Sometimes, the girls are not allowed to write letters when at the hospital. This is my reason for writing to you. I didn't know whether Lucy had been able to write or not and I didn't want you to worry.

I had the measles about six months ago and was sent to Bethesda, so I know something about the place. It is quite new and is supposed to be the most modern and well-equipped naval hospital in the world.

It certainly seemed that way to me. They have everything out there. I had three doctors and I only had the measles.

I don't know how long Lucy will be out at Bethesda. They keep you out there long after the time necessary. I guess they want to be very sure you're alright. Lucy went out on Thursday and she could come back tomorrow or in two weeks. You just can't tell. Edith and I wanted to go out and pay Lucy a visit today but decided against this idea, as Bethesda frowns on visitors. If we do go out, I'll write and tell you how Lucy is. However, as I say, she could be back at any time.

When I was at Bethesda I really enjoyed resting and I think Lucy will, too. It never hurts to relax a little bit, particularly when you do as much work as we enlisted WAVES do.

I guess I forgot to tell you that I am Lucy's roommate, one of them. The other one is Edith. I am fond of Lucy and I'm sorry this had to occur. Edith and I think that Lucy has the best sense of humor ever—it's wonderful—and she's so thoughtful, too. Always doing something for us. Lucy and I both went to IU and I am from Richmond, Indiana. I do hope this letter hasn't worried you.

Sincerely,

Frances

July 25, 1945

Dear Folks,

Yes, imagine it! Here I am propped up with pillows trying to write a letter in this hospital ward. It seems funny that I should be in the hospital no sicker than I am, but they keep you here for ages. They brought me here last Thursday evening. As usual, I was vomiting and couldn't stop. It was just like the time I went to Hunter and was so sick on the train with food poisoning. Anyway, I was really sick, but not sick enough to go to the hospital. The hotel doesn't have an infirmary, so they had the pharmacist's mate come from the Navy Department and take me down to the main naval dispensary.

From there they brought me out here. Of all the red tape! I had to sit up and tell where all my family was born—blah blah blah—until I almost passed out. If you were dying, you'd be lying on the floor tapping out information with your toenails before they put you to bed! Finally, I had an examination and then I had an I.V. to feed me glucose through my veins. They put a needle in my arm, and I had to watch the liquid trickle out of a bottle suspended above me. It's funny—your stomach doesn't feel full. Your skin feels sort of hot and prickly and your ears get dull. They fed me that way until Saturday noon, and then Sunday I got juice, a whole pitcher of orange juice, one of water, and another of milk. Boy, I really felt full then! Guess I'll be here for a couple more days till I get my strength back. Seems as if you never get out of this place. I'll have to go through 24 hours of red tape even after they've given me permission to leave before I can actually get out. That's the Navy for you.

I've needed so many things since I've been here but had no way to get them. I could use my shower cap, hairpins, etc. My hair is so straight it's pathetic!

I would've written sooner, but was pretty weak to sit up and write. Monday I received your letter, Mother, for one of the girls who is an "Up Patient" had messenger duty and stopped at the hotel for mail. There are three other girls out here from Hydro, but not in this ward.

I got such a nice letter from Richard so I already knew he was coming home. I was so excited, I didn't mind being sick as long as I knew he was coming home. I'm so happy he got my box at last. I must write to him.

Martha called me last week and I'm so thrilled. It was like a visit home getting all the gossip from her. I was supposed to meet Martha, Margaret Ann and Kathryn, and Dorothy Cockerham was to take us through Walter Reed Hospital. Well, that very day I got sick and had to come to this hospital instead! I'm really disappointed, for I was anxious to talk to Martha and have always wanted to visit Walter Reed.

You should see this hospital—it's really beautiful as it is very new and modern. It's in Maryland, but all the way across Washington from

Hydro, which is southeast. It's probably a good thing they sent me out here, for it's really the first rest I've had since I've been in the Navy. My eyes feel much better and I'm beginning to feel better than I've felt in months. The irony of it is on the day I got sick I had the day off to go see the civilian doctor who says I have a thyroid deficiency, which partly causes my eyes to be so bad.

Well, I'll write again soon. Virginia, I thought about you yesterday—Happy Birthday. I'll send your gift when I get back to the hotel.

Love to all,

Lucy

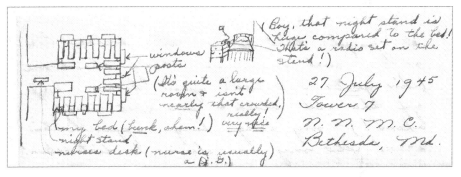

Lucy's drawing of her hospital room—July 27, 1945
N.N.M.C.—National Naval Medical Center

July 27, 1945

Tower 7 N.N.M.C Bethesda, MD

Dear Daddy,

This is a "pois'nal" letter to at long last thank you for the lovely gift of a bond and $5 for my 25th birthday! I'm really very prompt about thanking you, don't you think?[97] Well, I kept thinking maybe I'd get home in time to thank you in person, but seems as if that didn't materialize. Anyway, thanks millions—it certainly was wonderful of

---

97 Lucy's birthday—June 12.

you. You do so much for me, you and Mother both, and I always wish there were some way to tell you how much it always means to me.

Guess you've read about my being stranded here in a high white bed, with GIs all around me. You could probably top my best hospital story what with all the time you spent at St. Joseph's that time.[98] The doctors here all marvel over one thing about me—my long appendicitis scar![99] It's my one claim to distinction. I'm quite unusual you know, chip off the old block and all that stuff!

Some girls have been here for four or five months or even as long as a year with rheumatic fever, arthritis, etc. I realize every day how lucky I am to be so healthy. All my little ailments seemed silly when I came out here. Every few days one of the Red Cross ladies comes through and they are so sweet. One takes orders for supplies from Ship's Service, another gives out library books, and another brings around cord for weaving belts and making ornaments.

Miss *Berkley* has to take her pills now. I can't seem to pound it into people's heads that I'm Berkey without the L!

Haven't seen Martha yet, but I will as soon as I get out of here. Ah—there's a nice breeze blowing now—it's been hot all day following the storm last night. Bye for now, Daddy. Don't work too hard and I'll see you soon.

Lots of love,

Lucy

---

98   Lucy's father had spent a year in bed in 1935–36 following surgery for a lung abscess at St. Joseph's Hospital, Louisville, KY. He was 64 years old at the time this letter was written.
99   Lucy had an appendectomy at the age of five.

July 27, 1945

Dear Folks,

Life is just one meal after the other and one nap after the other here in the hospital. I'm still here, though really well enough to be out and they still won't let me get out of bed to go down to Ship's Service or even walk around. However, I guess the rest is doing me good.

This morning we had Captain's Inspection and worked like mad to get ready. Here in this naval hospital we get up and do our work even if we're bed patients. We have a Nursing Corps WAVE who comes in every morning and sticks a thermometer in my mouth and takes my pulse before I'm hardly awake and then at 6:00 a.m. yells, "rise and shine, hit the deck, everyone has to clean up and make her bed before 7:00!" At 7:30 we have breakfast. Mail call is at 10:00, lunch is 11:30, visiting hours 2:00–4:00. At 10:00 and 2:00 I get a multivitamin pill and a phenobarbital pill, at 4:00 mail call again, and 4:30 evening chow. Sick Call is at 9:00 in the morning when the doctor comes 'round and again at 7:00 p.m. The doctor who is officer of the day makes the rounds. 9:00 is lights out, but it's usually 10:00 before we can get to sleep, for some of the girls insist on talking. So, as you can see, it's a pretty busy day. When the doctor tells me I can get up, I'll be classed as an "Up Patient" and will have a detail in the morning—maybe dusting, cleaning the head, or sumpin' highly interesting. You never forget you're in the Navy!

Received your letter this afternoon, Mother, and was so glad to get it, as mail means so much here. Also got a letter from Lieutenant Don Curl, that Marine I got so disgusted with. He's overseas now and must be crazy to think I'd write him!

Still eating my chopped "dog food" and I'm sick of it, so I hope they'll change my diet soon. Our doctor, Dr. Stebbins, a former baby doc, is very nice, so maybe she'll change it, ahem!

Lots of love,

Lucy

August 1, 1945

Dear Folks,

Yesterday was the third anniversary of the WAVES, but here I was in the hospital, so I don't know what sort of celebration they had. Gee, I guess I'll get out Friday, but I think even that's too soon. I've been in bed so long I'm weak as a cat, and so darn silly. Honestly, I get so disgusted with myself! I'm an "Up Patient" now and go down to the Ship's Service on the first deck every afternoon. My knees are so wobbly and weak I can hardly move, and I guess I really look funny staggering along. Outside of the room where the fountain is located, there's a patio where we can sit outside and get some sunshine. I always sit there from 2:00 to 4:00, and that's really the only part of the day I enjoy. Mornings I have to dust about 44 bays and bedside tables and clean the nurse's bathroom. Boy, that is really a job! Takes me about an hour in all. Then I have to make my bed, dress, straighten my locker, etc., etc., etc. There's always something to be done.

I'll be so glad when Richard comes home and I can go on leave, for this summer has been so drab and draggy so far. I'm anxious to get home for a while.

Received your letter today and can report that they're not fixing any old troubles. If I ever told them about all my ailments they'd either laugh or keep me here for eight months! Soon as I am out I'll start thyroid treatments with the civilian doctor, and it'll be done in 1/4 the time it'd take the Navy to get around to it! Well, bye, out of news!

Lots of love,

Lucy

CHAPTER FIFTEEN
THE WAR IS OVER

August 12, 1945

Dear Mother & Daddy,

I'm just now getting around to writing again after being at the hospital. So much has happened in the last week I don't know what to think.

At Hydro, we listened to Truman's speech about dropping the bomb. There was absolute silence after the speech was over—none of us knew what to say it was so shocking. We'd heard that Japan was ready to surrender, and of course, none of us knew anything about these new bombs. Girls were crying and I just felt numb thinking about all the people that died in an instant. Truman says it's the greatest thing in history, but we're all wondering if other countries have this kind of bomb. I've always known Washington was a military target, but I never felt unsafe here until now. They say dropping the bombs will ultimately save lives, since our boys won't have to fight the Japs on their soil. We've heard such horrible things about the Japs and their cruelty to our boys, but it couldn't have been right to kill all those people. There's been horrible bombing all through the war, but this is different. All I've read says there'll be long lasting effects from radiation, too.

Rev. Hastings' sermon this morning was about "loving your enemy." When we're at war, that's so terribly hard to do, and I've sure tried. We're all anxious for the war to be over, and really, have been since the beginning. I know we'll talk about it at Young People's meeting tonight. I'm really interested in hearing what other church members are thinking.

On a happy note, I'm feeling well now and glad to be back at work. I've sure missed everyone and was glad to be missed by them. What a greeting when I returned!

Love,

Lucy

August 20, 1945

Dear Folks,

At long last I called home, and naturally I called while you were at the farm. However, it was good to be able to talk to Virginia and Eleanor.

I know Bob could brain me for not writing for so long. I'm anxious to know if he will get to finish his air cadet course—he was to have graduated the last of November. Surely they'll let him go ahead.[100] How about David? Have you heard if he's okay and stuff? Hope they don't stick any of the boys in the Army of Occupation. I don't know when I'll be out, probably in six months. There's so much scuttlebutt you can't believe anything you hear. We have to have 29 points for discharge and be mustered out. I have 24. It's ½ point for every year of your age and ½ point for each month in the service.[101] For sailors it's 44 points—the same setup except ½ point for every month of active combat duty. However, your officer can keep you if he feels you're essential, so there it goes.

Having peace is so unusual, we can't get used to it. Things unknown for the past two years are already appearing in stores, and this week

---

100 This is the last time Lucy mentions Bob and she never mentions his last name. As this relationship persisted for more than a year, it seemed more serious. But separation by months and distance likely meant the end of their time together. Lucy also dated other men during this time period.

101 Married women were decommissioned almost immediately. Approximately 1,800 WAVES stayed past their active duty. The official end date for WAVES was July 30, 1946.

we go on a 44-hour schedule which will change to a 40-hour schedule in October!

Tuesday night, the night of the announcement, Washington really went wild. Frances, June, and I went down to F Street and Pennsylvania Avenue and almost had our hats torn off, there was such a wild mob. Part of F Street was blocked off and it looked like pictures of New York with confetti and rolls of paper floating down from rooftops and windows and a mob going crazy. Everyone was kissing everyone else, officers were slapping guys on the back, and vice versa. One sailor had on a WAVES officer's hat and was trying to make an enlisted WAVE salute him. Newspapermen were atop a car taking pictures, whistles were blowing, and it took us almost an hour to move two blocks! What a night!!! Finally got in front of the White House, and I saw a WAVE officer who was one of my teachers at Hunter! After two years, we met in Washington in front of the White House to celebrate victory! I spoke to her and though she did not remember me she remembered my regiment, for that was when she first started teaching in the Navy. She's a darling girl and I didn't even salute her—but there was no saluting that evening. We had two days off—Wednesday and Thursday. Thursday I went on a moonlight cruise with a Marine who was wounded at Okinawa. His right arm is still bandaged and he can't move his fingers. He's at Bethesda.

Eloise Parr called and she and her husband are going to take me out to dinner on the 24th. I finally saw Martha one afternoon at Woody's and then Mary, Ann, Martha, and I had dinner at the Madrillon. It was so good to see Martha.

Lots of love,

Lucy

U. S. NAVAL BARRACKS
WEST POTOMAC PARK
WASHINGTON 4, D. C.

18 Sept. 1945
(Date)

Dept. __Hydrographic Office__

To: __BERKEY, Lucy M.__

Ser. No. __763-58-81__ Rate __Sp(X)3c__

Subject: Leave.

1. You are hereby granted __15__, days leave and __2__ days travel time, total __17__ days.

Commencing: __1700, 21 Sept. 1945__
(Hour)   (Date)

Expiring: __0800, 9 Oct. 1945__
(Hour)   (Date)
to report upon expiration to this command.

2. It is understood that your address while on leave will be:

306 East Walnut St.

Salem, Indiana

COMPLY WITH INSTRUCTIONS ON REVERSE HEREOF

(Executive Officer)

DEPARTED: __1700__ __21 Sept 1945__
(Hour)   (Date)

__(Signature of OOD)__

RETURNED: __0830__ __9 OCT 1945__
(Hour)   (Date)

__(Signature of OOD)__

Lucy's leave September 21—October 9, 1945
Courtesy of the National Archives

Eleanor, Lucy, Virginia
at home in Salem, Indiana
September 1945
Photographer unknown

Lucy and sister-in-law Mildred—September 1945
Photographer unknown

Miss Lucy Berkey, Sp. (x) 3/c
after enjoying her 17-day leave
with her parents the J. G. Berkeys left Sunday for Washington
D. C. where she is stationed with
the WAVES. En route, Specialist
Berkey was accompanied to Mitchell, Ind. by her parents and
aunt, Mrs. Fannie Thomas.

October 10, 1945—Courtesy of The Salem Leader

October 21, 1945

Dear Mother & Daddy,

Gosh, it was swell to talk to Richard on the phone after all this time!!! I am so glad he is home safely. And I just missed seeing him by ten days. Now I wish I'd scheduled my long leave for later, but none of us knew when he'd be home. How I wish I were home to hear all his stories. Please tell him to write and tell me everything! Here it's been over a year since Jonie came home, and I'm just as excited for Richard to be back.

The train ride back was fine—no problems this time. Maybe I'm finally getting used to it—ha! Could be because I was so relaxed after being home a while.

They're talking about keeping me here until January now. More girls have mustered out each week, and I'm really missing some of my good friends. Some left when I was home on leave, and I was sorry I'd missed the chance to say goodbye. Of course, the workload has changed so much since the war's been over. But, they're waiting for men to come back to work here, and all of them that have been in combat are due nice, long leaves. And they certainly deserve them!

Speaking of leaves, I think this is the prettiest fall I've seen since being in Washington. There's a nice crisp scent in the air, and I've enjoyed getting out and walking when the weather is nice. It was a lovely walk this morning to church—all of one block—but still beautiful. I have to head out to Young People's group in a few minutes. I just had to write and say how happy I am that Richard is home!

Much love to all, especially Richard!

Lucy

Dem 2/9-20-15M

IN REPLY REFER
TO FILE NO.

301-4

U. S. NAVAL BARRACKS

WEST POTOMAC PARK

WASHINGTON 4, D. C.

7 November 1945

From: BERKEY, Lucy M., Sp(X)3c, 763 58 81, USNR-W

To: Chief of the Bureau of Naval Personnel

Via: (1) Hydrographer
        (2) Chief of Naval Operations
        (3) Commanding Officer, U. S. Naval Barracks

Subj: Retention on Active Duty - Enlisted Personnel's Request for.

1. I became eligible for discharge on __Dec. 1945__ with __26__ points.

2. It is requested that I be retained on active duty until __15 Jan. 1946__.

3.

Lucy M. Berkey   Sp(X)3c   763 58 81
(Signature)   (Rate)   (Service No.)

- -

End-1   Date __7 November 1945__

To: Chief of the Bureau of Naval Personnel.

Via: (1) Chief of Naval Operations
        (2) Commanding Officer, U. S. Naval Barracks.

1. Forwarded, recommending approval. __BERKEY, Lucy M.__ is assigned
to a continuing billet.

2.

R.A. WARD Lt. Comdr. by direction

                                     Date __14 NOV 1945__

- -

* End-2

To: Chief of the Bureau of Naval Personnel

Via: (1) Commanding Officer, U. S. Naval Barracks

1. Forwarded, recommending approval.

2.

FINISHED FILE PERS 6901

MARGARET A. KOLLING
BY DIRECTION

* Optional

Courtesy of the National Archives

November 14, 1945

Dear Mother & Daddy,

I meant to write last night, but I was so tired from my weekend that I had to go straight to bed after work—and chow, of course!

Boy, I certainly had one wonderful weekend!! I left Friday after work. One of the fellows in the office took me down to Union Station in his car, so I really got started early. Got in New York at 10:00 p.m., and left for New Haven at 11:00, arriving there about 1:00 a.m. Got a taxi to Virginia's dorm at Yale and found I could stay right there for only 50¢ per night. Virginia has a nice corner room on the third floor. There are two large windows, one on each side and a double decker bunk. I got the upper, of course! There is a huge closet, two easy chairs, and two desks and dressers! That's because it's really for two girls, but Virginia is lucky enough to have it as a single. That building used to be a hospital, as you can tell by the wide doors. They've made it awfully nice and comfortable and home-like. There are three or four lovely rooms downstairs where the girls can relax or entertain guests. There's even a library. Also, Virginia has her own private mailbox with a key! She says the meals are delicious, though I didn't eat a single one there.

Saturday morning I was so dead from my train trip, I slept while Virginia went to class. At noon I met quite a few of her friends, all such lovely girls, and at 1:30 Thea Halloran, Virginia, and I left for Boston! Virginia had called me Thursday night and had asked me to go to Boston with them as Thea had said it would be okay. I decided to go ahead since I didn't want to wait till colder weather to go farther north. We passed through New London on the way, and just as we were crossing part of the bay, a submarine zoomed along, so we stared our eyes out! In Boston, we got off the train and walked about four or five blocks down to the Charles River. Thea told us MIT was just across the river and the famous "Shell" was not far away. We also saw the exterior of the Old North Church and Trinity Church. Then, on the streetcar, we passed the opera house and the art museum. Thea's mother is fat and jolly, blonde, and extremely intelligent. Her father has snow white hair, a wonderful sense of humor, twinkly eyes, and is a junior high school principal who specializes in languages. We discovered that Thea herself is pretty lousy with gray matter having finished at Boston University in three years by taking summer courses at Harvard. She majored in psychology but also finished a pre-med course, thinking she might like to become a doctor. She's been married two-and-a-half years, and her husband, who is quite wealthy, is overseas. Mrs. Halloran had a lovely meal for us. She had baked two pies and two cakes! They were all delicious, too. We sat around Saturday evening just talking and looking at Thea's college yearbook and her high school yearbook from the famous Girls' Latin School. Their home is lovely—a Dutch colonial. They live on the outskirts of Boston and it's sorta country-like. There are so many beautiful homes there. We had cake and cocoa before bed and slept rather late Sunday morning. For breakfast, there were griddlecakes and sausage, and she even fixed us some English muffins that were delicious. About 11:30, we drove out to Wellesley College to pick up a girlfriend of Thea's and bring her back for dinner. It's beautiful on that campus—all sort of a wooded estate. The buildings are quite far apart, each one on a knoll of its own. I noticed many bicycles, so I guess they make it to class on time! It was raining, so we couldn't appreciate it as much as if it had been a nice day. But then it rained all weekend, so we had to get used to it. It was also very cold in Boston, and Virginia and I almost froze to death in the back seat of the car.

Since Phil was in Boston on duty aboard ship, Virginia thought maybe we'd be able to see his ship. So that afternoon we drove down to the Boston Navy Yard and looked around. We saw lots of ships, cruisers, destroyers, etc., but didn't see his ship, which is a CA—a heavy cruiser. We left Lucia, the Wellesley girl, off at the bus station and then saw the main business district of Boston. We drove past Beacon Hill and down Commonwealth Avenue. It was so much fun seeing places and things you'd always just read about! Thea stopped for a few minutes to run into her sorority tea and say hello to her friends. We ate a chicken sandwich and delicious Bavarian cream back at the Halloran home and dashed for our bus. We missed it by a second and had to walk about five blocks to catch the streetcar. We got in about 11:00 in New Haven. The next morning, I went to nursing class with the kids. The class was on "Discharge of the Patient," mainly on social aspects. A medical social worker was there and she gave an interesting talk. After class I met the head nurse. She is really a gracious person, and seemed to think a lot of Virginia. Then, Virginia, Gale, Betty Jane, and I ate at George and Harry's at noon and had a very good meal. Then Virginia and I saw the Yale campus. I was disappointed in the campus itself, for it's a city college, and there's very little "campus" except in small grass plots in frequent quadrangles. The buildings are old and so beautiful and seem to have so much "atmosphere," as Virginia said. We went through the Memorial Library, and it is breathtakingly beautiful—the main lobby looks like a cathedral. The trophy room is extremely interesting, with everything imaginable, even old baseball caps and one lady's sash that was found in front of a hall in the mud after a football dance. We saw the Gutenberg Bible and many original books and documents. I'd like to see the whole place when I have more time. There were so many sailors and soldiers going to class, so they must be in a V-12 training program. We went to the Yale Co-Op, where Virginia had to get some small things, notebook tabs and stuff. That's a lovely store and so much larger than our bookstore at IU. We were getting so drenched from the rain, we decided to go back to the dorm. Anyway, Virginia was anxious to study for a test at 2:30. She had to wash a patient's hair (one of her classmates) while the patient was in bed. Later she said she was awfully slow, but did okay. I met her after class, and we saw the medical building across the street from the beautiful library. At 6:00 p.m. I left, and arrived in New York at Grand Central at 8:00, as the train was slow. I took a cab to Penn Station and couldn't get on the 8:30 train because there was such a mob of people. I almost suffocated in that station, for it was so warm in New York, and I'd come from such a cold place. Finally got on the 9:30 train and got in Washington at 2:10 a.m., so you can see why I slept till Monday night! That was really worth it, for I had such a marvelous trip, and I can really say I love New England. The air there is so invigorating. Virginia is really getting along beautifully, all the girls like her so much, and she's lucky to be getting such a good education.

Two weeks before that, I spent the weekend with Mildred Pittala, who's discharged, you know. We tried to get into Radio City Music Hall twice, and the line was two blocks long, so we didn't wait. I did get to see Broadway lighted for the first time! Well, I wanted to visit Virginia before cold weather, and had promised Mildred I'd see her before I left the East, so those things are accomplished. As for Thanksgiving, we don't know yet if we'll get Friday after Thanksgiving off. If we do, I'll be home Thursday morning. If not, I'll come Saturday morning. I'll let you know exactly when I'm coming. Tell Richard to perfect his square dancing and we'll paint the town red!

Lots of love,

Lucy

P.S. I don't want any of the things I sent home, Mother.

NHO 1083

NR

TRD₁-₁₀

HYDROGRAPHIC OFFICE
WASHINGTON 25, D. C.

IN REPLY ADDRESS NOT THE SIGNER
OF THIS LETTER, BUT
HYDROGRAPHIC OFFICE
NAVY DEPARTMENT
WASHINGTON 25, D. C.

REFER TO NO.

Op-43B8-hh

15 November 1945

From: Women's Reserve Representative
To: BERKEY, LucyM., SpX3c ED, V-10, USNR, 763 58 81
Subj: Appearance and Military Bearing - Commendation
        for.

    1.   During the time that you have been on duty here
it has been observed that you have consistently maintained
the highest standards of the Women's Reserve in your
appearance and military bearing.

    2.   It gives me great pleasure to commend you as one
of the outstanding WAVES of the U. S. Navy Hydrographic
Office in this respect.

Margaret Jones
Lt. Comdr., USNR-W

Copy to:
US NavBks

CHAPTER SIXTEEN
HEADED HOME

L ucy's letter of November 14, 1945 is the last known letter she
sent home. Her military records do not show any further leave,
so it's unclear whether she went home for Thanksgiving or Christmas
1945. She may have gone home on "liberty," basically a weekend pass.
A document in her record shows that on November 7, 1945, it was
requested she be retained on active duty until January 15, 1946. She
became eligible for discharge in December 1945 with 25.5 points.

On her discharge day, January 15, 1946, Lucy was given a booklet
called "Women's Reserve, United States Navy, Information Separation
Pamphlet." It included this commendation from WAVES Captain
Mildred McAfee: "A job accomplished, a victory won. As WAVES
have accepted their responsibilities as citizens in a nation at war, so
may they contribute their efforts to the fullest in building a world at
peace. Good luck and Godspeed." The booklet contained discharge
basics: payment, travel, insurance, records, and wearing of the uniform. It was unlawful to wear the uniform after arrival at home. It
ends with, "Goodbye WAVE, good luck Civilian."

9Y

BERKEY, Lucy Marian
(Last Name) _(First)_ _(Middle)_

763 58 81, Sp(X)2c V-10, USNR.
(Service No.) _(Rate)_ _(Class)_

US. NAVAL BARRACKS WASH. D.C.
(Present Ship or Station)

TRANSFER RECORD

Date Transferred **15 January 1946**

Authority **Pers-913-mm/NM(136) (P)**

ULTIMATE DESTINATION & DUTY

US. NavPersSepUnit, WR, NavalBarracks
Wash. DC., by reason of conv of govt
for disch. in accord with ALNAV
395-45. 25½ Pts. entitled to hon.
discharge.

_____DAYS LEAVE AND_____ _____DAYS TRAVEL ALLOWED

MARKS ASSIGNED UPON TRANSFER:

PROF. IN RATE	SEAMANSHIP	MECH. ABILITY	LEADERSHIP	CONDUCT
3.5		3.5	3.0	4.0

RECORDS IN MAN'S POSSESSION:

SERVICE RECORD	HEALTH RECORD	PAY ACCOUNT	CONT. SERV. CER.	PERS. EFFECTS
X	X	X	O	X

H. W. UNDERWOOD, Captain, USN(RET.
(Signature & Rank of Officer authorized to Sign) LHW

INTERMEDIATE REPORTINGS

Reported

Transferred

Reported

Transferred

REPORTING - ULTIMATE DESTINATION

U. S. PERSONNEL SEPARATION UNIT (WR)
U. S. NAVAL BARRACKS, WASHINGTON, D. C.

Reported At
(Name of Ship or Station)

Date & Time

RECORDS OFFICER
(Signature & Rank of Officer authorized to sign)

Courtesy of the National Archives

I'll Be Seeing You

NAVPERS-601 (Rev. 6-45)

BERKEY,   Lucy   Marian
(Last name)   (First)   (Middle)

763 58 81   Sp(X)2c   V-10 USNR
(Service Number)   (Rate)   (Class)

USNPSU (WR) Washington, D.C.
(Present ship or station)

17 January 1946

Discharged this date at U. S. NavPers-
SepUnit, Washington, D. C. with Hon-
orable Discharge, for convenience of
the Government in accordance with
       AlNav 442-45
Honorable Discharge Certificate
No. C2399187   issued.

Julia W. Wilson

     J. W. WILSON, Lieut.,W-USNR
     Records Officer.

Upon being discharged with an Honor-
albe Discharge, I acknowledge receipt
of the following:

Honorable Service Lapel Button, Honor-
albe Discharge Button, Honorable Discharge Emblems, Certificate of Satisfactory Service.

I have received the following instruction:

Concerning my rights and benefits as a
veteran.
That in order to continue my Government
insurance, premium must be paid direct
to Veteran's Administration.

Lucy M. Berkey
Signature of Dischargee.

Courtesy of the National Archives

2/21/2001

In 1938 I was graduated from Salem High School. I was studying in the library at I.U. when the news of Pearl Harbor was broadcast. My three brothers, Jonas, (Navy), Richard, (Army) & David (Navy) were soon in service and I was anxious to do my part. After a year of teaching art at Columbus, In. I was sworn in & received my boot training for the Waves at Hunter College in New York. It was in August, 1943.

After this Naval Crash Course ended I was stationed at the Hydrographic Office in Suitland, Md. My job in the Lithodrafting Section involved making chart corrections on existing zinc plates as well as preparation of new ones.

There were times for relaxation as well as work. A group of us even toured the White House in April of 1944. We had cake & punch with Mrs. Eleanor Roosevelt who personally welcomed each girl.

After the war we were asked to stay on until their former employees returned. In January of 1946 I was mustered out, grateful for all I had learned & experienced, quite an education.

Lucy M. Berkey, Voyles, Podoll

Lucy wrote about her WAVES service on February 21, 2001

EPILOGUE

Lucy returned to her parent's home in Salem, Indiana, and lived there until she married Harold (Hal) Voyles, Jr., on August 24, 1947. They left for Los Angeles on September 2nd so Hal could take a job with Columbia Broadcasting System (CBS). Lucy and Hal divorced in 1954. Lucy brought her artistic talents and skills to her work at Proctor & Gamble from 1955–1963. She married Carl R. Podoll on January 12, 1963 and remained in the Los Angeles area until Carl's death on October 29, 1999. Lucy returned to Salem in May 2000 to live with her sister Virginia. Lucy passed away on September 28, 2005.

In 1944, surveys of women indicated that 75–85% of the women working in wartime industries said they planned to stay in the labor force after the war ended. Those plans ran against the prevailing cultural values of the time. The WAVES acronym spoke to the temporary nature of their position—they were Women Accepted for Voluntary *Emergency* Service. The propaganda used to induce women into the military during World War II made it clear that war work was a situational change in women's responsibilities—traditional roles assigned by gender would resume at the end of the war. But many women who had been given the opportunity to work in traditional male roles did not want to return to the status quo. Women were proud of their work. They enjoyed earning equal pay, and they were excited to acquire new skills. They found satisfaction in their wartime jobs, and they knew their contributions to the war effort were immensely important to achieving victory.

While women's wartime work did not result in their liberation from their traditional, narrowly defined gender roles, it planted the seeds of the ideas that would grow into the women's movement of the 1960s and '70s. Stereotypical roles of women *had* changed during World War II. However, the government wanted to avoid widespread unemployment after the war, and that concern extended only to men. Discharges, layoffs, firings, and demotions removed women from their positions. The government aggravated the situation by cutting off federal funding for childcare services. Propaganda in magazines and newspapers directed women back into the home, portraying images of happy, content women raising large families in modern suburban homes.

80,936 women served as WAVES during World War II. They were parachute riggers, pharmacist's mates, instrument flying trainers, storekeepers, air traffic controllers, linguists, weather specialists, cryptologists, radio operators, clerks, dispatchers, lab technicians, decoders, mail room workers, mechanics, map makers, and much more. Having served dutifully and responsibly in these professional roles, many women found the thought of returning to the drudgery of homemaking unappealing, and possibly even unthinkable. There would be no going back. Throughout the 1950s, more and more women entered the workforce. Seven decades later, America continues to make progress toward gender equity in employment. While an amendment guaranteeing equal rights to women has yet to be added to the Constitution, the voices of women are becoming more strident, and incidences of sexual harassment in the workplace are being exposed all across the United States. Women from all walks of life are feeling empowered, coming out of the shadows to demand equal treatment. Every woman who returned from World War II military service came back a changed person, and some chose not to return to their previous life. When faced with the possibility of continuing to live an exciting and productive life, many women chose to remain in the cities where they had been stationed. Living, working, and socializing with other women created a camaraderie that had been unknown to most women prior to the war.

The women of Lucy's generation embraced their opportunity to show they were willing, able, dependable, loyal, efficient, and proud to do their part for the war effort. In doing so, they advanced the cause of women's rights. Many who served hoped that barriers to women's progress could be broken down. Because 350,000 women served in the military during World War II, government and military leaders were finally convinced that women had a place in the armed services. The Women's Armed Service Act of July 1948 allowed women to be sworn into regular active duty.

On the whole, though, most women who served in the reserves

during World War II were eager for the end of war and the return to peace. An unknown WAVES officer proclaimed, "One thing I know, I'll leave the Navy a pacifist and a feminist." In her 1943 book *The WAVES,* Nancy Ross asked: "Will a woman who has been taught types of guns and ships, planes and tanks, parachutes and weather maps, codes and strategies used in man's great periodic destructive games feel qualified to speak out at last on the subject of war's futility in a way she never has before—simply by virtue of her first-hand and technical knowledge of the tools of formal destruction? Or is it hopeless to expect that women can break the recurrent death rhythm of war if her great biological argument has not proved effective down the ages? How much longer will women be willing to go on risking their own lives to bring life into the world, only so that men can destroy it every twenty years?"

Women continued to be empowered in the Navy. In 1943, a woman could not hold a rank higher than captain. In July 2014, four-star Admiral Michelle Howard became the highest-ranking woman officer as Vice Chief of Naval Operations. As of this writing, the Navy website has a section called "Women in the Navy." Immediately under the heading is this paragraph:

What's it like being a woman in today's Navy? Challenging, exciting, rewarding, but above all, it's incredibly empowering. That's because the responsibilities are significant, the respect is well-earned, and the lifestyle is liberating. Moreover, the chance to push limits personally and professionally is an equal oppor-tunity for women and men alike.

Further down the page is the heading, "Take on a Role That Defies Convention," followed by:

The idea that certain jobs are better suited for men and men alone is redefined in the Navy. Stereotypes are overridden by determi-nation, by proven capabilities, and by a shared appreciation for work that's driven by hands-on skills and adrenaline. And women who seek to pursue what some may consider male-dominated roles are not only welcome, they're wanted—in any of dozens of dynamic fields.

I have a feeling that Lucy and the women of the WAVES would be smiling and proud to read these paragraphs on the Navy website. They made it possible.

Lucy—1946
Photographer unknown

ACKNOWLEDGMENTS

This project would not have been possible without my cousin, Carol Ann Martin Bucksot. In the summer of 2014, my brother, Eric, along with Carol Ann and I, had taken on sorting through the extensive collection of Berkey/Martin ancestral documents. At that time, I actually threw away the letters that comprise a large part of this book. Carol Ann had a gut feeling about the value of those letters and, thankfully, saved them from the garbage pile. I am deeply indebted to her for her love of family history and the many hours we have spent together sorting and researching our family history. Her support has been a driving force in turning Lucy's letters into book form.

I have been blessed with finding the right people at the right time to assist with research and proofread the manuscript. Researcher Elizabeth Terry was essential in photographing Lucy's military personnel record at the National Personnel Records Center in St. Louis, Missouri. Thank you to Archive Technician Patrick Fahy, of the Franklin D. Roosevelt Presidential Library, for digging deeper to find documents about Lucy's visit to the White House. Melissa Frew interviewed her mother, Eleanor Berkey Frew, Lucy's last living sibling, on several occasions. Eleanor's answers were extremely helpful in explaining some mysteries in Lucy's writing.

My sincere gratitude is extended to Rick Martin for serendipitously finding the rest of Lucy's wartime letters, her insignia, and other artifacts; Nina Berkey Seven and Kristin Berkey Adkins for providing information about their father David's service in the Navy; Jim Berkey for family historical details; Sara Brown for information about her aunt, WAVE Mildred Pittala; Museum Manager Cody Harbaugh, of the Bartholomew County Historical Society, for searching for Columbus, Indiana, school records; Lehman College Professor & Special Collections Librarian Dr. Janet Munch for sharing Hunter College WAVES primary sources, suggesting other sources, and sharing her article about WAVES history; Cindy Clague and Erik

Lohof for boundless encouragement; Holly Sullenger for information about the Crim family; Dr. Kathleen M. Ryan for sharing her dissertation, suggesting sources, and the wealth of information on her website "Homefront Heroines—The WAVES of World War II"; Kathy Wade, Washington County Historical Society, for genealogical information and Salem, Indiana, history; Meg Saxon for sharing photos and information about her mother's time in the WAVES; Nick Spark of Periscope Film for access to the WAVES movie, *Report to Judy*; and Ron Miner for sharing photos of his father's World War II Hydrographic Office maps.

Many thanks to the readers of the first draft for their comments and suggestions—Eric Berkey, Evan Berkey, Carol Ann Bucksot, Debra Janison, and Peggy Good. I am grateful to my editor, Lisa Ohlen Harris, for her encouragement throughout the research process and her tremendous attention to detail in making the manuscript a cohesive whole. Thank you to Patricia Marshall of Luminare Press for her skill and expertise in the publishing of this book. Thank you to Claire Flint Last for her wonderful cover design and meticulous care in the layout of this book.

This book would not have been possible without the financial support of these generous benefactors: James Abel, Teresa Allen, Leo Altmann, Dr. John Armstrong, Harriet Baskas, David Bergen, Todd Berkey, Evan Berkey, Eric Berkey, Jenna Berkey, Jason Bodnar, Javier Ignacio Tapia Bromberg, Wyatt Cates, Cindy Clague, Peter Dunn, Stephen Frew, Eleanor Frew, Melissa Frew, Debbie Harmon Ferry, Jenna Huntsberger, Eric Huntsberger, Debra Janison, Judy King, Margaret and Jim Knudson, Bill and Evelyn Kroener, Erik Lohof, Steve Long, Gloria Lutz, Dennis MacCoumber, Lynn and Dr. Mark Manship, Carol Ann Martin Bucksot, Garry Martin, Rick Martin, Sharon Medicis Michaud, Ron Miner, Sally Moore Goldman, Elizabeth Moyer, Dr. Janet Butler Munch, Gail Napier, Jennifer Nicklyn, Patricia Noel, Dr. Diane O'Leary, Mo Elizabeth O'Leary, Deborah Pattin, Elizabeth Pimper, Cheryl Pritchett, Carol Riley, Dr. Kathleen Ryan, Dr. Richard Schonberg, Lynn Semega, Nina Seven,

Janet Shadiow, Lorena Smith, Sally Starr, Dr. Al Stavitsky, Robin and Hugh Watson, Donna Weed, Jan Wolfram and Traci Yocom.

I am extremely grateful for the support and enthusiasm of my brothers, Evan and Eric, and my son, Eric. I couldn't have done this project without my husband, Michael, who encouraged me every step of the way. His knowledge of history, editorial advice, and patience has been exceptional.

BIBLIOGRAPHY

"2 Teachers to Leave System." *The Columbus Herald*, June 9, 1943.

"3 Air Fields Bring Influx of Workmen." *The Columbus Herald*, October 7, 1942.

"67 State Women Enlist in WAVES, Await Duty Call." *The Indianapolis Star*, October 3, 1943.

"100 Driven From Houses Here by Flooded Creeks." *The Columbus Herald*, March 24, 1943.

310 Publishing. "Greyhound: On the Road Through WWII and Beyond." http://www.americainwwii.com/galleries/greyhound-on-the-road-through-wwii-and-beyond/.

"5,300 Sign for Ration Books in City First Day." *The Columbus Herald*, February 24, 1943.

"43,000,000 Americans to Push Bond Sales During "Women at War Week" Nov. 22-28." *The Indianapolis Star*, November 15, 1942.

American Presidency Project. "Franklin D. Roosevelt Fireside Chat December 24, 1943 (transcript)." http://www.presidency.ucsb.edu/ws/index.php?pid=16356.

American-Rails.com. "The Monon Railroad, The Hoosier Line." http://www.american-rails.com/monon-route.html.

"Answers to Questions: Hydrographic Office Maps." *The Cincinnati Enquirer*, November 1, 1944.

Arbuckle, Alex, "1943 Bus Story: Wartime America Hits the Road." http://mashable.com/2017/02/04/bus-story/#fimGpJgVYkqu.

"Army Puts on Show for 3,000 City People." *The Columbus Herald*, November 18, 1942.

Barlow, Col. Cassie B., USAF, and Norrod, Sue Hill. *Saluting Our Grandmas: Women of World War II*. Louisiana: Pelican, 2017.

Becker, Paula. *HistoryLink.org.* "Knitting for Victory—WWII." http://www.historylink.org/File/5722.

Bell, Kevin. Phone interview by author. August 5, 2017.

Berkey, Jonas M. *World War II Chronicles of Jonas Martin Berkey.* Louisville: Self-published, 1994.

Berkey, Lucy Marian, 7635881, Enlistment Photo, Official Military Personnel File of Lucy Marian Berkey, Record Group 24, Bureau of Naval Personnel. National Archives at St. Louis.

Berkey Huntsberger, Karen. *Waiting for Peace: The Journals & Correspondence of a World War II Medic.* Oregon: Luminare, 2015.

Berkin, Carol, and Norton, Mary Beth. *Women of America: A History.* Boston: Houghton Mifflin Co., 1979.

Borrelli-Persson, Laird. "Mainbocher—The Most Important American Designer You've Never Heard of—Is Getting His Due in Chicago." *Vogue Magazine,* October 21, 2016. https://www.vogue.com/article/exhibitions-mainbocher-from-the-archives

Boettiger, John Roosevelt. "My Grandmother, Eleanor Roosevelt, A Conversation." Interview by Susan Ives. *The Living New Deal,* April 3, 2015. Audio transcript. https://livingnewdeal.org/full-interview-my-grandmother-eleanor-roosevelta-conversation-with-john-roosevelt-boettiger-and-susan-ives/.

Castellano, Nancy. *Looking Back at the WAVES: A Chronicle of 90,000 Navy Women of World War II.* Self-published, 2007.

"City Schools Go on Parade on Wednesday." *The Evening Republican,* May 1, 1943.

Cole, Merle T. *Cradle of Invasion: A History of the U.S. Naval Amiphibious Training Base, Solomons, Maryland, 1942-1945.* Calvert Marine Museum, 1984.

Collingham, Lizzie. *The Taste of War: World War II and the Battle for Food.* New York: Penguin Books, 2013.

Collins, Winifred Quick. *More Than a Uniform: A Navy Woman in a Navy Man's World*. Denton: University of North Texas Press, 1997.

Darnton, Eleanor. "WAVES Meet Test of a Year." *New York Times*, July 25, 1943.

Day, Deborah. "Cloth Survival Charts, Also Called Waterproof Handkerchiefs." Scripps Institution of Oceanography Archives, October 10, 1996.

Duis, Perry R. "Great Lakes Naval Training Station," Encyclopedia of Chicago. http://www.encyclopedia.chicagohistory.org/pages/543.html.

Fedman, David, and Karacas, Cary, "A Cartographic Fade to Black: Mapping the Destruction of Urban Japan during World War II." *Journal of Historical Geography 38*, (2012): 306-328.

"First Blackout to Be Thursday Night at 8:30." *The Columbus Herald*, March 10, 1943.

"Former Ball State Athlete Killed." *Muncie Evening Press*, January 17, 1944.

Franklin D. Roosevelt Presidential Library. "Day-by-Day Project: Franklin D. Roosevelt: April 4, 1944 Calendar Page."

Franklin D. Roosevelt President Library. "Letter from Congressman Lansdale Sasscer to Eleanor Roosevelt." Office of Social Entertainments Folder, Box 112.

Franklin D. Roosevelt President Library. "List of WAVES Attending White House Tea on April 4, 1944." Office of Social Entertainments Folder, Box 112.

Frew, Eleanor (Berkey). Video interview by Melissa Frew. February 19, 2017.

Frew, Eleanor (Berkey). Video interview by Melissa Frew. August 19, 2017.

George Washington University. "My Day, April 11, 1944." The Eleanor Roosevelt Papers Digital Edition. https://www2.gwu.edu/~erpapers/myday/displaydoc.cfm?_y=1944&_f=md056768.

Greenbaum, Lucy. "'History of the WAVES' Book Review." *The New York Times*, October 17, 1943.

Harvey, Edith, and Lissey, Jeanette. *Prepare for the Official Tests for WAACS, WAVES, SPARS and Marines: A Complete Guide and Instruction Book for Women in Military Service.* New York: Capitol Publishing Company, 1943.

History.com. "Jeanette Rankin Casts Sole Vote Against WWII." http://www.history.com/this-day-in-history/jeanette-rankin-casts-sole-vote-against-wwii.

"Hydro Happenings 1941-1946," Commemorative Yearbook, U.S. Navy Hydrographic Office, 1946.

"Is Army Major, Less Than 25 Years Old." *Garrett Clipper*, February 3, 1944.

"John Kooken is Now Captain in the U.S. Army." *Garrett Clipper*, October 12, 1942.

"Kingsbridge Astir at Navy Seizure." *New York Times*, January 14, 1943.

Keefer, Louis E. "The Army Specialized Training Program In World War II." http://www.pierce-evans.org/ASTP%20in%20WWII.htm.

Levine, David, "Remembering Camp Shanks." *Hudson Valley Magazine*, September 2010. http://www.hvmag.com/Hudson-Valley-Magazine/September-2010/Remembering-Camp-Shanks/.

Library of Congress. "On the Homefront: America During WWI and WWII, Volunteer Work." http://www.loc.gov/teachers/classroommaterials/presentationsandactivities/presentations/homefront/volunteer.html.

Life Magazine. pg. 33, September 20, 1943.

Look Magazine. Cover, September 5, 1944.

Mahin, Mary Elizabeth Cook. Phone interview by author. April 8, 2017.

"Man Does Shopping for 6,000 Women." *New York Times*, February 2, 1943.

"Married Men to Be Inducted in December." *The Columbus Herald*, November 11, 1942.

Martin, Virginia (Berkey). "Interview with Virginia Martin." Veteran's History Project WWII." Interview by Patricia McClain. June 28, 2001. http://memory.loc.gov/diglib/vhp/story/loc.natlib. afc2001001.00628/transcript?ID=sr0001.

"Mercury Falls to 11 Below for 6-Year Record." *The Columbus Herald*, December 23, 1942.

Munch, Janet Butler, "Making WAVES in the Bronx: The Story of the U.S. Naval Training School (WR) at Hunter College." *The Bronx County Historical Society Journal*, Vol. XXX, Number 1, Spring 1993.

Mundy, Liza. *Code Girls: The Untold Story of the American Women Code Breakers of World War II*. New York: Hachette Books, 2017.

Murdock, Maureen, MD and Bradley, Arlene, FACP. "Women and War." Journal of General Internal Medicine, March 2006.

National Archives and Records Administration. "It's a Woman's War Too! Powers of Persuasion: Poster Art from World War II." https://www.archives.gov/exhibits/powers_of_persuasion/ its_a_womans_war_too/its_a_womans_war_too.html.

National Archives and Records Administration. "World War II Records in the Cartographic and Architectural Branch of the National Archives." Compiled by Daryl Bottoms, 1992. https:// www.archives.gov/files/publications/ref-info-papers/rip79.pdf.

National Archives at St. Louis. *Wartime Rating Structure for Enlisted Personnel.*

National Council for the Social Studies. "Propaganda to Mobilize Women for World War II." *Social Education 58(2)*, 1994.

National WWII Museum. "Home Front Friday: Knit Your Bit." http://www.nww2m.com/2014/08/home-front-friday-knit-your-bit/.

National WWII Museum. "Ration Books: Rationing for the War Effort." http://www.nationalww2museum.org/learn/education/for-teachers/primary-sources/rationing.html.

National WWII Museum. "Take a Closer Look at Ration Books." http://www.nationalww2museum.org/learn/education/for-students/ww2-history/take-a-closer-look/ration-books.html.

Naval History and Heritage Command. "Recruiting Posters for Women from World War II." http://www.womenofwwii.com/recruitingposters.html.

"Navy 'Cruiser' to Visit City, WAVE, SPAR, Seabee Enlistment to Be Explained Here May 6." *The Columbus Herald*, April 28, 1943.

Navy Service: A Short History of the United States Naval Training School (WR) Bronx. New York: U.S. Navy, 1945.

"Navy WAVES." *Life Magazine*, March 15, 1943 cover.

Norman Rockwell Museum, Illustration History. "John Philip Falter." http://www.illustrationhistory.org/artists/john-philip-falter.

Official Military Personnel File of Lucy Marian Berkey. Record Group 24, Bureau of Naval Personnel. National Archives at St. Louis.

Parker, Mary E. "WAVES Beauty Routine." *New York Times*, August 8, 1943.

"Phi Beta Key to John Kooken." *Garrett Clipper*, December 9, 1940.

Phillips, Margaret (Bell). Phone interview by author. August 6, 2017.

"Picks 281 Colleges for War Training." *New York Times*, February 7, 1943.

"Pioneer Woman Doctor, Dorothy D. Teal, Dies." *The Columbus Herald*, December 13, 1985.

"Put Your Wartime Travel on a 4-Day Week." *The Republic*, May 25, 1942.

Roosevelt, Eleanor. "My Day: First Lady says British Women Prove Femininity Isn't Sacrificed to War Work." *Louisville Courier-Journal*, October 13, 1942.

Runyon, Damon. "Runyon Rushes to Champion the Women in Service." *Louisville Courier-Journal*, June 23, 1943.

"School Hours for Rationing Sign-Up Fixed." *The Columbus Herald*, February 24, 1943.

Ryan, Kathleen M. "From Propaganda to the Personal: WAVES, Memory and the 'Prick' of Photography." In *Oral History and Photography* edited by Alexander Freund and Alistair Thomson. New York: Palgrave MacMillan, 2011.

Ryan, Kathleen. "Homefront Heroines: The WAVES of WWII." Blog. http://www.homefrontheroines.com.

Ryan, Kathleen M. "Military Life: Coordinating WWII Magazine Publicity by the U.S. Naval Women's Reserve." *Journalism History* 40:4, 2015.

Ryan, Kathleen M. "Uniform Matters: Fashion Design in World War II Women's Recruitment." *The Journal of American Culture*, 37:4, 2014.

Ryan, Kathleen M, "When Flags Flew High: Propaganda, Memory and Oral History for World War II Female Veterans." PhD diss., University of Oregon, 2008.

Schumm, Laura. "America's Patriotic Victory Gardens," History.com, May 29, 2014. http://www.history.com/news/hungry-history/americas-patriotic-victory-gardens.

"Sees WAVES, SPARS Enlisting Negroes." *New York Times*, February 3, 1943.

"Serve Your Country in the WAVES." *Argus-Leader*, June 30, 1944.

"Shops Run for WAVES and SPARS." *New York Times*, April 18, 1943.

"Signing for No. 2 Ration Books Starts Feb. 22." *The Columbus Herald*, February 17, 1943.

Smithsonian National Postal Museum. "Laundry Box." https://postalmuseum.si.edu/collections/object-spotlight/laundry-box.html.

"Stage Set for Navy Cruiser." *The Columbus Herald*, May 5, 1943.

Stars & Stripes. "Navy's Highest Ranking Female Office to Command Europe, Africa." May 20, 2016. https://www.stripes.com/news/navy-s-highest-ranking-female-officer-to-command-europe-africa-1.410582.

"State Set for Ration Sign-Up." *The Evening Republican*, November 18, 1942.

Stephenson, Gertrude. *Gone…But Not Forgotten*. Evansville: Self-published, 2005.

Stephenson, Gertrude. *Heroes Among Us*. Evansville: Self-published, 2005.

Stremlow, Colonel Mary. "Free a Marine to Fight: Women Marines in World War II." http://2hzxr1lyvt537ichs3vglb28.wpengine.netdna-cdn.com/wp-content/uploads/2016/01/Free-a-Marine-to-Fight-Women-Marines-in-World-War-II.pdf.

Sullenger, Holly. Phone interview by author. August 7, 2017.

"The More Women at War: The Sooner We'll Win." *Statesville Daily Record*, March 2, 1944.

"Third Ration Book to Be Issued Through Mail." *The Columbus Herald*, May 12, 1943.

U.S. Census Bureau. "Suitland Federal Center." https://www.census. gov/history/www/census_then_now/suitland_md/suitland_federal_center.html.

U.S. Coast Guard. *Tars and Spars, The Coast Guard Show*. Playbill for tabloid musical revue, 1943.

U.S. Navy. *The Story of You in Navy Blue*. WAVES Recruiting Booklet, 1942.

U.S. Navy. *Women in the Navy*. https://www.navy.com/navy-life/ winr.html.

U.S. Office of Price Administration. *Rationing in World War II*. Booklet, Washington, D.C.: 1946.

Vassar Historian. "Mildred McAfee." Vassar Encyclopedia, http:// vcencyclopedia.vassar.edu/alumni/mildred-mcafee.html.

Walters, Lindsey. "The Girls in Blue: National Mobilization and the Feminization of the Armed Forces in WWII." *Gateway History Journal*, Vol. XV, 2015: 76-92.

"War Charts Define Seven Seas." *Shiner Gazette*, June 10, 1943.

"War Jobs Await 5,000,000 Women: They Must Be Recruited by End of 1943." *New York Times*, Sept. 25, 1942.

"WAVES: Hydrographic Office December 23, 1942 to July 30, 1944," U.S. Navy, August 1944.

"WAVES Play Big Part in Navy Hydrographic Office Program." *The Palm Beach Post*, May 14, 1944.

"WAVES Uniforms." *Life Magazine*, September 21, 1942.

"WAVES, SPARS Get Paid." *New York Times*, March 6, 1943.

Webber, Scott E. *Camps Shanks and Shanks Village: A Scrapbook*. Historical Society of Rockland County, 1991.

"Weekend Parties Honor Soldiers." *The Evening Republican*, September 21, 1942.

Witkowski, Terrence. "The American Consumer Home Front During World War II." Association for Consumer Research, https://www.acrwebsite.org/search/view-conference-proceedings.aspx?Id=8204.

Woloch, Nancy. *Eleanor Roosevelt: In Her Words*. New York: Black Dog and Leventhal, 2017.

"Women at War, Interallied Information Center." *Louisville Courier-Journal*, October 13, 1942.

Women's Memorial. "History Highlight: Women Veterans and the WWII GI Bill of Rights." https://www.womensmemorial.org/history-highlight

WWII Escape Maps. "History of WWII US Cloth Escape Maps." http://www.escape-maps.com/escape_maps/history_of_wwii_us_cloth_escape_maps.htm.

WWII Escape Maps. "WWII History of U.S. Navy Rubber Life Raft Charts." http://www.escape-maps.com/escape_maps/history_of_wwii_us_navy_rubber_lifeboat_charts.htm.

Yellen, Emily. *Our Mothers' War, American Women at Home and at the Front During World War II*. New York: Free Press 2004.

Films

Boot Camp in the Bronx. Film interview with Nancy Lynch Castellano, New York Historical Society, Published September 25, 2012. https://www.youtube.com/watch?v=r5Vzaodprm8.

Crowds on F Street During VJ Day Celebration in Washington, DC. News footage, 1945. https://www.youtube.com/watch?v=HJOETdUL6so.

Dear Boss: Navy WAVES Recruiting Film. U.S. Navy Film #MN-7400, 1943. https://www.youtube.com/watch?v=tdra6kuJqPM.

First Impressions of Civilian Employees. U.S. Navy Training Film, Atlas Education Film Company, 1944. https://www.youtube.com/watch?v=ADWhOXjIyI4.

Fight Waste! War Film Bulletin No, 13. War Activities Committee of the Motion Picture Industry, 1943. https://www.youtube.com/watch?v=GaDhA7eVRHs.

Here Come the WAVES. Directed by Mark Sandrich. Los Angeles: Paramount Pictures, 1944.

Homefront Heroines: The WAVES of World War II. Directed by Kathleen M. Ryan. Documentary, 2012.

It's Your War, Too. War Department Film 958, Documentary short, 1944. https://www.youtube.com/watch?v=QGp93ijzok4.

Nation Celebrates. Universal Newsreel, 1945. https://www.youtube.com/watch?v=66EOCMdEqCI.

Personal Hygiene for Women, Part 1. U.S. Navy Training Film, Audio Productions, Inc., 1943. https://www.youtube.com/watch?v=gcqt1cly5dg.

President Truman's Announcement of VJ Day. World Wide Newsreels, 1945. https://www.youtube.com/watch?v=05XtKblztGE.

Report to Judy. United States Navy Recruiting Film, 1944. https://www.youtube.com/watch?v=Rk1v2VgxNAM.

Supervising Women Workers. U.S. Office of Education Training Film, 1944. https://www.youtube.com/watch?v=3cfHOrFKKcM.

That Men May Fight. U.S. Navy Recruiting Film, 1944. https://www.youtube.com/watch?v=PazHV_shhFU.

The Navy Way. Directed by William Berke. Los Angeles: Paramount Pictures, 1944.

The War. Directed by Ken Burns & Lynn Novick. Walpole: Florentine Films and WETA-TV, 2007.

The War Ends in Europe. United News Company Newsreel, 1945. https://www.youtube.com/watch?v=7zL-sBxVk_I.

The World Today Newsreel: Navy WAVES: Women Accepted for Volunteer Emergency Service. Los Angeles: Twentieth Century Fox, 1943. https://www.youtube.com/watch?v=DpjYTwGuoGs.

WAVES Celebrate Second Birthday. United News Newsreel, 1944. https://www.youtube.com/watch?v=aFvIBXR9S-M&feature=youtu.be.

Women in the U.S. Navy: Ladies Wear the Blue. U.S. Navy Film, 1974. https://www.youtube.com/watch?v=HW_p_pvc0_g.

Washington, D.C., VE Day, May 8, 1945. News footage, 1945. https://www.youtube.com/watch?v=Z18gWcwa9FI.

Audio Recordings

General Eisenhower: D-Day Broadcast June 6, 1944. https://www.youtube.com/watch?v=1pT6dBYXASE.

Complete Broadcast D-Day CBS Radio June 6, 1944. Internet Archive. https://archive.org/details/Complete_Broadcast_Day_D-Day.

Complete Broadcast D-Day NBC Radio June 6, 1944. Internet Archive. https://archive.org/details/NBCCompleteBroadcastDDay.

George Hicks Reports From the Deck of the USS Ancon. London: Blue Network, June 6, 1944. https://archive.org/details/NBCCompleteBroadcastDDay.

World War II Radio Broadcast, April-June 1945. https://www.youtube.com/watch?v=yUAZq2O1pn8.

INDEX

ASTP program, 35, 42
atomic bomb, 213
barracks H, see WAVES
Berkey
    David, xiii, 42, 57, 59,
        63-64, 87, 89, 95, 101,
        134-135, 145-146, 151-
        152, 185, 197-198, 205,
        214, 235
    Eleanor, xiii, 4, 64, 95, 100,
        103, 107, 110-111, 114,
        121, 129, 152, 185, 191,
        214, 217, 235-236
    Jonas (Jonie), xiii, 2, 4, 6, 9,
        11, 13-14, 17, 21, 23-24,
        26-27, 42, 87, 89, 100,
        111, 117, 121, 135, 137,
        143, 145, 151-152, 168,
        170, 172, 174, 180, 184-
        186, 202, 219
    Josephine, 80, 92, 97, 101,
        107, 178-179
    Mildred McBride, xiii, 6, 14,
        17, 87, 96, 121, 129,
        135, 152, 168, 171, 179,
        218
    Richard, xi, xiii, 4, 8-9, 13,
        17, 21, 26, 35-36, 42, 87,
        89, 95, 100, 104, 109,
        111, 121, 126, 129-133,
        137, 145-146, 150, 152,
        154, 168, 170, 174-176,
        179-180, 184-185, 188-
        190, 197-198, 200, 202,
        205, 208, 212, 219 , 224
    Virginia, xiii, 6, 10, 20,
        21-22, 42, 77, 87, 100,
        103, 107, 114, 123, 129,
        143, 152, 180, 185-186,
        189, 193-194, 197-198,
        202, 209, 214, 217, 221-
        224, 230
Bethesda Naval Hospital, 206-
    207, 209, 215
black women, 45
boot camp, see WAVES
Bryan, Admiral George Sloan,
    see Hydrographic Office
Cadet Nurse Corps, 40, 42,
    223
Camp Atterbury, 2, 6, 8, 13, 18
Cantrell, Cecil, 80, 93, 97, 101,
    111, 137
Columbus, Indiana, 1-2, 6, 14,
    18, 59, 92, 124
Crim, Kathryn, 80, 92, 111,
    115, 125, 137, 208
Crim, Margaret Ann, 80, 92,
    111, 115, 137, 208
Cunningham, Leonard, xiii, 6,
    8, 10-13, 15, 17, 21, 23-24
D-Day, 149
enlistment requirements, see
    WAVES